Religion & the ARTS

the

in Education

Dimensions of Spirituality

EDITED BY DENNIS STARKINGS

Hodder & Stoughton

A MEMBER OF THE HODDER HEADLINE GROUP

Acknowledgements

The publishers would like to thank the following for permission to reproduce copyright photographs in this book: p121 reproduced courtesy of Bridget Riley, London; p123 Art Institute of Chicago, USA / Bridgeman Art Library; p126 Michael Holford; p127 Rene Magritte, The Museum of Modern Art, New York; p74 Paul Gaugin, Albright-Knox Art Gallery, Buffalo, New York - A Conger Goodyear Collection, 1965; p77 Wassily Kandinsky, Stadtische Galerie im Lenbachhaus, Munich; p78 Franz Marc, Offentlich Kunstammlung Basel, Kunstmuseum; p79 Copyright by DACS 1993, London, Paul Klee-Stiftung, Kunstmuseum, Berne; Piet Mondriaan, Rijksmuseum Kroller-Muller, Otterlo. Other photographs have been supplied by authors.

The publishers would also like to thank the following for permission to use copyright material: The Hibbert Trust for the passage on page 37; Peters Fraser & Dunlop Group Ltd for the extract from *The Mersey Sound* by Roger McGough, reproduced on page 167.

Every effort has been make to trace and acknowledge ownership of copyright. The publishers will be glad to make suitable arrangements with any copyright holders whom it has not been possible to contact.

British Library Cataloguing in Publication Data

Religion and the Arts in Education
Dimensions of Spirituality
I. Starkings, Dennis
375

ISBN 0-340-57146-2

First published 1993
Impression number 10 9 8 7 6 5 4 3 2 1
Year   1998 1997 1996 1995 1994 1993

Printed in Great Britain for Hodder & Stoughton Educational, a division of Hodder Headline PLC, Mill Road, Dunton Green, Sevenoaks, Kent TN13 2YA by St Edmundsbury Press, Bury St Edmunds,

CONTENTS

Foreword

by Professor Ken Robinson

The Department of Arts Education at the University of Warwick provides undergraduate and graduate education for teachers of art and design, music, drama, English, history and religious studies. The department conducts research both within these disciplines and across them. This book has grown out of a particular series of explorations into the common ground between religious education and the arts. Some of the papers in this book have grown directly from a unique in-house seminar series on Religious Education and the Arts. Others have been commissioned as a result of that series, to broaden and complement the debate. Collectively, the papers are concerned with conceptions of and relationships between the areas of religious experience, spirituality, artistic creation and understanding.

At other times and in other cultures there have been intimate relationships between the arts and religion. The artistic traditions of Western Europe are closely interwoven with the growth and influence of Christianity in particular. In Islamic and other religious cultures the arts have had similarly intimate roles in articulating and representing the feelings of awe and profundity that religions answer to.

In Western European cultures the relationships between religion and the arts are no longer routinely strong. One reason is the declining influence in this century of organised religion on the structure and organisation of social life. A second is the emergence of artists as a separate professional group, for the most part following lines of individual inspiration and creativity rather than those set down by the demands of patronage. If, in society at large, religion and the arts have become distanced from each other, in education in particular they are often entirely divorced. A specific reason for this is the increasing specialisation of knowledge in the contemporary world and the corresponding fragmentation of the curriculum into a variety of separate specialisms. On this basis the debate between teachers is often not so much about what they have in common in education but what is distinctive about their teaching that merits a separate place in the curriculum. This book is an attempt to buck that trend.

The National Curriculum in England and Wales was brought into being by the 1988 Education Reform Act. A principal aim of the National Curriculum is 'to promote the moral, spiritual and cultural development of pupils at school and in society'. This emphasis on spiritual and moral development clearly indicates an important role for religious education in schools. But it also implies a powerful role for the arts. As some of the papers in this collection make clear, the arts are deeply concerned with questions of value, of purpose and of meaning in human existence and to this extent they overlap with the fundamental questions of religious practice and belief the world over.

This is a book of explorations and connections. It might take as one of its axioms, Raymond Williams' observation that the study of culture is not of the various aspects of social life as separate processes but of the connections and relationships between them: of how religion interacts with politics, with law, with economics and with the arts and how all of these interact with each other. One of the expectations of this collection of papers is that by laying bare some of the fundamental and common processes of religion, the arts and spirituality, there may be a greater unity of purpose in the curriculum in general, in aiming to meet the needs and interests of the pupil as a whole.

Professor Ken Robinson is Chairman of the Department of Arts Education at the University of Warwick.

GENERAL INTRODUCTION

——————

This book comes in the wake of the 1988 Education Reform Act and its concern for spiritual development in education. Under its Chairman, David Pascall, the National Curriculum Council committed itself to articulating the spiritual dimension of all schooling and to supporting the distinctive contributions of religious education.[1] From the NCC we had *Religious Education - A Local Curriculum Framework*, and then (in April 1993) *Spiritual and Moral Development - A Discussion Paper*. Under the new School Curriculum and Assembly Authority (as the successor to NCC) discussion is likely to continue - as will the development of practical arrangements governing school policy, assessment and inspection.

Within a public debate concerning the spiritual dimension of education, this book offers a distinctive emphasis. It places religious education in the context of arts education. At the University of Warwick religious education has for some sixteen years been a part of the Department of Arts Education. When staff seminars set out to explore notions of the spiritual it was as though they gave form to relationships between RE and the arts that had hitherto been implicit in our shared experience. One way to put it is to say that those meetings disclosed a shared sense of the spiritual values to which David Pasacall drew particular attention - qualities of inspiration, imagination, affirmation and contemplation, and the importance of the WHY questions.[2] The nature of this convergence is significant for the wider public debate now taking place. It has not meant identity of personal views on religion, the arts or any other matter. Rather, it has meant a community of concern for what we corporately offer in our educational system. However one initially regards the spiritual dimension, the shared enquiry drives us back to fundamentals, to questions about why and how we teach and the impact we have.

The nature of 'spirituality' is explored in this book across the field of arts education not by imposing some predetermined notion of the spiritual upon all contributors, but by inviting people to explore spirituality's implications from their own point of view. Some of our writers tackle the definition of spirituality directly. This needs attention because the notion of spirituality is disputable and 'protean in its forms'.[3] Others look into their own disciplines for concerns essentially related to spirituality. It drives them to look for fundamental concerns, for what their curriculum subject may contribute to wholeness of life. Finally there is a section devoted specifically to religious education

2

in which (alongside writers whose background is specifically in RE) specialists from other areas contribute their insights. This does not mean that those other specialists consign spirituality exlusively to the fields of religion and religious education. Nor does the existence of a separate RE section cut off RE from the rest of the book or from the rest of the curriculum. Rather, the composition of this section acknowledges the relatedness of disciplines and a continuity of concern across the book as a whole.

ENQUIRING INTO THE SPIRITUAL

The notion of spirituality has been traditionally a notion of the religious life, with its expressions ranging from personal devotion, to public liturgy and the arts and general culture of societies. At the outset, we should note the range and dynamic of this religiously grounded spirituality. Christian spirituality has always had an interactive and exploratory character, has been an adventure into understanding the true way of things. Based on revelation, it has been a constant dialogue with cultural forms and ideas. Some religiously committed people (and indeed some opponents of religion) will perhaps suppose that a spiritual concern ceases to be relevant outside the social influence of religious forms. Others will hold to the traditionally religious notion of spirituality but be more tolerant of secularity as perhaps an interim and ambiguous phenomenon. They will see it as something inconclusive and somehow awaiting the reconstruction of religious forms. So be it. It must at the very least be a duty of public education to keep open the questions on which human history alone can decide.

But what are we to say about personal and corporate spiritualities now, in an age when faiths and cultures are thrown into ever-increasing contact, mutual influence and contradiction, and when (for much of the western world, at least) formal religious adherence seems less prevalent than it was? What are we to say about that profoundly important aspect of the modern world whereby arts and sciences have progressively assumed independence from formally religious inspirations? Here we are speaking not only about further challenges arising within the traditionally religious notion of spirituality. We are talking about whether there is some personal and corporate concern (a concern perhaps for wholeness and integration of life, for shared and fundamental values) that is an aspect of all human life. Faced with a divided world, our minds confused by the fragmentation of competing ideologies, we have perhaps been silent for too long in English education about personal and corporate values - about the way we prepare our children (in all subjects of the curriculum) to face the world with courage and purpose.

If we are to make a start on meeting this challenge we shall need to look into the fundamental concerns of curriculum subjects with an eye to the way in which they meet human needs. The approach of this book is to be open to what Norman Gibson happily calls 'the interrogative impulse' - inviting writers to pursue the nature of the spiritual in their own ways and in their own contexts. If we begin by allowing for diversity it is because sensed diversity is one of the issues before us. But the goal is a unity of educational purpose from which to meet the needs of our pupils as they come to terms with the world. There is an option open to all people of goodwill whose children are educated in the same society. It is to recognise the diversification of our human quest

3

for meaning and for the integration of personal and social life - to recognise that where the arts (for example) appear to have achieved a status independent of religious inspiration they may not have ceased to carry the aspiration that is the hallmark of a spiritual quest. If this is so, we can expect the language of spiritual exploration to be diversified, to be apparently secular, or to have incidental reference to the religious, or to represent a readjustment of the way we understand religion and the arts. The explorations of this book exclude none of the options so far mentioned. Their reliance on 'the interrogative impulse' gives primacy to the WHY questions at the heart of any spiritual quest.

THE STRUCTURE OF THE BOOK

A word must be said about the structure of a book in which authors have been free to express their own concerns and to assume the range of reference that they themselves have felt necessary. The book has been organised into those sections that the editor has found most useful in providing his own introductions across a challenging range of material. This brings us to the role of the editorial pages. Exclusively the responsibility of the editor, they offer his personal commentary on the issues as they develop; and hopefully they will help readers to find pathways through the issues. But the editor's own sense of how issues relate to each other may not necessarily represent the most interesting, the most just or the most significant interpretation of his colleagues' work. The safeguards against his giving too personal an interpretation lie in the summaries that precede each individual chapter and, of course, the chapters themselves.

Readers have a range of options in using this book. Topics of interest to specialists can be traced in the the titles of individual chapters and through the chapter summaries; and then one possible overview of the sections (or of the book as a whole) may be traced across the editorial introductions. At the end of the book there are some suggestions about the relatedness of themes and topics.

REFERENCES

1. See the speeches of David Pascall - to the Religious Education Council for England and Wales (7th May 1992), and to The Association of Religious Education Advisers and Inspectors (10th July 1992).

2. Speech of David Pascall to The Association of Religious Education Advisers and Inspectors (10th July 1992).

3. For a thoroughgoing critique of various usages see Ann Henderson's 'Spirituality and Religious Education' unpublished M.Phil thesis, University of Warwick, 1990.

INTRODUCING
THE
SPIRITUAL

Introduction

Statutory concern for the spiritual development of pupils is not an invention of the 1988 Education Reform Act, for in this respect it reaffirms the Act of 1944. Now however there may be a difference - a new administrative determination to give the spiritual dimension practical and substantive meaning in education. If this is to be effective across the whole curriculum and in the religious education of a plural society, we may need to think of human spirituality in new ways. Ideas of spiritual development depend on our notion of spiritual values. Our operative educational understanding of spiritual values needs to be a consensual development. It needs to bear discernible relation to the component value-systems and those of society as a whole. Though it will involve values that are transcendent, it needs to be built by enquiry and from the ground upwards.

Consider, for example, the traditionally religious focus of spiritual values. Fifty years ago it was possible to argue the spiritual significance of education exclusively in Christian terms and according to Christian conceptions. The difference now is certainly not that the voice of Christian spirituality ceases to be important and influential: it is that (however tolerant it may be) it may not be heard by others and so cannot provide an exclusively governing framework for a religiously plural society. To speak more broadly of the issue, it may once have been possible for religious conceptions to govern all aspects of life including the arts. That is not now very obviously the case. Autonomy is commonly claimed for the arts as for science, so that a specifically religious language (or framework) of spirituality may not now govern all others for all citizens. To focus on the area of education with which this book is concerned, it may be that aesthetic experience and an autonomously aesthetic language of values offers an alternative. The first chapter explores distinctions between religious and secular varieties of spirituality, arguing for the authenticity of secular spirituality as a notion and suggesting that the two are inter-related. The second chapter explores the distinction between belief and unbelief in terms of a distinction between religious and aesthetic outlooks.

When (in 1925) Basil Yeaxlee discussed the spiritual in education, his outlook was displayed in the following words:

> We are committed to the faith that the spirit of man answers to the spirit of the universe. Spiritual values are those which belong to the human person in common with the universe known also as personal.... [1]

Readers will recognise the Christian language and conviction of one of religious education's leading figures. Within a Christian framework Yeaxlee's approach was generous and astute. As Professor Elias points out, Yeaxlee did not think that a 'spiritual atitude' always coincided with religious commitment: outside the religious communities of meaning there were people concerned for spiritual values in their commitment to remedying social and economic injustice. Nor did he think that all religions were spiritual: religions could, for example, be superstitious. Nevertheless, it has to be observed that these admissions allowed no ultimate independence to secular perspectives. Since the spirit of man 'answers to the spirit of the universe', secular spiritual values were ultimately pulled back into the orbit of Christian theism. And of course the highest accolade went to religion. In Professor Elias's commentary on Yeaxlee, 'what true religion adds to the spiritual is a conscious relationship to the soul or centre of the universe.....Religion is thus spirituality, coming to fullest con-sciousness in persons'.[2] This seems to have been the pattern of things in 1944. The great William Temple's vision of the schools as suffused by religious values was structured on lines not very different from the outlook of Yeaxlee.[3]

Some fifty years on, it remains important not only to believers but to everyone else that spiritual values be not merely decorative but woven into the fibre of experience and understanding. But the question as to how this can be done is our contemporary problem, for no single theological framework is universally acceptable. There are those of course, and they are represented among the writers of this book, for whom the ultimate framework of understanding is Christian and for whom new problems and new awareness are referred to a theology in part established and in part evolving. Their contributory voice is important, their claim to attention undeniable. On the other hand, the Education Reform Act requires due attention to other world religions, just as our society at large requires respect for all conscientious beliefs. Across the whole field of arts education, and not only in the area of RE, there are religious voices that claim authenticity and independence in their own terms and not by reduction to other frameworks. Buddhism, for example, proposes a spiritual path whereby belief in God is probably ruled out through the teaching of *anatta*, and is at least discountenanced as falling within the spiritually misleading range of 'views and opinions'. Islamic voices call for values in education differing in their emphasis and application from the Christian.

Secularity too is a deeply conscientious matter. Those for whom no God seems to answer in prayer, will express aspirations (and appreciations of the fibre of experience) that are distinctive and which will resist reduction to religious perspectives. Of course it may be important no less for believers than for humanists or secularists in these ambiguous and confused times to avoid closing too early the circle of conviction that

Yeaxlee demonstrated in a Christian form. On all sides there is a need to remain open to the lessons of experience, and flexible in the response to it. In this, William Temple was exemplary. "I am putting this crudely," said Temple on one occasion, "but I believe our Lord is much more interested in raising the school leaving age to sixteen than he is in acquiring an agreed Religious Syllabus." [4]

Spirituality Now - a Beginning

It has been suggested that the religious and the secular outlooks fall within the range of an enquiry into contemporary spirituality, and that the one must not be prematurely reduced to the outlooks or terminology of the other. For this reason, Starkings seeks to draw a map of spirituality's overall landscape. He tries to define and to respect the distinction between the religious and the secular, to assert their independent authenticity, but also to show how the spiritual journey of individual men and women may cross the boundaries. That art and religion have coincidental concerns is represented in the authorities on whom he draws, but without definitionally appropriating the arts to either a religious or a secular framework. When David Jenkins approaches the distinction between belief and unbelief through the investigation of art forms, he naturally chooses those that are contextually religious. By close attention to the aesthetic structure of the Christian mystery plays and the Taz'iyeh he provides an original and distinctive account of the divergence between religious commitment and secularity. What for some people is a contextual experience of religion, is for others a textually contrived and staged experience of ideas.

While both Jenkins and Starkings offer different elaborations of the distinction between religious and secular perspectives, Starkings argues for their frequent relatedness in personal experience, for a necessary continuity between the two. To the extent that this later argument hold good, Jenkins' secularity may be an authentic component of the spiritual in contemporary terms.

References

1. Basil Yeaxlee, *Spiritual Values in Adult Education*, Vol.1 p.3, quoted in John Elias, 'Basil Yeaxlee: Educator of Adult Spirituality', *British Journal of Religious Education*, Vol. 7, No.3, Summer 1985, p.105.

2. John Elias, 'Basil Yeaxlee: Educator of Adult Spirituality', British Journal of Religious Education, Vol. 7, No.3, Summer 1985, p.106.

3. Archbishop William Temple's role as an architect of the 1944 educational settlement is well known. *Christianity and the Social Order* was published by Penguin in 1942.

4. Quoted in Iremonger, *Wlliam Temple*, Oxford, 1948, p. 275.

DENNIS STARKINGS

THE LANDSCAPE OF SPIRITUALITY

The problem is how to take an overall view of spirituality - a notion which, having religious origins, is now meaningfully applied outside religious frameworks. On the one hand, the author resists the assumption that all art and meaningful living is but a surrogate religion. On the other hand he holds to the distinctiveness of (for example) Christian spirituality. He suggests that while the religious kinds of spirituality find their focus and authentication in the distinctive experience of worship, secular spirituality is authenticated in a progressive integration of life's experience. Secularisation may be a provisional, relative and ambiguous phenomenon. The religious and the secular are related to each other through the contemporary experience of living across essentially distinguishable frameworks of meaning - a situation in which the arts are universally relevant as makers of meaning.

It had been apparent as far back as 1944 that a society divided as to the status of 'religion' was likely to be less divided when talking about 'the spiritual'. Citing an astute political use of this in the 1944 Education Act (whereby teachers became responsible for contributing to spiritual development) Jack Priestley noted more recent evidence from David Hay that many who were reluctant to profess religion nevertheless confessed to having had 'spiritual experiences.[1] Priestley's own important article, 'The Spiritual in the Curriculum' took a correspondingly panoptic view of spirituality's educational significance and potential.[2] Talk about human spirituality surmounted the religious and secular divide. Representing a fundamental concern for meaning and value, talk about spirituality might help us to talk about issues such as the aims of education. At the very least, talk about 'spirituality across the curriculum' might help us to stop talking so drearily and exclusively about curriculum bits and pieces.

But there is an initial obstacle to be overcome if a concern for the spiritual is to be so generously productive in education; and it has to do with those distinctions and resistances between the religious and the secular that Priestley did not deliberately explore. At worst, this current educational concern for the spiritual may come to seem

✓ like a compulsory baptism of the secular, or (from the religious point of view) a dissolution of religion into a generalised earnestness. This danger should lead us to take seriously a view that contrasts with Priestley's inclusivist view of spirituality. It is the view that insists on professed religion as spirituality's traditional and perhaps essential vehicle. On this view, other understandings of 'spirituality' are at best derivative and subordinate, and may even be parasitic and invalid. Such narrowness of perspective is ultimately wrong, I think; but there is something to be learned from it. The challenge for anyone who wishes to form a view of the nature of spirituality that is sufficient for the comprehensive purposes of a national educational system is this - to draw such a map of spirituality's overall landscape as may relate spirituality's distinctively religious forms to its broader and secular manifestations.

RELIGION AND SPIRITUALITY

The notion of 'spirituality' relates traditionally to the lived experience of religion - not as something exclusive and feeding on itself, but as something evolved by faith in its engagement with the world. It is not the same as knowing about dogma, doctrine or church history, though knowledge has something to do with it. It is not even the same as personal devotional experience, though attention to a personal or subjective element brings us perhaps nearer to the target. As traditionally understood, spirituality seems primarily to represent an achieved state of all gathered knowledge and experience within the religious life. It has corporate as well as individual manifestation - displaying (from one case to another) distinctive qualities of sensibility in form, style and tone. Its appreciation calls for an approach very close to the way we appreciate art - demanding, for example, some sensitivity to the founding tradition, and a willing attention to its distinctive 'voice'. It is no mere accident therefore that the distinctive timbre of a religious spirituality can be discerned not only in the personal qualities of life but in the arts. It is thus, for example, that we speak of Anglican spirituality as evidenced in devotional life and in poets such as John Donne or George Herbert. Finally, of course, the personal and corporate spiritualities of religion are interdependent. The spiritualities of shared religious traditions interact with their own past, with current apprehensions of the world, and with each other - in short, they live or die - through the spirituality of persons. At the public level, spirituality's relative vitality can be traced in the transactions of public worship, private prayer and personal living, and may be evidenced in outcomes as wide-ranging as the creation of historic liturgies, the structure of a society's public institutions and the arts of a community.

WORSHIP - AND THE LANGUAGE OF THE SACRED

To speak of Christian belief as a matter of personal or corporate spirituality is to speak of it as a lived experience. More specifically it is to understand the role of worship in shaping such a world view. Religion as Leszek Kolakowski insists, "is not a set of propositions deriving their sense from criteria of reference or from their verifiability". Rather, "the language of the Sacred is the language of worship". It is meaningful only "in acts which believers interpret as communication with God: in ritual, in Prayer, in mystical encounter".[3] T.R Martland similarly suggests that religious dogma and doctrine are statements of fact only within the worship context:

> Men form them in the spirit of worship, formulating that which their religious activity discloses... Their function is to call for a commitment, a call to let this holy object, or that holy place, direct him who is interested to what he must see. This dogma or doctrine derives its authority from the system into which it fits and into which it leads men. Its truth is a truth-to that particular system.[4]

Kolakowski elucidates the dynamics of this. In the language of the Sacred (established through the experience of worship), "the understanding of words and the feeling of participation in the reality they refer to merge into one" - so that "'belonging to' precedes all proofs, which therefore are never proofs in the sense acceptable to a criminal court or to the editor of a scientific journal". It follows that "particular components of the language of the Sacred" will look absurd outside the worship-context.[5] "The gift par excellence of religion," is, says Kolakowski, "the world endowed with meaning".[6] But this meaningfulness is established in a special way. Religion contrasts with "everyday and scientific discourse" in that understanding and believing are a single act, unified in the worship context.

Public liturgies are clearly not the only things that Martland and Kolakowski have in mind when they refer to worship. On the other hand, shared rituals exemplify the reality of participation (Kolakowski's 'belonging to') whereby knowing and believing become a single act. Certainly the sense of participation that might have been obscured in earlier times has been underwritten in modern liturgical reform. The Christian Eucharist, for example, can be regarded as a participative drama. It celebrates various 'moments' in the Christian story of salvation (such as the Last Supper, the crucifixion and the Messianic Banquet) and makes them present in the experience of the worshipful community. In much the same way as secular drama suspends our ordinary sense of time and place, so Eucharistic worship may make present different 'moments' of the salvation story through a shifting sense of time and place. Personal involvement in worship means identifying with the story that it makes present. It means (all in one moment or movement of understanding and believing) adopting the story as one's own or - to put it another way - becoming a full member of a religion's spiritual and cultural family. But this does not mean that the believer sees all this as 'performance'. A profound element in the divine story of Eucharistic worship is participation in a present awareness of the direct and saving action of God; and Kolakowski observes that participation unifies understanding and believing where rituals are "taken as the genuine recreation of an original event, and not as acts of remembrance alone".[7] To complete the point, "In acts of worship, especially in ritual," he says, "religious symbols are not conventional signs or images; they work as real transmitters of an energy coming from another world... In particular circumstances, defined by the religious tradition, signs are - instead of simply representing - what they signify."[8]

The Truth of Religion and the Truth of Art

There is then the drama of the liturgy, celebrating the affirmations of faith. It may indeed by the case that the truth of religion is essentially the truth of art. Developing an argument of this kind, Martland observes that art and religion do not illustrate established and otherwise demonstrable interpretations of experience. Rather, they establish perceptions from which experience is subsequently understood. Proust, for example, sees women who pass in the street as Renoirs. "Such," he says, "is the new and perishable universe which has just been created. It will last until the next Geological catastrophe is precipitated by a new painter or writer of original talent."[9] The act of worship and the work of art are both 'performative'. That is, they make a difference, so that the world is understood in new ways. Both art and religion have their degenerative, past-affirming and conservative counterparts, characterised by Martland as craft and magic respectively; but a positive and transformatory power distinguishes both art and religion in their authentic forms.[10]

In an example particularly comvenient for this present discussion, Martland comments of Leonardo's 'Last Supper'. It is not, he says, "about the last supper: rather the painting itself is the actual 'Last Supper'; that is, it presents to the world a new understanding of that supper-event which is true to its inherited characters and they to it, a new understanding which the world now takes seriously and from which it continues its exploration into the supper's meaning."[11] If this is true of a painting of the Last supper, it is not less true of the act of worship that celebrates it. Worshipful experience determines the precedence of God in a new understanding of the world. Such precedence of God in Christian experience of the world is fully consistent with the observable fact that some notion of 'God' can be derived from the cultural and religious tradition of mankind. As Martland observes in speaking of the work of art, it too emerges from a cultural tradition, and that is how we first recognise it. But religious acts (like works of art) perform their own renewed understanding, intervening in that tradition and changing it.

THE AGNOSTIC ELEMENT OF FAITH

Martland makes another relevant point. The fact that art and religion make possible adventures into new territory, explains why there are no criteria for determining when a work of art is completed or what it means, and why "religious claims are so often proclaimed in terms of an insufficiency".[12] Powerful as they may be in placing the awareness of God before all other experience, moments of Christian worship do not deliver God bound and captive into the worshippers' hands. As a matter of personal spirituality, Christians know both less and more about God than their opponents seem often to think. They know less, in the sense that Christian tradition always assumes God-in-himself to be greater, even perhaps radically different, from the 'God' apprehended in any personal experience. Here, the role of Revelation is often misunderstood. It does not exhaust the mystery of God, but declares what (in human terms) is needful for the converted and devoted life. Notice the dynamic implicit in such a statement. Revelation is to be grappled with. It is to be adopted and applied in the adventure that returns ultimately to God as a mystery. In these terms, the Christian experience of God is an experience of ultimacy and insufficiency. And yet at the same time Christians know more than their opponents readily allow. They know the reliability and foreshadowed presence of god, made real to them in the experience of worship and going before them in their experience of the world.

This pattern of knowing and 'unknowing' is the hallmark of all profound Christian spirituality and not just its Orthodox forms; but Orthodoxy offers prime evidence of it. St Gregory of Nyssa gave this account of that is called, 'the way of unknowing':

> Imagine a sheer, steep crag, with a projecting edge at the top. Now imagine what a person would probably feel if he put his foot on the edge of this precipice and, looking down into the chasm below, saw no solid footing nor anything to hold on to. This is what I think the soul experiences when it goes beyond its footing in material things, in its quest for that which has no dimension and which exists from all eternity. For here there is nothing it can take hold of, neither place nor time, neither measure not anything else; our minds cannot approach it. And thus the soul, slipping at every point from what cannot be grasped, becomes dizzy ad perplexed and returns once again to that which is conatural to it, content now to know merely this about the Transcendent, that it is completely different from the nature of the things that the soul knows.[13]

That this sense of human insufficiency nevertheless amounts to knowing something is affirmed by St Dionysius the Areopagite:

> Emptied of all knowledge, man is joined to the highest part of himself, not with any created thing, nor with himself, nor with another, but with the One who is altogether unknowable; and, in knowing nothing, he knows in a manner that surpasses understanding.[14]

This encounter with *something there* brings us to take account of a complementary approach - one that is often designated, 'the way of knowing'. It registers in positive images this mysterious something that is otherwise rather paradoxically encountered through 'the way of unknowing'. Psalm 104 is a famous example, and Gerard Manley Hopkins' poem, 'God's Grandeur' is another. In each case, contemporary imagery displays the experienced presence of God as underpinning or going-before all mundane experience. Though such imagery affirms a sense of divine creative and transformatory power, it would be mistaken to assume that this 'knowing' represents a sudden access of human sufficiency. Rather (through acknowledging divine supremacy over a fallen world), it admits a sense of 'possibility' to the understanding of human life.

A SPIRITUALITY OF THE SECULAR?

It is worship that shapes the distinctive world-views and private languages of religious communities. Ultimacies such as Nibbana or the Kingdom of god are foreshadowed in the language of that experience, but are the mysterious destinations of a life's journey. All of this is the very condition and context of the spiritual life as we have understood it in the past, and it would seem not to exist outside religious communities. Some caution at least would therefore seem to be advisable if the notion of spirituality is to be applied to personal or corporate life in avowedly secular contexts. To attribute the coherence, commitment and direction of a religious spirituality to the less predictable and determinate varieties of secular living might be to devalue the linguistic and intellectual currency to no-one's ultimate advantage. It might be to sanctify the secular at the price of evacuating religion. To a challenge posed in this way - that is, from historically established usage - there is no satisfactory answer except to say that the historical perspective fails in so many ways to interpret our contemporary experience.

The everyday circumstantial evidence for this lies in claims that are made for the spiritual value of music, ballet, painting or drama independently of religious contexts. Such claims may be more than a propagandist device to ease money into the Arts Council bank account. They may really express a substantial contemporary conviction that through these and other human activities we reach out towards some wisdom, some humanity, some integration of our life experience.

It may be the chief lesson of the religious spiritualites that they win recognition not by confessional attachment as such but through their authenticity as integrations of life's experience, spirituality's shining examples are recognised in the arts, the religions, even the politics of the world and across the boundaries of cultures and religions. In them we recognise an achieved state of wisdom and humanity, a charisma, a giftedness not inevitably granted by attachment to creed or ideology. Religiously committed people are inclined perhaps to honour such giftedness by calling it a religious disposition - and so it may be, in the sense of potentiality or by association. But there are some clear cases of shining spiritual giftedness standing deliberately apart from religion to varying degrees. They would include Stevie Smith, whose brilliant lecture to the St Anne's Society is a most moving document of a spirituality deeply engaged with Christianity but standing deliberately apart from it.[15]

It has been suggested that an authentic spirituality is primarily recognised by its integration of life's experience rather than by its confessional attachment. If this be so, it places the traditionally religious alongside other recognisable modes of spirituality rather than at their head. Mircea Eliade explained the human discovery of significance in the world in terms of two notions - the sacred and the profane.[16] The profane world was in this context the world of chaos and unmeaning, whose time was the evenly limitless and impersonal time of the chronometer and whose space was boundless and amorphous. The sacred world was the meaningful world whose time was shaped into epochs, histories and personal moments of significance and whose space was marked out by thresholds, discontinuities and centredness. It was, by this account, the temple on the holy mountain that focussed the placement and history of a people in the world - an example reminding us that Eliade was explaining the nature of religion. But this account of religion may be in truth an account of all discernment of personal and collective meaning in societies. It may apply to societies in which religion is but one of the expressions of identity, where a single religion no longer over arches the thought and institutions of the community and where resistance to religion is conscientious and significant. Consider, for example, how we mark out what is sacred to us in everyday life - the importance of the thresholds that preserve our personal space and to which other come by invitation and using the ritual signs of greeting. Consider the special significance of time spent waiting for someone we love, or of time marked out in our memories as the history of family and friends. In all these ways we 'found a world' for ourselves, working some meaningful story out of our place in the world. The rituals that serve our attributions of significance to places and persons (the handshake, the kiss, the family or friendship meal, for example, are there in the common life before they are present (no doubt with special significance) in the practice of religion. So too is the personal life-story, well or ill-adapted as it may be to the circumstances and aspirations of all kinds. How else could ritual or story, the urge to found a world, be known or recognised as significant in religious contexts? How else could the adequacy, visionariness or futility of religious forms be recognised or evaluated unless there were already an aspiration grounded in everyday needs and experiences? Subject to the proper condemnation of unrighteous Mammon,'the world' deserves in certain respects better appreciation than it gets from the religions generally.

There may therefore be spiritual journeying, a spiritual life, a spirituality no less authentic for being only marginally or residually related to formal religion. Or (to put it another way) there may be a pervasive and conscientiously sensed quest for meaning that finds its resolution only for some people in formally religious contexts. Like the spiritualities of formal religion, such spiritualities are delivered and affirmed through shared institutions, rituals and traditions. In speaking of religion, it was suggested that a unity of knowing and believing was established through participation in the experience of worship. A parallel process is apparent in the growth and confirmation of secular outlooks - with the important difference, of course, that other things replace the formalised ritual context of worship. Social institutions such as friendships, the family, the school, the world of business and the professions, all contribute to establishing the intellectual and moral configurations of the inhabited world. Their force is such that they too establish a unity of knowing and believing, at depths commonly too profound to be described as conscious choice. They too are refined by a dimension of aspiration, transcendence and ultimate 'unknowing'. This commonly arises in what we might call 'the conscious art of living', whereby (amidst all the influences operating upon us) we make our choices that define ourselves and the world we inhabit. It is specifically represented also, of course, by the speculative adventures of art. There may be (according to the various standards people will wish to apply) a profound difference between the powerful or inspired manifestations of the spiritual life and the banality of our everyday endeavours; but this divide will not always fall along the division between the secular and the religious.

SECULARISATION AND ITS AMBIGUITIES

We are living, it seems, with secularisation - with the progressive removal of ideas and institutions from religious connection, influence or control. Like that other famous phenomenon, 'the rise of the middle class', it has been a pretty constant historical companion and of equally uncertain import at any given time. Secularisation is a relative thing, and a tendency. A secularised society such as that of Great Britain is not one that has passed any universal judgment on matters of religion. It is one that has adjusted to common sense - as in state funding of the schools or hospitals that the churches could no longer sustain, or when allowing people to vote despite attending the wrong places of worship. As these instances may already suggest, secularisation is ambiguous in its significance. We cannot easily know whether some apparent retreat or religious influence is an ultimate collapse of religion or a phase in renewal, the stimulus to some new institutional growth or theological understanding. In truth, the boundaries between the religious and the secular are only provisionally distinct, and are subject to flux; and the Christian who lives and thinks within a Christian framework cannot do so exclusively or without reference to other frameworks of meaning. Out of this and the common life of a society come new formulations in religion as in anything else.

In all of these processes the arts seem to occupy important middle ground. They clearly have a significant role across the spectrum of human spirituality. For some Christians, the arts may reflect the divine creative power and be related perhaps to an incarnational theology. For others, who find themselves in accidental or occasional relation to the power of religious conceptions, art may be explained as a spiritual Odyssey with a more or less determinate relation to traditional religious frameworks. There are certainly art-theories of this kind. Where there may be no professed contact with the ideas or symbols of formal religion, the arts may be assumed to stand entirely free from religion as makers of meaning. But they are nevertheless makers of meaning. Against this whole background, it is not the religious or the secular account of the arts that is most relevant to spirituality. It is rather the finally ambiguous (or multivalent) status of the art process. The human spiritual process (whether in its religious or its secular forms) itself aligns with the arts in having ultimate indeterminacy - so that there are no external criteria for determining its satisfactory completion.

CONCLUSION

The formally religious and the variously secularised spiritualities have been presented as distinct positions, with some concern for their dynamics and with the suggestion that there is movement within and between them. But though the religious and the secular spiritualities do indeed represent positions held (often tenaciously) by different people, they just as commonly represent positions battling for supremacy within the hearts and minds of individual man and women. Indeed, it is essential for believers that this should be the case. If it were not so, Christian theology and spirituality would fail to live and grow in relation to the world. It can of course correspondingly be argued that convinced secularity will be enfeebled by a determined exclusion of religious insights and possibilities. Most importantly for the argument of this chapter, it would be strange to refuse the term 'spirituality' for processes of the personal and corporate life which bring people to moments of choice. As between the religious and the secular world-views, there remains what Kolakowski calls an 'ontological option'.[17] This means that we can choose, or may be influenced, to think and to live on one set of assumptions rather than another. Equally, of course, we may be led to revise our understanding of their relationship. The job of religion and the arts in education must have something to do with sustaining the dynamics of such options.

REFERENCES

1. Hay, D. (1982) p.128.

2. Priestley, J. (1985a) and see also (1985b)

3. Kolakowski (1982) p.165

4. Martland, T.R. (1981) p.119

5. Kolakowski (1982) p.165

6. Kolakowski (1982) pp. 159

7. Kolakowski (1982) p.167

8. Kolakowski (1982) pp. 165-166

9, Quoted in Martland (1982) p.13

10. See Martland (1981) p. 118.

11. Martland (1981) p. 118

12. Martland (1981) p. 16 and see page 93

13. Quoted in Ware (1979) pp. 29-30

14. Quoted in Ware (1979) p. 31

15. Smith, Stevie (1981) p.168

16. Eliade, M. (1959)

17. Kolakowski (1982) p. 157

BIBLIOGRAPHY

Acquiviva, S.S. (1979)   *The Decline of the Sacred in Industrial Society*, trans. P. Lipscomb, Blackwell

Eliade, M. (1959)   *The Sacred and the Profane: the Nature of Religion* (tr, W.R. Trask), New York, Harcourt Brace

Hay, D. (1982)   *Exploring Inner Space*, Penguin

Henderson, Ann (1990)   *Spirituality and Religious Education*, M.Phil The sis, University of Warwick (unpublished)

Kolakowski, P. (1982)   *Religion*, Fontana Paperbacks.

MacIntyre, A (1967)   *Secularization and Moral Change*, Oxord University Press.

Martland, T.R. (1981)   *Religion as Art - An Interpretation*, State University of New York Press, Albany.

Pratt, V. (1970)   *Religion and Secularization*, St. Martins Press

Priestley, J. (1985a)   The Spiritual in the Curriculum, in Souper. P. (ed), *The Spiritual Dimension of Education*, Occasional Papers Series No.2, University of Southampton Department of Education, 1985, pp 27-48.

Priestley, J. (1985b)   Towards Finding the Hidden Curriculum: A Consideration of the Spiritual Dimension of Experience in Curriculum Planning, *British Journal of Religious Education*, Vol.7, No.3, pp. 112-119.

Smith, Stevie (1981) Some Impediments to Christian Commitment, A Lecture to the St. Annes Society, December 1968, reprinted in Stevie Smith, *Me Again*, edited by J. Barbera and W. McBrien, Virago, pp.153 - 169.

Ware, K. (1979) *The Orthodox Way*, Mowbray, London and Oxford.

Dennis Starkings is a Lecturer in the Department of Arts Education at the University of Warwick and joint editor of *Resource*, the journal of the Professional Council for Religious Education. Joint editor of *The Junior RE Handbook*, published by Stanley Thornes, he has published articles on a range of topics including the teaching of Christianity and Buddhism with reference to the arts - one of them translated into Thai and published in Bangkok.

DAVID JENKINS

"AND SHE SUPPOSING HIM TO BE THE GARDENER....." SPIRITUALITY, THE ARTS AND THE OPEN SECRET

Where religion intersects with culture (as in the medieval mystery plays) aesthetic enquiry may be able to penetrate the 'open secret' of religious belief. In the context of early Christian Gnosticism, the author explains the tension between surface events (the sjuzet) and the deeper or hidden truths (the fabula) underlying them. He explains the interplay of these two elements in the mystery plays and how (building on an established Christian tradition of allegorical interpretation) the plays present the 'open secret' of belief. From an aesthetic point of view the devices that play sjuzet against fabula - as when Adam is linked with Christ, and then with the gardener at the empty tomb - are structural, textual, and dramatically contrived. After exploring the same thesis in terms of the Persian Taz'iyeh plays, the author concludes that the religious and aesthetic may represent variously related or ultimately alternative responses.

As I write, on Easter Sunday in Suva, Fiji, I am reflecting on this morning's large Methodist gathering in Sukuna Park. The agreed tone was one of joyful surprise, although one dependent upon a kind of dramatic re-enactment; for the news, of course, was no surprise at all: Christ was Risen, promised "first fruits (why is it all so much more potent in Handel's *Messiah*?) of them that sleep". The congregation was enjoined to look "in sure and certain hope", as *The Book of Common Prayer* puts it, to the Resurrection of the Dead. Such "hurrahing in harvest", although revealed openly to babes, remained opaque and impenetrable to this observer.

And the azurous hung hills are his world-wielding shoulder
Majestic - as a stallion stalwart, very violet-sweet!
These things, these things were here and but the beholder
Wanting;......... [1]

How then to understand it? The dominant metaphors of the spiritual life are those generating both expectancy and the sense of achievement - conflicting yearnings both for the journey and the city that are quite beautifully dissected in Italo Calvino's *Invisible Cities*. It displays also a paradox at the heart of our notions of the spiritual life, in that it is held to be both intensely private and definitionally shared - so that we are uncertain as to whether we should talk about faith or about faith communities. These dimensions of journey and destiny, of the private and the public, are of course inextricably linked and somehow mutually validating. For religion to go beyond religiosity it must presumably foster and sustain inner convictions, and indeed the presence of these is conventionally the basis upon which a public demonstration of faith is allowable. Interestingly, this requirement of spiritual integrity parallels the view that no would-be artist can deploy mere technique to transform a mediocre human insight. Thus Helen Gardner, crossing the boundaries of art and religion in introducing the Divine Poems of the 17th century metaphysician John Donne, declared famously that even with a formidable wit at his disposal, the divine poet was "in permanent danger of overspending his spiritual capital".[2] Since the boundaries between spirituality and aesthetics are at least permeable, and in both directions, it may be that an analysis of the aesthetic can illuminate the validating processes of the spiritual life in Sukuna Park.

Within this deeply shared and intensely private journeying and sense of discovery, what is it that makes the openness so transparent for those who belong and yet leaves the secret so unfathomable to those who do not? I look for the answer with reference to my interest in medieval religious drama - an area where spirituality intersects with culture and where the issues become more accessible to analysis. I think the answer lies at the border where the spiritual merges with the aesthetic, where technique influences the way spiritual capital is invested and disposed. The heart of this is how we respond to the tenuousness of the narrative link between the *sjuzet* and the *fabula* - or, in other words, to the tension that exists between the surface of descriptive instances and the deep truths held to lie behind them.[3] In effect, the remainder of this chapter is a development of this single point. I shall try to make the agenda manageable by confining my detailed comment as far as possible to one mystery cycle, now referred to by scholarly consensus as the *N-Town Cycle*, although it began life (in Block's Early English Texts Society Edition) as *The Ludus Coventriae*, because it was once (wrongly) supposed to be the missing Coventry Plays. But the argument begins a little further back and travels finally to other corners of world culture.

OPEN SECRETS

Though the drama of medieval Christianity is my principal sustaining example, a clear and powerful case of disjunction between the surface (of descriptive instances) and the deep truths (held to lie behind them) appears in early Christian Gnosticism. The discovery of the fifty two Coptic tractates in a jar in the Upper Nile Valley in 1946 took thirty years to appear in a full edition, following a millenium and a half's invisibility after being buried for their own or their owners' protection; and comment about their contents may serve to explain the importance of "the open secret" as both a spiritual and a textual matter. The relatively recent publication of the entire *Nag Hammadi*

Library has opened the debate on what Gnosticism stood for.[4] It may also confirm a suspicion that the church has shown extra-sensory imperception in adjudicating successive heresies, getting matters wrong more often than chance alone can explain.

The central tenet of Gnosticism is that we are strangers in an alien world. The faithful are necessarily estranged from ordinary society, with which they profoundly refuse to compromise. Salvation is through *gnosis*, or secret knowledge. The *fabula* is deep, mystical, transcendental; the *sjuzet* through which it must be perceived or gleaned is more like the mere surface paint through which Leonardo's *Notebooks* reveal him striving unceasingly for the illusion of depth.[5] Amid the distracting clatter and clutter of everyday life, the wonder is that men (and they are men) perceive the mystery at all, that great wealth has made its home in such poverty. Hopkins makes an identical point in *The Windhover: To Christ Our Lord*, in which nature is depicted as replicating the hinted secrets in miniature, offering microcosmic cameos of the universal *fabula*. Just below the surface of the ploughed field or the dying ember lies a hidden treasure store:

> No wonder of it: sheer plod makes plough down sillion
> Shine, and blue-bleak embers, ah my dear,
> Fall, gall themselves, and gash gold-vermilion.

Both the poems of Gerard Manley Hopkins and the gnostic texts are striving to declare how the "secret" might become "manifest". The *Gospel of Thomas*, quite explicitly a compendium of "secret sayings", hints at ways in which all might be revealed, not as on the Mount of Transfiguration, but inwardly, without recourse to street theatre. Yet the disciples' questions to the Risen Christ show them to be embarrassingly stuck at some formalistic level. ("Do you want us to fast? to pray? to give alms? to regulate our diet?") Typically for a gnostic text, *The Apocryphon of James* (apocryphon = secret book) treats Jesus as a kind of Zen master, customising his insights to the spiritual progress of his various disciples, for in Gnosticism as in aesthetics, knowledge or appreciation involves a dialogue between "out there" truths and "self-knowledge". Self-location is critical, as is the notion of levels, although these matters are not quite reduced to questions of connoisseurship and taste. The spiritual life is conducted in a way not entirely removed from standard accounts of reader response theory.[6] The gospels of Gnosticism, although not entirely good news, are constantly teetering on the edges of philosophy and art. The Logos myth is reworked in *The Tripartite Tractate* to suggest three distinct kinds of human being. The *hylics*, like Madonna's *Material Girl*, live in a basically materialist world. The *psychics* are poised slightly uneasily between the worlds of spirit and matter - their pre-Marxist false consciousness hopefully relieved by occasional penetrations. Top marks go to the spiritual *pneumatics*, whose daggers are entirely air-drawn but who were wickedly misappropriated by T.S. Eliot:

> Grishkin is nice; her Russian eye
> Is underlined for emphasis;
> Uncorseted her friendly bust
> Gives promise of pneumatic bliss.

Although you wouldn't guess it from Eliot's "Whispers of Immortality", the spiritual gnosis of the pneumatics is pretty potent poetic stuff too, full of irony, paradox and metaphysical conundrums. This is particularly noticeable in the strangely-titled, "Thunder, Perfect Mind".

Since the "She" of my title, who supposed herself in conversation with a gardener, is of course that "composite saint" Mary Magdalene, it will tie my piece together a little if I record Mary's appearance in *The Nag Hammadi Library* in a tantalising and evocative fragment of a *Gospel of Mary*. The slightly piqued disciples request to be told what "hidden words" Jesus had used on that occasion. As in art, so in the spiritual life; there is a tendency to marginalise women's achievements. Peter, barely able to suppress his irritation that Jesus might have revealed anything privately to a woman, is reproached by Levi with the bald statement that, "He loved her more than us" - an observation to be held perhaps in tension with the canonical, "Lord thou knowest that I love you", and its cryptic rejoinder, "Feed my lambs".

THE AESTHETICS OF MEDIEVAL DRAMA

Although there was not a strong interest in the Middle Ages in constructing a distinctive theory of aesthetics, the arts (particularly drama and iconography) were seen, beyond initial uncertainties, as sensuous aids to worship. The medieval mystery plays were illusions created by devices, and were put on, as Bill Tydeman and others have indicated, in a very "stagey" kind of way.[7] The *fabula* of deep truths conveyed by the plays totally transcended its pageant waggons and the narrative antics of the street-theatre's apparent *sjuzet*. In both the theology and the staging of the *N-Town Cycle*, the incarnation was itself a device producing an illusion, and the two forms of commentary intersected. Finding their purposes compatible, cultures tend to run the spiritual and the aesthetic in tandem. My argument, stripped bare, is that it is this commonality of purpose in playing the *fabula* of deeper truths against the *sjuzet* of descriptive instances and 'business' that allows us to collapse the spiritual into the aesthetic or (if we wish) vice versa.

A foreshadowing of the resulting spiritual and aesthetic issues can be traced in the pre-medieval history of aesthetics.[8] Plato's "doctrine of forms" echoes the dichotomy between *sjuzet* and *fabula* - although his denunciation of poetry and representational art seems to put him among the Philistines. The arts fared a little better in Aristotle's *Poetics*, where tragic drama was held to purge the emotions of pity and fear. This formula however has only limited usefulness to those trying to construct an aesthetic account of medieval drama. Partly this is so because of the soundly alleged "impossibility of a Christian tragedy". Where suffering and death are transcended by resurrection and the coming of the Kingdom, all things end in the dance of comedy. But the formula is of limited use also because of the cogency of Gerald Else's argument that *catharsis* is a structural rather than a psychological construct, a matter of what happens, formally, in the plays, not of some inner purgation experienced by the audience.[9] This weakens our ability to argue that Aristotle saw tragedy as turning theatre-going into a quasi-spiritual experience, and that medieval drama finally proved his point.

A more promising strand linking classical aesthetics to the medieval era resides in continuities that can be traced in an implicit theory of interpretation. The work of Homer, as poet and seer, was increasingly held to be open to deep, but rather fanciful, allegorical interpretations and increasingly perceived as carrying profound truths hidden in symbol and allegory. Consider here the peculiar problem posed to Christianity in having a double set of texts. At its roughest, the dilemma of the hi-jacked Hebrew scriptures (turning them into the Christian *Old Testament*) was solved by giving to them the treatment given to Homer, evolving styles of interpretation that transcend their literal or received meanings.[10] Understood in retrospect, in a Christian perspective, the secret truths of the *Old Testament* reveal themselves through typological and allegorical forms of exegesis. As in solving a good crossword clue, the truth once revealed could not have been otherwise. Jonah's experience in the whale's belly in this mode "prefigures" the Harrowing of Hell, an association offering the iconic leviathan hell-mouth to the medieval stage. Such figurative interpretations were legitimised by St. Augustine in terms of their capacity of facilitate spiritual growth.[11] The ultimate inspiration for this theory of interpretation was John Cassian's four levels of meaning to be found in the scriptures - historical, typological, tropological and analogical.[12]

The open secret of the Mystery Plays

Rosemary Woolf's account of typological interpretation as a device in the *Abraham and Isaac* episode is complemented by the work of Martin Stevens across the N-town cycle as a whole.[13] The extent to which the mystery cycles are written in acordance with patristic notions of the salvation history of man, and how those notions largely determine the choice of episodes, has been better understood since Kolve's work.[14] The "core" included *The Creation, Adam and Eve, Noah, Abraham and Isaac, The Shepherd Plays, Herod, The Birth of Jesus, The Temptation in the Wilderness, Christ before Pilate, The Crucifixion, The Harrowing of Hell* and *The Last Judgement.* Although the guilds, responsible for the production of the cycles in each of the major locations except N-Town, were religious organisations, they also embodied the notion that craft skill was itself to the glory of a God who chose earthly incarnation as the step-son of a carpenter - so that, at York, the nails of the crucifixion ("large and long") are commended *as craft objects.* Attempts were made at various levels of audacity to match guilds and plays. At Chester *The Deluge* was given to "the drawers of water from the Dee", while the York sausage makers were entrusted with the entrails that spill forth from the hanging of Judas.

Although rooted in medieval life, the plays have in common a juxtaposition of *narrative time* (the sequence of the plot), *contemporary time* (medieval England) and *figurative time* (the non-time of the divine plan). It is at this last level that the *fabula* can best be understood, although exemplified at the other levels. Erich Auerbach's defining work *Mimesis*, important to the entire argument I am trying to develop here, has this to say about figurative time:

> An occurrence on earth not only signifies itself, but others that it predicts or confirms. The link is oneness in the Divine Plan. [15]

Both the theology and the texts are elaborated to resonate with a particular kind of thematic repetition. The underpinning theological concept is the doctrine of *recapitulatio*, a concept which demands that Christ re-iterates Adam, restoring by repetition. It avoids the worst crudities of a "barter" theory of the redemption by emphasising the continuity of God's providence.[16] Something of its flavour is caught in the iconography of the period, so often a bridge between the theology and the drama. The *Holkham Bible Picture Book* uses emblematically the "pelican in piety", the bird pecking its breast to succour its young with little fountains of blood.[17] The strict allusion is to Psalm 101 ("I am a pelican in the wilderness") but the *fabula* references Jesus, justifying the usual non-literal "placement" of the bird's nest on the holy rood tree, itself often sprouting foliage. (The dead tree of the second Adam brings life, while the live tree of the first Adam brought only death). But in the "Fruit Forbidden" of the *Holkham Bible* the pelican tops Eden's tree. Only to the uninitiated would this be an inappropriate placing, since the trees have a mystical unity. (Indeed some of the legends of the holy rood assert *physical* continuity, the rood growing from the pip of Adam's apple). Such complex reverberations appear at time almost capable of exponential growth. The *Arundel Psalter* has a "Tree of Life with Nicodemus" that playfully turns him into spiritual fruit, referring back to the "you must be born again" episode. Similarly a phallic Rod of Jesse, perhaps the ultimate icon of a disinterested autoeroticism, displays its arboreal genealogy of Jesus and manages to get in on the symbolic act.

A number of important issues arise from the use in medieval drama of the doctrine of *recapitulatio* and the invitation to typological and allegorical interpretation, all of which were already part of the "mind set" of the contemporary believer. In the first place we can dispose of the old accusation of "naive anachronism", which must rank as one of the least discerning misjudgements of all time. More interesting is the extent to which the structure lends itself to that most sophoclean of ironies in which the audience knows the end from the beginning. Neat examples abound, as when Herod in *The Slaughter of the Innocents* boasts "He will die on a spear" even as the audience references Longinus as its bearer. The Methodists of Sukuna Park received their news in the same spirit. A more tricksy issue in speculative poetic hands is what might be termed the limits of typological decorum. A willingness to stretch the metaphor to embrace Rahab the hospitable harlot as a type of Christ (her red hair like Christ's blood in Marlowe's *Dr. Faustus* "streaming in the firmament") must be somewhere near the outer edge, but what about the "mock nativity" of the stolen sheep in Mak's wife's cradle in the Wakefield *Second Shepherds Play*? Such pressing the boundaries apart, the more one looks the more one sees the "open secret" everywhere.

The theme at the heart of the *N-Town Cycle* most pertinent to the argument of this chapter is its systematic development of the notion of "pious fraud".[18] The conflict between Jesus and Satan dominates the cycle, but the characterisation is conceived of in a rather daring way, reflecting an earlier classical aesthetic. Cornford distinguishes a traditional opposition between the *eiron* (from which we get the word irony) and the *alazon*. The *eiron* is understated, concealing his true identity behind a disguise. The *alazon* is brashly overstated, a braggart in a Herod-the-Great kind of way.[19] In the *N-Town Cycle* Jesus is the *eiron*, but his understatement is given a twist by the imposition on the plays of a speculative theological framework, the so-called "deception of Satan" theory of redemption.[20] Satan has acquired mankind by malignant fraud and must be out-duped in return. Presented with the "open secret", he must see the *sjuzet* but miss the *fabula*. Patristic sources for this theme are suggestive, for example Gregory of Nyssa's metaphor of the fish hook in *The Great Catechetical Oration*. Satan is tricked by the humanity of Christ, but it is the divine Logos playing the line:

the deity was hidden under the veil of our nature, that, as is done by a greedy fish, the hook of the deity might be gulped down along with the bait of the flesh.

The equivalent in chess is the sealed move, known only to the player who has made it. In the plays, the theme is worked through consistently in *The Betrothal of Mary*, *The Trial of Joseph and Mary* ("By my father's soul here is great gyle!"), *The Temptation in the Wilderness* (after which Satan declares, "His answers were marvellous. I knew not his intention/ whether God or man be he I can tell in no degree"), *The Descent of the Anima Christi into Hell* and somewhat equivocally in an incomplete *Last Judgement* play. But the fanciful theology surrounding pious and malignant fraudulence is most fully developed in an exquisite *Christ and the Doctors* play in which the boy Christ ("twelve years old" through his mother but "everlasting" through his Father) turns the temple episode into a theological set-piece. He explains the *Logos* as a *Logos Pediagos*, a divine teacher restoring knowledge in kind. A nice exchange occurs with one of the doctors:

Doctor	What need was it for her to be wed
	To a man of so great age
	Lest that they might both go to bed
	And keep the law of marriage?
Jesus	To blynd the devil of his knowledge
	And my birth from him to hide
	That holy wedlock was a great stoppage
	The devil in doubt to do abide.

To a believer, the spiritual frisson associated with the process of disclosure through which one possesses the open secret is inseparable from the aesthetic judgements involved in appreciating the plays.

One final example will perhaps make my choice of title for this chapter more clear. Stanley Fish offers a brilliant exposition of a sermon by Lancelot Andrewes, delivered on the 16th April 1620.[21] Fish sees the sermon as an example of what Roland Barthes calls "replete literature". The sermon, based on the Biblical narrative, deals with the appearance of the risen Christ to Mary Magdalene. Although constructed in narrative terms, it is really an insight into the *fabula*, seen as a vast mesh of fitness, agreement and correspondences within a "storehouse of equivalent and interchangeable meanings". Even in "supposing Him to be the gardener", Mary is *cleared of error*. (Jesus is the second Adam, can weed the tares of sin from the human heart etc. etc.). Fish realises he is dealing with "structural homiletics", a world in which all affirms everything else in a colossal secret, adding adroitly that "in the universe of the sermon it is impossible to make a mistake". And indeed contemporary alabaster carvings and lists of stage props for medieval plays allow Jesus a floppy gardener's hat and a spade, restoring literalism through an appropriate *sjuzet*.[22]

How common is the open secret?

At this point it is worth asking whether the complex configuration of spiritual and aesthetic impulses analysed above characterises medieval religious drama through some quirky historical accident, or whether there are "generic features" likely to be encountered elsewhere. Comparative theatre ethnography suggests it would be illuminating to turn to the traditional Persian Taz'iyeh play in order to test the insights in another setting. Taz'iyeh has an evident similarity to the medieval mystery cycle, in relation to which it can be said to be the Shi'ite equivalent, based on the events surrounding the massacre at Kerbela in the sixty-first year of the Muslim calendar and the associated cult of Imam Hussein which is celebrated on the first ten days of Muharram. Taz'iyeh plays centred on Kerbela and its proximate events include *The Majilis of Imam Hussein, The Massacre at Kerbela, The Majilis of Hoor, The Majilis of Qasm, The Majilis of Ali Akber and The Majilis of Mokhter.* The Taz'iyeh texts are only marginally accessible, although the *Corolli Collection,* which includes the 1055 Taz'iyeh manuscripts, is likely to inform future critical studies.[23]

Consider again Cornford's distinction between the understated *eiron,* (concealing his true identity behind a disguise) and the brashly overstated and braggart *alazan.* In the Christian mystery plays the concealed *eiron* Christ was able to deceive and triumph over the braggart *alazan* devil. It is clear that in the Taz'iyeh (as in the mystery cycle) *alazan* antagonists are made to look "shabby and ridiculous" by frivolous or buffoon-like behaviour - for example, Shemr's brave boast, "I will rope the necks of his weeping children like gazelles". In the debate between Shemr and Ibn Sa'd in *The Martyrdom of Abbas,* they are depicted as "two old fools rather than military commanders". Shemr stoops constantly to contemptible behaviour, quaffing illicit hooch at strategy sessions in his field headquarters, and putting up his personal body-count by beheading a corpse. Gaming-boards and wine-jars litter Yazid's court in Damascus where Imam Hussein's surivors are held captive. In H*agrat-e Abbas* Shemr employs the cultural device of the "declaimed challenge", but somewhere in the middle the vaunting comes out wrong:

> At times I am sweet as rock sugar, at times I am like the venom of the serpent. I am the calamity of Kerbela, the offspring of menstruation and adultery. Look upon me: I have seven nipples on my chest like a dog.

Both the medieval mystery play and the Persian Taz'iyeh came out of deeply religious communities. Both theatres were popular, indigenous, even *avant-garde* in their time, and had strong ritual elements, with everyday stage-props as standard ways of triggering the right responses. Both were subject to social, artistic and iconographic influences.[24] Both medieval religious drama and the Taz'iyeh plays are constantly "prophetic" in their use of figural time and the capacity it gives to anticipate sacred events. In both traditions, however, some plays are prophetic in a more explicit sense. The N-Town *Prophet's Play* follows the tradition of the Latin *Processus Prophetarum* in introducing a sequence of Old Testament figures who tell of the coming of Christ. A similar spirit is found in *The Majilis of Zakariza* (Zakariza was the father of John the Baptist), a play largely given over to prefigurations of the tragedy of Kerbela. It is this figural view of time that allows Kerbela to appear as a *tableau vivant* juxtaposed within a variety of plays ostensibly about other matters. There are differences, of course, and one of them is that in spite of the Lament of the Three Marys sequences in the mystery plays, the Taz'iyeh is much more consistently wedded to an aesthetics of weeping, whilst less rich in humour and incidental social irony. Finally, an issue related to the arguments of critics like Kolve and Frye, is whether it is possible to root comparisons in some "formalist" account of cyclic religious drama as a genre, linked perhaps with what Chelkowski calls "archetypal elements".[25] Certainly there are thematic parallels. Mankind's salvation-history underpins the Christian mystery plays and also the Taz'iyeh, where Imam Hussein intercedes on behalf of the faithful. Both, too, are rooted in the scholastic tradition of their respective religions. Andrzei Worth's account of the Taz'iyeh tradition (contrasting it with the fate-driven Asharite puppet plays) is that it is rooted in Mutakallimin scholastic theology, which celebrates free will within the divine plan.[26]

CONCLUSION

Both the Taz'iyeh and the mystery plays are theatres of allusion and illusion, "redemption dramas", perhaps founded in some deep-seated myth of re-integration. Both spawn their doubting characters and disbelievers. Medieval religious drama had its Doubting Thomas, forced to re-crucify Jesus with his own (finger) nails. The Shi'ite equivalent is the anonymous dervish in *The Poor of the Desert and Mosa* who disputes the need of Hell until confronted with the problem of where else to send Shemr. Ultimately both dramatic traditions are confirmatory of the "open secret" they espouse, theatres of disclosure in which aesthetic and spiritual judgements coalesce, a believers' stage on which all the signifiers confirm the *fabula* and reaffirm it as the shared property of the faith community.

There are, of course, theories of the arts and spirituality that take a more meanminded view of the capacity of the human race to generate complex mythical meanings and explanations. A recent attempt by Michael Gazzaniga to root the so-called "inevitability of religious beliefs" in the way human beings are wired up produced little by way of convincing neurophysiological inference, beyond the murky thought that those suffering from "temporal lobe syndrome" find that their injured brains nurture intensified religious convictions, inexplicably packaged with hypergraphia (a compulsion to write) and bizarre sexual activity.[27]   Aspects of the factoid life of Mary Magdalene, of course, embrace all three, and Freud was interested in gospels and gardens too.[28] "Seek ye first the Kingdom.....and all these things will be added unto you"? Perhaps, but there is a suggestive link that takes one back to my opening remarks. Writing and sex are, like the spiritual life, essentially both shared and private, sustaining their own particular open secrets. But at least the link with the arts is an antidote to the slow seeping poison of the unvivid spiritual life, its tendency to slide into the banal cliches of an unexamined religiosity.

---| REFERENCES |---

1. "Hurrahing in Harvest", *The Poems of Gerard Manley Hopkins*, 4th ed., 1967, (ed. Gardner and Mackenzie) Oxford University Press

2. Helen Gardner made this observation in the context of Dr, Johnson's aphorism, "Let no pious ear be offended, if I advance, in opposition to many authorities, that poetical devotion cannot always please." See Gardner, Helen (ed.),*The Divine Poems of John Donne*, Oxford University Press 1978

3. In their studies of narrative, the Russian Formalists attempted to distinguish between the story or *fabula* and the plot or *sjuzet* in literary language. Frank Kermode took this concept further and broadened its connotative potential towards the emblem of great universal themes of human experience (*fabula*) and the particular narratory instance of example (*sjuzet*).

4. Robinson, James *et al.* (eds), 1984

5. See Catherine King, *Leonardo*, Unit 13 of A201 *Renaissance and Reformation*, Open University Press,1972

6. See for example Eagleton, Terry, (1983) pp 74ff, and Thompkins, Jane ed. (1980)

7. See Tydeman, William (1978)

8. See Beardsley, Monroe (1975)

9. See Else, Gerald (1957)

10 For the relationship between the intentional fallacy and threats to the "autonomy" of a text, see James Kinneary, "The Relationship of the Whole to the Part in Interpretation Theory and in the Composing Process", *Visible Language*, XV11, 2 (1983) pp 120-141.

11. St. Augustine, *De Doctrina Christiana*, Book 1V, translated by Sister Theresa Sullivan, Catholic University, 1930

12. John Cassian's *Collationes* (XIV, 8, Migne, Vol. 49 Cols 963-64) takes "Jerusalem" as its worked example.

13. Woolf, Rosemary (1986) and Stevens, Martin (1987)

14. Kolve, V.A. (1966)

15. Auerbach, Erich (1957)

16. See Turner, H.E. (1952) and 1 *Corinthians* 15, 47.

17. See Hassell, W.O. ed. (1954) and Ferguson, George (1954)

18. The idea was a familar one. See J. Steadman "Satan's Metamophosis and the Heroic Convention of the Ignoble Disguise", *Modern Language Review*, 52, 1957.

19. Cornford, F. M. (1934)

20. See Timothy Fry, "The Unity of the Ludus Coventriae" in *Studies in Medieval Culture Dedicated to G.R.Coffman* (Studies in Philology XLV111, 1951)

21. Fish, Stanley (1980)

22. See W.L.Hildburgh, "English alabaster carvings as records of medieval religious drama" *Archaeologica*, XC111(1947) pp 51ff. In the York Winedrawers "Jesus (as a gardener) speaks". The Coventry Cappers Play of *The Resurrection and Descent into Hell*, which includes the appearance to Mary, has a spade as one of its properties.

23. In discussing Taz'iyeh I am particularly and transparently indebted to the impor-

tant studies made by Peter Chelkowski (see Bibliography) and to a research student of mine, Reza Alemohammed. Chelkowski's book is the proceedings of an international symposium on Taz'iyeh held at the Shiraz Festival of Arts, Iran.

24. For example, the historical influence of processions, particularly as they affect the spatial organisation of cities, can be traced through Masoud Kherabadi's *Iranian Cities: Formation and Development* (1991). For literary, musical and iconographic influences, including the traditional so-called Quhuekhancha paintings see Chelkowski (1979); while issues concerning "poor theatre" can be followed in Grotowski (1969).

25. See Kolve (1966) and Fry (1957).

26. Andrzei Worth in Chelkowski (1979). For the implicit theology behind the puppet play tradition, see Jamil Ahmed, "Theatre and Islam" *The Dhaka University Studies*, Part A Vol.47 No.2 December 1990.

27. See "The Inevitability of Religious Belief", Ch.11 of Gazzaniga (1985), and Stephen Waxman and Norman Geschwind "Hypergraphia in Temporal Lobe Epilepsy" Neurology, 24 (1974) pp 629-36.

28. The word 'factoid' is of course borrowed from Norman Mailer, who coined it to cover autobiography when it seeks to be true to myth rather than history, notable in his own *Marilyn* (Monroe).

BIBLIOGRAPHY

Auerbach, Erich (1957): *Mimesis: The Representation of Reality in Western Literature*, translated by Willard Trask, Doubleday, New York

Beardsley, Monroe (1975: *Aesthetics from Classical Greece to the Present: A Short History*, Macmillan

Calvino, Italo (1974): *Invisible Cities* Secker and Warburg

Chelkowski, Peter ed.(1979):*Taz'iyeh: Ritual and Drama in Iran*, New York University Press

Cornford, F. M. (1934): *The Origin of Attic Comedy*, Cambridge

Eagleton, Terry (1983): *Literary Theory: an Introduction*, Basil Blackwell,

Else, Gerald (1957): *Aristotle's Poetics: The Argument*, Cambridge

Ferguson, George (1954): *Signs and Symbols in Christian Art*, Oxford University Press

Fry, Northrop (1957): *Anatomy of Criticism*, Princetown, N.J.

Gazzaniga, Michael (1985): *The Social Brain: Discovering the Networks of the Mind*, Basic Books, New York

Grotowski, Jerzy (1969): *Towards a Poor Theatre*, London, Methuen

Fish, Stanley (1980): *Is There a Text in This Class?: the authority of interpretive communities*, Harvard University Press

Hassell, W.O. ed (1954): *The Holkham Bible Picture Book*, London, Dropmore Press

Kolve, V.A. (1966): *A Play Called Corpus Christi*, Stanford University Press

Robinson, James et al.eds. (1984): *The Nag Hammadi Library in English*, E.J. Brill, Leiden

Stevens, Martin (1987) *Four Middle English Mystery Cycles*, Princeton

Thompkins, Jane ed. (1980):*Reader-Response Criticism*, Baltimore

Turner, H.E. (1952): *The Patristic Doctrine of the Redemption*, Oxford University Press

Tydeman, William (1978): *The Theatre in the Middle Ages*, Cambridge University Press

Woolf, Rosemary (1986): *Art and Doctrine: Essays on Medieval Literature*, Ambledon,

David Jenkins is Professor of Education and Psychology at The University of the South Pacific at Suva in Fiji - having been until recently a Professor of Arts Education at the University of Warwick. His experience ranges from school teaching to teaching and research at the Universities of Keele and East Anglia, the Open University and the New University of Ulster. He is General Editor of the Open Books Curriculum Studies series.

Personal and Cultural Dimensions

INTRODUCTION

This section is about the personal and cultural dynamics of spirituality. Peter Hastings' chapter describes a Christian's spiritual journey across the boundaries between cultures and religions. It is a journey towards the renewal of what it means to be Christian - not least in education. When Steve Attridge then explores the making of myths - myths of 'otherness' and myths of ourselves - his work may be regarded as in one sense a commentary on the processes underpinning Hastings' argument. Attridge suggests that the making of myths is a broadly human activity through which we come to some organised understanding about ourselves and the world. He regards spirituality in education as, 'a shared set of concerns between those educative processes which seek to inform, change and enhance the lives of children in our schools'. Finally, the patterns of spiritual development considered in this section exemplify creativity - a process characterised by Brenda Lealman as the making of new worlds via the disturbance of equilibrium, connection-making, and attentive waiting or receptivity.

Christian obedience to divine revelation may in some hands appear to be a force for inertia and conservatism. It has in other hands been a driving force, making Christian intelligence and commitment the engine of transformation. Of the two historical possibilities it is arguably the latter that is the more authentically Christian. There are two aspects to this revelation. One the one hand it is transcendent. The person and the teachings of Jesus Christ are a revelation of the divine, an authoritative disclosure of things transcendent and beyond the everyday world, a challenge to the world order. On the other hand, this revelation is immmanent. It takes place in the world and must be truly of the world if it is to be heard at all. When Jesus taught in parables he used characters and situations accessible to his hearers, but only to blast them into thinking the hitherto unthinkable. There is a human need to which all spirituality responds in its pursuit of the hitherto unthinkable and unimaginable.

Hastings' apparent radicalism arises against this background. Substantial matters of the faith have been re-expressed from one age to another in terms comprehensible within the surrounding culture - not thereby submitting to it but restoring conditions in which the challenge of Christian values may be heard. The doctrine of The Holy Trinity, for example, was not a formulation of the earliest Christians. It was a development marking Christianity's emergence from the Jewish world via the culture and ideas of the Greeks. Administrative structures (and correspondingly magisterial conceptions) now considered characteristic of Catholicism owe much to the power, the culture and the legal forms of the Roman Empire. At times, the Christian emphasis has lain upon divergence. That Catholic and Protestant Christians developed divergent emphases on matters of belief, church order and personal piety is a fact that owes much to rising nationhood and to cultures diversifying in distinct economic and cultural settings. But in our own time, the thrust of cultural divergence is balanced in Christian thinking against the ecumenical movement and a yearning for some greater unity of Christian mind and purpose. Against this background Hastings' apparently radical approach to the received tradition of the West testifies to an ancient tradition of creative catholicity.

In the latter part of the nineteenth century there began a dramatic shrinking of the world due to the impact of new technologies. It established the background of economic, social and intellectual imperialism from which our modern world still struggles to emerge. Steve Attridge explores the dynamics of this and discerns a similar dynamic in the imaginations of children as they come to terms with the world. In the context of just one minority culture, that of the Inuit, Brenda Lealman sharpens our sense of what may be lost to us if we emerge cynically untouched by the visions of other cultures. But the problems of implicit or explicit imperialism concern all three writers in this section. For all of them it is an issue in the meeting of cultures and the shaping of personal visions. Be it a matter of conception or misconception, the process is continuous from the meeting of cultures to the encounters of children with the world around them. On the matter of the truth or adequacy of these encounters, there are relevant chapters elsewhere in the book. In the final section of the book when Robert Jackson talks about the arts of interpretation, he is very far from talking about arbitrary subjectivity. He is concerned to establish a method. Clive Erricker's emphasis on the personal functions of myth-making offers an implicit standard in its concern for personal health and social well-being. The two writers perhaps offer different kinds of test. However, both have some relation to the concerns of Hastings, Attridge and Lealman. It is that the reality of interpersonal and intercultural encounters is a matter of continuously adjusted responses and that some responsibility for these lies within the orbit of education.

PETER HASTINGS

CROSSING THE BOUNDARIES IN CULTURE AND RELIGION

While teaching in Uganda, the author encountered the emotional responses, the verbal and body-language of other cultures. As a committed Roman Catholic he spells out the challenge of all this to the thought-forms of a Christianity and a political outlook grounded in the European tradition. Christianity must rediscover its capacity to re-think the language and ideas of the faith; but this is not just a matter of appreciating the diversity of hitherto alien cultures and thought-forms, or of admitting their de facto representation in the United Kingdom. It is a matter of building new dimensions of change and growth into our own home-grown educational outlooks. In the context of his experience as a head teacher in England, the author considers how all pupils might be liberated towards more creative patterns of self-understanding, aspiration and faith.

In the context of religious education, why do we reach out to other cultures? Is it to learn from them, to teach them, to pool the thoughts of the whole human race in a shared search for truth, to present them with a packaged "answer"? And, if the last, has this packaged answer any more real roots in our culture than in any other? Are we approaching tribes, generalised groups called cultures, peoples, or individual persons?

In discussion of these questions I must declare an interest; I am a believing and practising Roman Catholic and this rightly affects my standpoint, preoccupations and understanding of values. I do not accept as Christian the authoritarian procedures of Rome, the manipulation of children or adults (although I have no doubt that we can each be found guilty of manipulation) nor, as an educator, would I attempt to hand over a definitive packaged answer to any question. I would hope to be establishing a desire to search for truth, to increase the participation of all in the activities of knowing and loving, which I believe to be the already existing participation of every person in the life of the Trinity, and to enable each person to be open to the question, if and when it comes, "What do you think of Christ?" All those rooted in a revealed religion have the strength and the handicap that this brings. All that I write is in this context.

CONTRASTS

Long before I went out to Africa I was deeply interested in the history and rights of African peoples. I was a member of the Africa Bureau, wrote articles in a small newspaper I then owned in opposition to the imposition of the Central African Federation, took Dr. Hastings Banda (as he then was) on a short speaking tour, and was asked by Dr. Banda to run an opposition newspaper in Salisbury, studied the position of colonial protectorates in international and constitutional law, and advised Benedicto Kiwanuka (later the first Prime Minister of Uganda and finally the Chief Justice murdered by Amin) who helped to advise the deposed Kabaka.

Alongside this I attempted to build up a picture of African history. The "African" history taught in Africa was nothing more than the history of the European exploration, conquest and administration of Africa. This was the equivalent of describing an account of the Viking raids, wanderings and conquests in England as a "History of England". To replace this I burrowed in the recorded versions of tribal oral traditions, anthropologists' accounts of tribes, such archaeological records as I could lay my hands on and the Hakluyt Society volumes. It was slow work and much at a very introductory level. Nevertheless it helped me to appreciate something of the antiquity, growth, stability and continuing legal traditions of Africa's past kingdoms.

I thought that all this constituted a good preparation for teaching history, and perhaps some theology (I had been a speaker for the Catholic Evidence Guild) in East Africa, but most that I had read and learned was of "cultures", "legal systems" and generalised "peoples". When I started a three year contract as a teacher in pre-Amin Uganda and met "persons" acting as individuals within a culture of which I had barely touched the outer skin, I rapidly suffered shocks. I told a class a tragic and painful story and the room was filled with a great burst of laughter. Startled and puzzled, I suggested tears as more appropriate. Embarrassed, one student said: "You told the story so vividly - we laugh when something is vivid, even though it is not funny". This was reinforced shortly after when I heard of a man, in the midst of a laughing crowd, roaring with laughter while he wrapped a carpet round a woman screaming from the pain of her burning clothes.

In those same weeks I drove one night to Kampala. On the road ahead there were cars parked facing me with headlights full on. Going cautiously through the glare I was just able to swerve, stop and halt the traffic behind me to save a man lying drunk in the road. The occupants of the parked cars were leaning against them and watching. I called to them and asked for help in carrying the man to safety on the side; they all jumped into their cars and drove away. I almost physically forced a man at a mud built roadside tavern to help me. I recounted this to a colleague who told me that he, driving the same road, had seen a badly driven tractor topple sideways, pinning the driver beneath it. He stopped and tried to extract the man but could not do so. There was a crowd of locals watching from the bank's height and he called to them for help. They took to their heels. I was told that the reason for this apparently unfeeling behaviour was that any African assisting such a casualty would be accepting family obligations for the future, and might end up paying not only, like the Good Samaritan, hospital charges but the school fees of the injured man's children and much more besides over the years. Compare this with Christ's parable and one can see that strong social pressures made the Samaritan's role too stringent to accept - even in this area, where most of the local people were Christians, and many were second or third generation Christians.

I had to recognise that the emotional responses, the body language and verbal language with which persons expressed these, together with the fabric of social customs and obligations and the behavioural responses which these made acceptable, were not simply statements of familar thought in a different language from my own, but expressions of a cultural outlook with which I had no contact, concerned with ideas I had never met and lacking language corresponding to the ideas grown in me by my upbringing. I could not reach persons without a common culture, theirs or mine or a shared hybrid.

Not body language alone, but verbal language was missing. Words seemed to be missing - my African colleagues were either well or dying: there seemed no way of saying that one was a bit under the weather or having an unpleasant attack of malaria. Even the purpose of language was different. A European asks a question in the hope of obtaining information; an African may, in his cultural context, answer the question in order to conceal that information. Either way it was a shock when transfered into the other language. If I, speaking Luganda, asked in the standard greeting (regretably about the extent of my Luganda): "Where have you come from?" I accepted happily the answer: "From over there", followed by: "Where are you going to?" "Over there." The Baganda do not hand out in any casual manner information which might give another power over them. If I spoke in English, I forgot their cultural response and would be irritated by "Over there"; in English I wanted facts. For them too it was a shock; one man asked me, in English: "Where have you come from?" When I, in my English culture, replied: "From Kisubi", he appeared to have been struck on the jaw; when he had recovered and asked: "Where are you going to?" my reply, "To Kigezi", produced a stunned silence. Only afterwards did I suddenly realise what I had done.

RECOGNISING DIVERSITY?

In those days we were still locked in the belief that the intellectual world was confined to Europe, while laughing at old Imperial China for considering that there was nothing of importance outside China. The "Club", to which I did not belong, was confined to Europeans. Outside the school community or the University, we met at first no Africans socially at the houses of our friends. The school in which I taught was a Catholic mission school, very much in the shadow of Belloc's "Europe is the Faith and the Faith is Europe". In that mind-frame there were few who saw a need for crossing culture barriers, unless for others - to be ruled by us, accept our ways, be baptised, wear clothes, learn table manners and an acceptable European language. So we taught English literature, English and European history, European art, debased notions of English citizenship and English political and constitutional practice. In the course of this we gave them English as a bridge between the tribes and as an international language, which had its value, but atrophied the development of their own languages and so of the thought of their people.

We know how Matteo Ricci and his fellow Jesuits failed to carry Rome into the project of stating the Christian message in the terms of Chinese thought and culture, and regret the wasted centuries since. Now the mood is changing. Buddhism, Hinduism and the Tao have come into fashion. In the present mood of the world even we British, perhaps even Rome, can see the need for the study and understanding of cultures as different from our own as the Indian and far Eastern cultures. These have the status given by art and antiquity; we recognise their importance. We may not do very much in consequence; but, at least in theory, we accept that these may have something to teach us. So we should. John the Baptist was named by Christ as his forerunner, one who was preparing the way of the Lord and announcing that the fullness of time was come. I was raised in the tradition that there were many other forerunners; that, through the ages of man's existence, there had been a preparation and that all these preparations and forerunners were to enable the nations to fulfil themselves in Christ: Socrates, Aristotle and Vergil were suggested - each a source of our Graeco-Roman culture.

In these days we are able to recognise Buddha and Confucius no less than Socrates. These would not be forerunners preparing for the fulfilment by Christ of the Judaic culture into which He was born, nor of our culture, formed by Graeco-Roman philosophy, theology and law, but for the fulfilment of theirs. So a trickle has begun of those who are attempting to cross the barriers and live the implications of Christ's message as these might be seen in the fulfilment of another culture. Such was the work of Bede Griffiths, once a Benedictine monk in England and in Scotland, in his ashram, offering Christ to the East to fulfil itself in Him in its own way, and offering us insights from the East that we had lost or never had. If we accept our share, we may find value in the undefined expanses which have gone from our sight through the grinding of the syllogism and of ever more exclusive definitions.

Bede Griffiths offers us an example of what is for our gain:

> In Asia we are confronted with the great tradition of an ancient wisdom, which is part of the inheritance of our common humanity. The question is, how do we relate this ancient wisdom, this perennial philosophy as it has been called, to our own tradition of Christian faith?

> In the first place Asian religion challenges us in our very conception of God. Christianity, and with it the other Semitic religions, Judaism and Islam, all believe in a personal God, a creator who transcends the world and rules it from above... In the Asian religions, on the other hand, Buddhism does not allow for a creator God at all. Chinese religion speaks rather impersonally of Heaven (tien) and of Tao, the Way. Hinduism, though it allows for a creator God, prefers to speak of Brahman, the infinite, eternal reality beyond word and thought, which is the origin and the end of the universe.

> Perhaps the essential difference between the two outlooks is that for the Semitic religions God is essentially transcendent, separate from the world, while in Asian religions, God, or the first principle of being, is essentially immanent. It is the 'ground' of being, the inner reality which sustains the whole creation. Thus the Upanishads, the earliest text we have in Hinduism, says: 'In the beginning this' (meaning the whole universe) 'was Brahman, one only without a second'. This language is often interpreted as a form of pantheism, but in reality it is not pantheism, by which is meant that all is God, but pan-en-theism, which means that God is in all things. This is strictly orthodox Christian doctrine. St.Thomas

Aquinas, a doctor of the middle ages, asks in what sense God is in all things, and he answers that God is in all things first of all by his power, because he 'upholds all things by the word of his power'. But then he says he is not in all things at a distance, because there is no distance in God. He is therefore in all things by his presence. He then says he is not present in all things by a part of himself, as there are no parts in God, therfore he is in all things by his essence. In other words, God the creator is in every particle and sub-particle of matter, in every living thing and in every human being by his very essence. For a Christian this means that the Trinity is in the whole creation, in every part of it. Oriental doctrine helps us therefore to realise an often forgotten aspect of our own Christian faith." [1]

These cultures, of which notice is now taken, have the status and prestige given by art, great buildings and thousands of years of written records and literary achievements. What about the smaller and less articulate cultures? Are they recognised too? I remember first thinking of this when a Dominican priest and friend, with wide experience of Africa, sadly mused to me that the missionaries he knew were unable to understand the notion of the ritual killing and eating of kings in certain tribes as being a part of the long preparation of Africa for the reception of the message of Christ. Similarly, the British troops that stormed into Benin in order to rescue missionaries and found every roadway lined with the bodies of the dead, were unable to understand that this came from an idea of sacrifice for which the missionaries ought to have viewed their message as the completion and fulfilment. Instead, from the viewpoint of our culture, it was simply seen as mindless cruelty and produced the title: "Benin - City of Blood".

CATHOLIC REFLECTIONS

A major problem for all Christian churches was, and is, how to offer Christ's message to Africans in the context of their own language and culture while leaving the philosophy and theology of the Greeks and Romans behind in Europe. Christ's message had, in its first years, to be separated from the Jewish culture and explored within the European, it now needs to be separated from that Graeco-Roman culture of Europe and explored within the very different cultures of Africa and Asia. That requires the recognition that the Graeco-Roman edifice built in Europe is not part of the message Christ brought but, at most, one culture's expression of it; that African tribes have their own valuable cultures through which to develop a different, but equally valid, expression of that message; that this requires language, African language - at Pentecost each person heard the simple, undeveloped message in his or her own tongue, not in the ancient language of the Jews nor in any international tongue such as Greek or Latin.

Some of the difficulties facing missionaries in translating their message into African languages are discussed by Professor Hastings of Leeds University.[2] The message that missionaries took to Africa was not the plain, unvarnished message of Christ; it was the message of Christ, brooded over and amplified through the linguistic and artistic exploration of 2000 years of European cultural development. Professor Hastings presents a picture of the choice and imposition of words by early missionaries and translators to represent European concepts to Africans for whom those concepts did not exist, and for whom the subsequent understanding of the imposed words probably did not exist either; surprisingly he even offers a slight defence of the use of incomprehensible words.

Uncomprehended words acquire their own meanings and, far from spreading the culture out of which they originally emerged, may become the bastion of something utterly opposed to the aims of that culture. Hitler and Stalin were "democratically" elected by popular votes. Even by the end of the last century Sir Henry Maine had shown that "popular government" in Latin America, with regimes installed by the army and ruling by the power of the army, while retaining the trappings and the language of Britain or of France, was the product of a different culture in which the British or French models could not be nurtured; so it has remained until this day.

In our own land it may reasonably be asked what "democratic" means in a system in which a government elected by little more that a third of the votes available can carry through nation shaking changes in the teeth of the representatives of the remaining two thirds. Perhaps popular government exists in neither Europe nor Latin America, but to use the words associated with the structures as though they represent the same realities in each system is to destroy communication. Certainly the subsequent history of former British territories in Africa does not suggest that the political ideas the British, in their culture, imagined that they were packaging were actually those received by Africans in theirs.

There is a fascinating account of a very courageous attempt to do these things; to slough off the Graeco-Roman skin and to offer the message of and about Christ, stripped down to its original bones, to a pagan people in their own terms to clothe in the flesh of their own culture.[3] This people is the Masai, a naked cattle people who have rejected European culture and will walk in Nairobi viewing it as European tourists might view Katmandu. Vincent Donovan was able to recognise in Masai actions the expression of the very ideas he believed that he had been sent to bring. When a Masai son quarrels with his father, wishes for forgiveness and is granted it, he comes with his friends to his father who spits upon him; it is the spittle of forgiveness and signifies what it achieves as Christians believe that water does in baptism.[4] In the same way, a handful of grass offered and accepted between disputing Masai is a sign of peace, indeed it is peace as the spittle is forgiveness. [5]

Respecting this culture as having its own fulfilment in Christ and its own expression of that fulfilment, Donovan took them from Abraham to Christ. Like so many matters of importance, that was simple but not easy, requiring great integrity. He spoke of the High God, who is not a tribal god but God for all tribes, and is the God for whom Abraham had to leave his land to find, and now the search is for the Masai. "This story of Abraham - does it speak only to the Masai? Or does it speak also to you? Has your tribe found the High God?" Donovan, about to give a glib answer, suddenly thought of the tribal gods of the French and the English and the Americans, who are always on their side and against their foes; he had to reply: "No, we have not found the High God. My tribe has not known him. Let us search for him together." [6]

Finally, he respected this culture so totally that the Eucharistic liturgy that he gave to them was simply the account of Christ's words and action with the bread and wine on the night before He died; all else was for the Masai to express and each village had its own expression. [7] This was a very sensitive approach. Back in this country, what have we learned? Certainly there is a considerable, but far from universal, movement towards dialogue with cultures other than our own as both necessary and desirable. The Catholic community, perhaps unsurprisingly, is still ambivalent, but is producing some very open thinking with which most concerned with Religious Education in a multi-cultural society, other than those who are fundamentalist, would agree:

> First of all we must foster the concept of Britain as a multi-cultural, multi-faith society - a pluralist society in which different communities have equal rights and deserve equal respect. This is especially important because British racism is reinforced by ethnocentric attitudes which treat Muslims, Hindus, Sikhs as strange or exotic outsiders... Secondly, children must over the years be given sufficient information about the major world religions to enable them to relate to these faith communities as a familiar part of their world. Bits of information can actually be counter-productive - reinforcing the notions of other faiths as strange and different - even funny. Most important, however, as early as possible our children must begin to learn the art of dialogue - sharing their stories and hearing from others their different stories... The difficulty is that we have so few educational contexts in which Catholic children and children of other faiths can be together and get to know one another and in which appropriate discussions of another's religious traditions can be fostered as a natural part of the learning process. In this respect, Catholic schools which for various reasons have accepted pupils from other faith communities have a particular potential for creative experiments in multi-faith education." [8]

This recognition of many cultures, of their value and dignity, must be important, but does it in fact focus our attention on the obvious - even if previously ignored - ethnic cultures and divert each culture from the recognition of its own internal diversity? When those we meet wear different clothes, are different colours, speak different languages, it is not difficult to recognise that these differences need consideration and acceptance, that those with different backgrounds must work at the interface if relationships are to grow and peace and love be fostered.

At present multi-cultural concern is really multi-ethnic concern, and that is multi-colour concern. All this is vital; but is concentration on these concerns blinding us to an equally urgent problem even closer to home? A friend of mine was, some forty years ago, particularly interested in the number of mixed-racial Catholic marriages in the U.S.A. between black and white partners. She remarked on the comparative stability of these marriages compared with marriages of unmixed race. She believed that this was achieved because the clear differences between the partners had forced a hard look at the adjustments which had to be made by each for the other's culture. In the course of that hard look many differences were recognised which might otherwise have emerged awkwardly later; whereas a white Catholic doctor's son marrying a white Catholic doctor's daughter might simply not consider the possible existence of the cultural differences, some very deep, which almost every couple possess, until great hurt and harm had been done.

It may be that our eyes in this country, whichever may be our own culture, are so fixed on those whose appearance clearly indicates another culture, that we are blind to those within our own doors - our children. There are many parents today concerned at their failure, and the failure of teachers from whom they may expect help, to transmit to their children their family culture as they see it: Sikh, Moslem or Christian, Presbyterian or Catholic. It may be at first hurtful, yet ought we not to recognise that our children may meet, and choose to grow into, a culture different from our own - and still love us and we them? Education, including religious education, is not only to help us to tolerate the culture of others, but also to enable us to challenge and change or even reject that into which we are born.

We can be very obtuse about recognising a different culture. Mine is, or was, legal with a dusting of old Catholic county, Ampleforth and Oxford, holidays with jealously sought privacy, reading and walking hills, officer and being my own boss, and very competitive. This has been an influential culture, perhaps, but not one that could be regarded as the common inheritance of the British people. Yet it was so regarded, with many bows towards the altars of Shakespeare, Jane Austen, Constable, Habeas Corpus and the singularly misdescribed "democracy".

So, when I became a headteacher and saw before me all those delightful faces and all white like me, despite all that I had been through and said, I found myself offering them a curriculum that would produce something resembling my culture. Then I wondered why there were elements of disaffection. There before me were cultures I had not recognised, and, if I had, would have regarded them as inferior to my own, not acknowledging their values and merits and achievements. There were Irish Catholics, with their own sub-cultures; there were engineering, council house, "clevers are not liked in our part of the town" cultures; horse cultures (including racing), football cultures and endless others. Suddenly I recognised this, and what was I to do? I remembered Schumacher's advice: "Find out what they are doing and help them to do it better". I attempted to act on this; whether I succeeded is another matter, but I certainly became as proud and delighted with the riding instructor, the jockey, the dedicated plasterer and the racing car builder as with those who achieved what I had originally offered in the way of, perhaps narrow, academic success.

The consequence of this was that I was felt to be encouraging children to develop career prospects and lifestyles with which parents were not always happy as being outside their own culture. However, every child will grow these days into a culture different from that of parents. Since the 1944 Education Act every generation has become more highly educated and qualified, academically or technically, than the one before it. Additionally, vast and indigestible opportunities have flooded the young - the car, the package holiday, electronics, the computer. All this has inevitably produced new youth cultures which parents, teachers and - in the context of religious education - churches, have to recognise, study, accept and speak to in words and images which have meaning for the recipients.

In a society which has increasingly departed from adult religious activity while demanding conformity to religious practice on the part of its children, the intellectual search on which those children now embark may cause considerable shock to parents with a religious affiliation, but a shock which perhaps ought to be changed to a cry of welcome. "Many a man, brought up in the glib profession of some shallow form of Christianity, who comes through reading Astronomy to realise for the first time how majestically indifferent most reality is to man, and who perhaps abandons his religion on that account, may at that moment be having his first genuinely religious experience." [9] This does not apply only to those with glib and shallow religious experiences.

In no field is the recognition and addressing of the new cultures born under our noses more urgent and emotive than in religious education. Images from the past continue to speak the thought of the past and sometimes misrepresent the thought of the past. Christians took over from the Egyptians the picture of the Judgement and the mouth of Hell, an image that I suspect is with us still and that we could well have done without. On the other hand, the picture of the Ancient of Days, with a big white beard, has certainly lost its significance as a representation of wisdom and strength, as of Charlemagne, at 200 years old (really of timeless age) cleaving his way through his foes. Now, such a representation is not understood and has entered the comic area.

Are these images part of a culture that this generation of young can accept? The costumes? The crowns (Do our children really have an idea of Kingship? Are they republicans?)? Will the picture of a child bridegroom leading the swathed figure of his child bride on a string attract or repell? What of the cults of private miraculous visions? Lay these alongside the images of the young world - the music , the hair, the dress - can the one pass to the other? The Sacred Heart already appears as a gang badge on the backs of leather jacketed, foul-mouthed thugs. If we need images then they must be images acceptable to this new culture and convey the intended message with weight - not be received as a bad joke. Will the culture of today's young give popular nourishment to the images we offer?

What should we do? I suggest, and not just for Christians, that we might consider something on the lines of Vincent Donovan's work with the Masai. We ask for creative thought in writing, in art, in music, in drama - why should we not give to the young who have their own culture, like it or not, the year of decultured exposition, questioning and discussion that Donovan gave and then say: "Clothe that in your own expression"?

The results would be varied and some might be startling; the details, perhaps, a nightmare for dedicated liturgical lawmakers. There are many who are fearful of change, however controlled that change may be. The thought of uncontrolled change, leading literally God knows whither, might send some into a dead faint because they trust neither the thought processes and judgement of believers other than themselves nor, as Christians would hold, Christ's promises that He and the Spirit will guide us always. I am not afraid since I actually believe those promises and accept that it is not for me to know the outcome. In fact, for whatever faith and for whatever the aim of any religious educator, the task of helping and encouraging the young to evolve, with their elders or without them, new expressions for new cultures is vital; one does not put new wine into old wineskins.

I have written as I have confessed, from the position in one of the many subcultures of the Catholic church, but I believe that the same problems face all. Whether in England, Wales or Ireland, in the Punjab, Pakistan or Bengal, if we are to live together in peace and dignity, we must try, by crossing culture barriers, to understand and respect each other. As urgently, if we have truth we wish our young to consider in the rapidly changing context of knowledge and lifestyles in which we all live, we must accept that we need to change to produce expressions that will be nourished by new cultures and, in return, nourish them.

I will leave the final comment to a possibly surprising source:

> "There are some people," Smiley declared comfortably,"who, when their past is threatened, get frightened of losing all they thought they had, and perhaps everything they thought they were as well. Now I don't feel that one bit. The purpose of *my* life was to end the time I lived in. So if my past were still around today, you could say I'd failed......Frightened people never learn, I have read. If that is so, they certainly have no right to teach." [10]

REFERENCES

1. Griffiths (1989) p.5.

2. Hastings (1989) pp. 98-121.

3. Donovan (1982) p. 30.

4. Donovan (1982) p. 59.

5. Donovan (1982) p. 121.

6. Donovan (1982) pp. 44-6.

7. Donovan (1982) pp. 119-28.

8. Religious Education in a Diverse Society (1987)

9. Lewis

10. Le Carré

BIBLIOGRAPHY

Donovan, V.J (1982)	*Christianity Rediscovered, An Epistle from the Masai,* London, SCM Press.
Griffiths, B (1989)	*Christianity in the Light of the East,* The Hibbert Lecture 1989, quoted by kind permission of the Trustees of The Hibbert Trust. (Copies are available from the Hibbert Trust, 14 Gordon Square, London WC1H OAG, £1 post free.)
Hastings A (1989)	*African Catholicism, Essays in Discovery,* London, SCM Press.
Le Carré (1991)	*The Secret Pilgrim,* London, Hodder & Stoughton
Lews, C.S. (1993)	*Miracles,* Fount Paperbacks
Maine, H (1899)	*Popular Government,* London, John Murray.

Religious Education in a Diverse Society, a paper prepared by a Working Party for the attention of the Catholic Association for Racial Justice and the Committee for Community Relations of the Bishops Conference of England and Wales, March 1987.

Peter Hastings is currently an Associate Fellow in the Department of Arts Education at the University of Warwick. Widely travelled, with an enormous range of work-experience, he was for twenty-one years Head of Bishop Bright Grammar School and its successor, the Trinity Comprehensive School, in Leamington Spa. He there participated in the Schools Council Music Project and the Gulbenkian Arts in Schools Project, while pioneering new courses in Theology, Philosophy and Theatre Studies.

STEVE ATTRIDGE

FICTIONS OF OTHER CULTURES

Justifying his approach to spirituality as the quest for personal integration and wholeness, the author sees spirituality in education as, 'a shared set of concerns between those educative processes which seek to inform, change and enhance the lives of children in our schools'. At the heart of this pervasive spirituality there is an encounter between identity and otherness. This theme is explored first as an encounter between West and East in the writings of De Quincey, disclosing ethnocentricity and a tendency of such narratives to mythologise ideas of the self and the world. Pursuing the theme into the experiences of childood, the author explores imaginative story-making as the reciprocal force through which the child (using symbol and metaphor) organizes experience of the world and is organized by it. The author demonstrates this active spirituality of childhood in some vivid examples, showing the importance of meanings that children apprehend and share with us in the form of story.

Ged saw...a fearful face he did not know, man or monster, with writhing lips and eyes that were like pits going back into black emptiness....In silence, man and shadow met face to face, and stopped.

Aloud and clearly, breaking that old silence, Ged spoke the shadow's name, and in the same moment the shadow spoke without lips or tongue, saying the same word: 'Ged.' And the two voices were one voice.

Ged reached out his hands, dropping his staff, and took hold of his shadow, of the black self that reached out to him. Light and darkness met, and joined, and were one......He laughed. 'The wound is healed,' he said, 'I am whole, I am free.' Then he bent over and hid his face in his arms, weeping like a boy. [1]

Coming at the end of Ursula Le Guin's *A Wizard of Earthsea* the above passage is the apotheosis of a distinct genre in twentieth century fantasy literature, that in which the puzzle of the self is a constituent element of plot and action. Ged's journey to the farthest reaches of Earthsea is, of course, an inward journey, and the central quest is not for a belief, a god or an ideology, but for integration and wholeness, the coexistence of ostensible contradictions within a human form. Ged, whose name is a stroke of the pen away from God, is only truly Ged when he names the shadow as himself. The symbolism of the shadow self is not part of the story of Ged, but is the story. Also, the use of sentence structures, such as 'And the two voices were one voice" and the incantatory repetitions in sentences like "Light and darkness met, and joined, and were one." clearly align the story with a tradition of sacred storytelling. Having embraced the Other, the "man or monster", the shadow self, Ged himself becomes a metaphor of wholeness, as his friend, Vetch realises:

> And he began to see the truth, that Ged had neither lost nor won but, naming the shadow of his death with his own name, had made himself whole: a man: who, knowing his whole true self, cannot be used or possessed by any power other than himself, and whose life therefore is lived for life's sake and never in the service of ruin, or pain, or hatred, or in the dark. [2]

The story is, I would argue, as much a spiritual story as it is a fantasy adventure novel. In saying this, the term "spiritual" is always in danger of collapsing into generalities. For it to have some useful currency it is necessary to give the term some boundaries. The Oxford English Dictionary catalogues its etymological complexity, but among the many entries under "spiritual" are: "applied to material things, substances, etc., in a figurative or symbolical sense;.... of transcendent beauty or charm;.... characterised by or exhibiting a high degree of refinement of thought or feeling."[3] Whilst such entries do not help to define the term specifically, they do suggest an approach to it. Specifically religious and aspects of secular education, particularly in the arts, may both lay pedagogical claim to the making and understanding of figurative and symbolical meanings, the transcendent, and refinement of thought and feeling. Given this etymo-logical common ground, it may be useful to think of the spiritual as a shared set of concerns between those educative processes which seek to inform, change and enhance the lives of children in our schools.

Ged's shadow self is an image of Otherness, and my purpose in this chapter is to suggest the broad context of ethnocentricity in the literary encounter between the West and the East. I shall also discuss how the Otherness engendered by such narratives is paralleled in childhood encounters between self identity and otherness which find expression in story. At the heart of these processes is a tendency to mythologise about ideas of a self and the world it inhabits. This tendency, often dependent upon metaphor in story as a generator of meaning, has implications for a distinctive view of religious education. I am also concerned to claim the need for a greater attention given to the culture of childhood, which is both principal victim and recipient of adult meanings in the family, schools and the world beyond. By attention, I do not mean looking at what and how children learn through the myopic lens of our own pedgagogical preferences, but giving an enhanced status to the meanings children make and occasionally share with us, through story.

OTHERNESS

Edward Said's book, *Orientalism*, was published in 1978.[4] It has been very influential on thinking and writing about the concepts of Occident and Orient and has generated supportive and reactive viewpoints. Said's basic premise is that since the Middle Ages,

46

Western culture has largely written about, governed and shaped the Orient as the "Other." The effect of this is to fix its inhabitants in the position of object, thereby confirming the subject, powerful position for Westerners, who retain a cultural and narrative authority. Essentially, a demonology is created, a myth of Otherness in which individuals and whole cultures are potential threats unless governed by the civilised West. Said is not discussing overtly racist or jingoistic utterances, but supposedly more neutral works, such as history, philology, administration, as well as literature, which collectively form a discourse, a "style of domination". The traffic between imaginative, academic and administrative conceptions of the Orient conspire to relegate it to a position of inferiority, a demon which is there not to be cast out but to be taught its place. What is insidious about this, Said argues, is that it is not a specifically conscious activity, but is embedded in the very language, methodologies, scholarship and administration of Western culture. This constitutes a powerful cultural myth within which, as I shall indicate, individuals can create their own personal mythology.

In the nineteenth century, the etymology of "Orient" assumed pejorative associations. To "orientalise" meant to make vague, loose, especially in the realms of thought, as opposed to Western ostensibly pragmatic, hard headed rational thought.[5] Orientalism works in a variety of ways: fixing peoples in an unchanging past tense so that they are seen to exist outside "civilised" history; making of them a textual entity; creating them through simple oppositions (eg. black and white); denegrating the cultural practices and religious beliefs of indiginous peoples; writing of people as children, thereby naturalising colonial relationships in terms of parent and child, teacher and pupil. This is a slow, historical process, occasionally sharpened by warfare during which the metaphorical and rhetorical languages of antagonistic belief systems erupt, as I have argued elsewhere.[6] The assumed adulthood of the West confronts the supposedly volatile infancy of the East. What happens in the orientalising process is the creation of a story within and from which individuals, communitites and even nations behave "as if" the story were true. I take this to be the case also with religious belief and practice, within which behaviour is governed by the moral, ethical and practical tenets of a story or group of stories which have defined, illustrated and perhaps illuminated the given religion. As such, narrative content and conventions are metaphors for the idealised life, be it Christian, Moslem or Hindu.

What is at stake here is not only how what we call narrative mobilises meaning, but what it may reveal about possibly unconscious tendencies - in individuals, cultures, and relations between the two. As Michael Bell states: "The shaping of experience by narrative, indeed the very impulse to tell stories, may suggest primordial, but subliminal, processes underlying even the apparently independent planes of reason or evidence."[7] This "impulse" has, I think, a double effect. Narrative suggests something technical, a conscious manipulation of language, usually according to certain rules and conventions, which are then availabe to criticism. Indeed, it is the assumed existence of recognisable structures and codes in narrative upon which much contemporary critical theory stakes its ground. These elements are the "evidence" that narrative is present, and is available to the scrutiny of reason. It may also be that the more nebulous "primordial" and "subliminal" elements which inform the making of narratives also constitute some kind of evidence and are discernible to certain kinds of criticism, albeit speculative and provisional. It could be said that certain readers and critics of religious

47

narratives are primarily concerned with what is subliminal and possibly latent in the text, with what is not specifically articulated but is implicit.

Critics of Orientalism often stress the subliminal impulses which are taken to inform certain writings. To be more specific, I shall consider one text, Thomas De Quincey's *Confessions of an English Opium Eater*,[8] to suggest how a personal mythology is an informing presence in the book, and that this has implications for values and beliefs in education. *Confessions* was written in 1821, in the context of the opium wars when the "problem" of China was a subject of much public debate. De Quincey is premised by the title of the book as the quintessential opium eater, the English addict imprisoned by an Oriental vice, and the book is both an articulation of the addictive hell and, as the term "Confessions" suggests, a purgatorial and rhetorical attempt at release from that state, or at least from the isolation of it. The theological associations of De Quincey's "confessions" ground what is a literary text within a spiritual framework. For a confession to be authentic it has to be, in some sense, "true", and by borrowing a Christian term, writing for a secular market and seeking to engage the Chinese "problem," De Quincey's "truth" will be not only a private confession but a public pronouncement, uttered with the authority of someone who is both a man of letters and an addict whose suffering constitutes an experiential knowledge of the exotic but dangerous hell that is for him, in some fundamental sense, China. As the educated, suffering "eater" of opium, which acts as a metaphor for China itself, De Quincey has experienced all, and will now share the story.

In the *Confessions*, metaphors of integration, development and progress are associated with the West, metaphors of decay and stasis associated with the East. The accumulation of such metaphorical patterning creates a discourse of subjugation of the East to the West, a rhetorical map underpinning De Quincey's opium addiction and which suggests that his own development, like that of his nation, has been tainted by contact with the Orient. This is his purpose, conscious or otherwise: to establish difference to the extent that his opium problem may be set at some distance, as part of the problem of the East. Having consumed the worst of the East, he will attempt to rid himself of it with the language and thought of the West in a kind of literary exorcism.

There is a moment in the *Confessions* when De Quincey discusses the problems of defining the happiest period in a man's life. His own was in 1816 and he proposes the term "lustrum" to define such a period. However, lustrum not only means a period of time (four or five years in antiquity) but is believed to be the root of the French luere (to wash) and has the further meaning of purificatory sacrifice, something performed by Roman censors for the people after the census had been taken.[9] These etymologies suggest a ritual of purification, a time of clarity after having ordered things, and we may read the *Confessions* as just this - the ritual of story as a purificatory telling. Into this time of clarity, when De Quincey had ostensibly achieved domestic and mental order in the quietude of his lakeland cottage, enters a figure designated only by race - the Malay:

> The servant who opened the door to him was a young girl born and bred amongst the mountains, who had never seen an Asiatic dress of any sort:....the girl...came and gave me to understand that there was a sort of demon below, whom she clearly imagined that my art could exorcise....In a cottage kitchen...stood the Malay...he had placed himself nearer to the girl than she seemed to relish...as she

gazed at the tiger-cat before her. And a more striking picture there could not be imagined, than the beautiful English face of the girl, and its exquisite fairness, together with her erect and independent attitude, contrasted with the sallow and bilious skin of the Malay, enamelled or veneered with mahogany, by marine air, his small, fierce, restless eyes, thin lips, slavish gestures and adorations....as I had neither a Malay dictionary, nor even Adelung's *Mithridates*,...I addressed him in some lines from the Iliad; considering that, of such languages as I possessed, Greek, in point of longitude came nearest to an Oriental one. He worshipped me in a most devout manner, and replied in what I suppose was Malay. On his departure, I presented him with a piece of opium....I was struck with some little consternation when I saw him suddenly raise his hand to his mouth, and (in the school-boy phrase) bolt the whole...The quantity was enough to kill three dragoons and their horses....[10]

I have quoted at length because it is an important passage, coming at the centre of the book, the core of the *Confessions*. The Malay then constantly reappears as a "fearful enemy" in what De Quincey calls his "Oriental dreams", which are peopled with "unutterable slimy things" and "cancerous kisses".[11] So, the Malay is used in the text as a cause that leads to certain effects, in this case the Oriental poisoning of reason and sleep.

In the passage quoted above the first question to ask is: why is he called the Malay? Why not the Oriental, or Chinese, or Asiatic? Especially given that De Quincey freely uses these terms elsewhere. Perhaps because the word shares the root "mal" (bad) and linguistically resembles malady, or malaise, acting as a metaphor for both De Quincey's opium addiction and for the ensuing inner malady of his dreams. The Malay then comes to signify both obsession and disease, both of which may be said to possess their victims. This reading is supported by the rhetoric of illness and demonology in the passage: "a sort of demon.... sallow and bilious....fiery eyes". The Malay is there at the centre of the *Confessions*, which is De Quincey's story and personal history, a writing out of the addiction as confession and warning to readers who belong to his own culture; is there at the centre of De Qunicey's happiest year, a physical manifestation of the Orient, but one who is also cast as a spiritual agent, the lucifer of his dreams. In this sense the Malay is a sort of metaphorical monster, a Caliban whom even De Quincey's Prosperonian art cannot, as his serving girl assumes, exorcise. His art is in fact language, and he resorts to Greek, a home of rhetoric and linguistic order, but even the *Iliad* cannot make human contact with the Malay, thereby confirming his Otherness and alienation from the cradle of civilised culture.

The Malay "bolts" a huge amount of opium, suggesting immense appetite and this links with later references to De Quicey's dreams, in which a prime fear is of being consumed by the "monstrous scenery" of the East. The cultural myth of a voracious and overpowering east is clearly at work here, but what we are reading, of course, is how that myth has furnished De Quincey's interior landscape. The rapaciousness of the Malay and the monstrous "Nilotic mud" of De Quincey's dreams are part of an imaginary structure, born in culture but borne now by his own psychology. We are now back in the territory of the primordial, the subliminal, but with further points to make about them. The ethnocentricity of the culture which De Quincey inhabited, its writings, paintings, histories, geopolitical theories, creates a climate of ideas which then furnishes further ideas and art works, such as his own. In this sense, we can reasonably say that in some important way, culture becomes personality. The social becomes the personal. The personality acquires and holds beliefs generated by culture and develops them according to its own particular circumstances; in this case, those of the opium addict, with its attendant distortions and caricaturing exaggerations. Here, the subliminal and primordial are not simply nebulous terms indicating an inherent and primitive mind set, nor are they indicative of unconscious recesses which cannot be properly discussed because of their hidden nature. They start to become objects of knowledge, available to criticism and understanding, when we examine their manifestations as stories, writing, telling, and confessions.

Before developing these points further, it is also important to note that De Quincey is a *belles lettres* figure in the literary canon and his works are part of a cultural tradition, studied and reproduced in educational institutions. If we are to understand and teach them properly, we also need to locate their historical contexts and discuss the kinds of beliefs inherent in the rhetorical structure of such works. Moreover, if we are to enhance our understanding of the function of story in relation to experience, we need to match a technical grasp of narrative structure with a speculative awareness of the kinds of impulses, desires and repressions which are latent in a given story.

THE RECIPROCAL IMAGINATION

I have indicated above how the representation of Otherness in a narrative indicates relationships with self and others which are rooted in culture and are then expressed as personal experience. These are essentially imagined relationships, in the sense that they are what Raymond Williams calls "mental conceptions" [12] which hold a tension between "copying" what is there as well as being able to "see" what does not literally exist. These imagined relationships constitute a personal mythology which may give us some clues regarding what it is like to be the teller; how he organises the world symbolically and metaphorically can tell us something of how he organises his own experience and how the creation of a story in turn organizes him. It is a dynamism of reciprococity. In the *Confessions* De Quincey creates the figure of the Malay, already a cultural sign of the decadent East before his book was written, not simply as a metaphor for his worst imaginings, but as the embodiment of them. As the psychotherapist Miller Mair writes, in *Between Psychology and Psychotherapy, a poetics of experience*, we are "used by the metaphors of our culture."[13] but equally, we reveal ourselves in our stories:

> All our stories are expressions of ourselves even when they purport to be accounts of aspects of the world. We are deeply implicated in the very grounds of our story telling. [14]

So we can say that when we use metaphor in story, there is a complex relationship between that which is borrowed from our culture and that which individuates and reveals us, as tellers of the tale. This forms a relational aesthetic between that which is already there and that which is being lived and articulated.

OTHERNESS AND CHILDHOOD

I wish now to consider a child's storytelling in order to see what metaphors and what kinds of Otherness are present, and how these might reveal ways in which the child is "deeply implicated" in the grounds of his own storytelling. The child, J, had evinced great interest in stories from an early age. After his parents separated, when J was 3 years old, he experienced disturbances and traumas which often caused him bewilderment, confusion, and pain. A pattern of stories also evolved. Some were painstakingly written, some were dictated to an adult who acted as scribe, then illustrated by J, and some were taped. One story, which was made into a book and illustrated by J, is called "The Little Boy and the Dragon" and begins:

> Once upon a time there was a dragon. He lived in a cold place. Nobody ever played with him because they thought he would be too fierce. So he went for a walk over the hills and far away. He met a little boy who said he'd been lonely in this world too. They'd both been the same - lonely, lonely.

They befriend each other, partly by sharing jokes, then the boy takes the dragon back to his parents' home. At first they reject the dragon and there is domestic fear and a great deal of hiding and jumping out of windows to escape, but through the boy's persistence the parents learn to accept the dragon as part of the family:

> After twenty days they got used to him. They decided to keep him and lived happily ever after. 'Night night' said the little boy. 'Night night' said the dragon.

Another story, recorded whilst J told it to a friend and an adult concerns a little boy who goes with his parents to the outskirts of a "wild wood" where there is no grass, but lots of "little buggy things." The boy leaves his parents and enters the wood where he meets the hostile "Fungus Mungus", a smelly and ostensibly repugnant creature which is hostile towards the boy. Eventually they become friends and again the boy takes the monster back to his parent's home; they are terrified of Fungus but the boy reconciles them to it, and the domestic gap is bridged. Several other stories retell a variation of this: a family picnic, the little boy leaving his parents(often after they have forbidden him to go into the wood) and going into the wood where he encounters a monster. When J obtained his own dog in reality, the dog became part of the story as the boy's sole companion when he leaves his parents, although J never named the "little boy" as himself. Eventually a moment of shorthand evolved, in which the story was reduced to essences; J simply wrote on a piece of paper: "The monster   J   My dog   daddy mummy". J left the piece of paper on his father's desk and this was the first time he had actually named himself.

What can we make of these stories in terms of metaphor and Otherness? Firstly, it is important to identify what general patterns are manifest in the stories, in order to see how these frame specific elements within them. Clearly, the ritual of telling was significant: establishing that this was story time and place, gathering the necessary materials, such as pen, paper or cassette recorder. This formalising of real time and place is significant in establishing that a particular kind of experience is about to be entered, one which may be part of the flow, or fragmentation, of everyday life, but is also different - in the same way that a framed picture is part of the visual compass of a wall, but draws attention to itself as different, as a focus for a more intense visual experience. For J, the stories were both a private experience (in that they presumably had personal meanings) and a shared ritual, involving a public use of language with himself as storyteller and one or more others as scribe, listener, audience. However, the terms public and private suggest distinct spheres of experience and it is more useful to designate a third area, that of storytelling ritual, in which private and public coalesce and meanings are made which allow the articulation of communal meaning (the surface reality of the story) yet retain the possibility of more private and oblique realities. Arguably, a similar thing happens in religious practices, such as public prayer, readings, talks, though I would not wish here to state any easy equivalance. However, if, as in De Quincey's case, the *Confessions* are a public articulation of personal experiences, then I would claim that the same process can be at work in other forms, such as J's stories. Both require careful reading to discover any hidden agenda. It was also important to J that his stories transcended the ephemeral by being written down, illustrated, made into books or recorded, which suggests a desire to communicate something and give it substantial and lasting shape in a form which does not require the rational and perhaps inappropriate burden of making it explicit.

The content of the stories does suggest definite patterns. In each one the little boy feels compelled to leave the parental domain and enter a threatening environment where he encounters the unknown and unfamiliar, befriends it, returns and acts as mediator so that the family can assimilate the unknown. Like Ged in *A Wizard of Earthsea* it is imperative to the story that the boy is alone at an edge where known reality blurs and the encounter with the monster is both an experience of aloneness and a means of return to the known world, having gained something - new knowledge, a new friend, a newly experienced self. The fracture of J's sense of family and its component relationships meant that he literally had new realities to comprehend in hitherto uncharted territory, and it is surely likely that story offered both the form and the freedom to explore these. It is not that story solves the problem, but it does offer a way of travelling through it.

J's monsters, like the image of the Malay in the *Confessions*, have elements which prefigure the stories themselves. The dragon and Fungus are part of the currency of existing literature which J borrows to furnish his own story. They also embody Otherness - metaphors for that which is unknown, possibly dangerous, yet very much there to be encountered. For De Quincey, it is personally and politically imperative that the Other be represented in ways which confirm his difference and strangeness, although as I have indicated, the writer is actually creating a metaphor for his own mental state, which is also a spiritual state, given the confessional terms with which De Quincey chooses to frame his story. For J, the imperative is reconciliation, and wholeness for the family unit, which in real life, has gone badly awry for him, with an accompanying threat to his sense of self. If both De Quincey and J are "deeply implicated", as Mair states, in their own stories, then we can see contrary impulses at work; in the *Confessions* metaphor is used to establish distance and difference (albeit unsuccessfully) and, in J's stories, it is used to re-establish integration, if only for the duration of the story. Like Ged, J has to claim the monster as his own if he is to survive in any satisfactory way, whereas De Quincey clearly feels survival depends upon keeping the danger firmly outside himself. Metaphors here may be seen as part of a strategy for the management of self. The imaginary relationships in J's stories gain a particular dynamic when we realise that in his own life, certain hitherto real relationships had now become imaginary.

Clearly, the kind of intertextualising I am offering is open to criticism. How can a nineteenth century text by an eminent writer be compared with stories told by a five year old child in the late twentieth century? However, it is precisely these differences which throw into relief similarities, particularly the role of metaphor in story making, and which can help us to be aware of the significance of story in the making of individual identities. The impulse, primordial or otherwise, to tell stories, indicates our common ground, a thread which weaves through history and across cultures, canons and curriculae. It is a fundamental starting point for educators. The storytelling process is what Jack Priestley, in referring to the value of reflection, calls "the ebb and flow of the individual relations with the world."[15] If we can intertextualise individual stories, we are also constructing foundations for interchange between personal mythologies and the world of public and collective stories, and this is perhaps the space in which religious mythologies become pedagogically alive.

I am arguing here too for a view of metaphor which is experientially and phenomenologically based, rather than confined to the terrains of the purely semantic or decorous. The referential status of metaphor is complex, but if we approach metaphors in stories as particular conceptions of the world in ways which I have already outlined, then part of what we are attempting is an imaginative identification with the situation of the teller. If we pursue this process further, then it is not that metaphor constitues a representation of the world, but, for the teller of the story, the world is metaphoric. As Samuel Levin states: "metaphors should be taken literally" if we are to understand a "particular conception, one that transgresses our standard view of reality."[16] It may then transpire that Otherness is ourselves.

References

1. Le Guin, Ursula (1979) pp.164-65

2. Le Guin, Ursula (1979) pp165-66

3. Oxford English Dictionary

4. Said, Edward (1978)

5. Oxford English Dictionary

6. Attridge, Steve (1986)

7. Bell, Michael (1990) p.172

8. De Quincey, Thomas: (ed.1971)

9. Oxford English Dictionary

10. De Quincey, Thomas: (ed.1971) pp.90-91

11. De Quincey, Thomas: (ed.1971) p. 109

12. Williams, Raymond p.158

13.   Mair, Miller p.77

14.   Mair, Miller p.257

15.   Priestley, Jack (1985)

16.   Levin, Samuel p.2

BIBLIOGRAPHY

Attridge, Steve (1986):   "Dis-Oriented Fictions", in *Encounter*, February 1986

Bell, Michael (1990):   "How Primordial is Narrative", in *Narrative in Culture*, ed. C. Nash, Routledge

De Quincey, Thomas: (ed.1971) *Confessions of an English Opium Eater*, Penguin

Le Guin, Ursula (1979):   *A Wizard of Earthsea*, in *Earthsea Trilogy*, Penguin

Levin, Samuel (1988):   *Metaphoric Worlds: Conceptions of a Romantic Nature*, Yale University Press,

Mair, Miller (1989):   *Between Psychology and Psychotherapy* (a poetics of experience), Routledge

Priestley, Jack (1985):   'The Spiritual in the Curriculum', in Souper. P. (ed), *The Spiritual Dimension of Education*, Occasional Papers Series No.2, University of Southampton Department of Education, 1985, pp 27-48.

Said, Edward (1978)   *Orientalism*, RKP, 1978

Williams, Raymond (1979): *Keywords*, Fontana

Steve Attridge is a Lecturer in the Department of Arts Education at the University of Warwick, and has lectured and published on the theme of Orientalism and on children's storytelling. A published poet, he won an Eric Gregory Award for poetry. A Community Playwright in Coventry for two years, he has published a novel based on his six-part drama series for BBC Children's Television. Other commissions are in hand.

BRENDA LEALMAN

DRUM, WHALEBONE AND DOMINANT X: A MODEL FOR CREATIVITY

In the drum-dances and the traditional sculpture of the Inuit there is the pervasive sense of an underlying reality awaiting release. Inuit creativity relates to an underlying mystery that is seen as 'given' and which emerges through the artistic process. Inuit conceptions of creativity contrast with the western which (by celebrating 'artistic intention' and the imposition of images) have become open to accusations of mere mystification and banality. Sadly, Inuit conceptions are now vulnerable to the ready-made meanings of the western mass media, to market forces, and to the treatment of art as a mere commodity. The author finally considers whether the traditional Inuit approach to creativity has any messages for western education. Through the creative imagination (as disturbance of equilibrium, connection-making, and attentive waiting or receptivity) new worlds are made possible.

The raw arctic: towers, spires, ice bastions; mountains, tight folded into each other. Great cliffs and screes, icecaps and glaciers. Nunassiaq, The Beautiful Land, the north eastern territories of Canada. A land of dwarf willows, bilberries and lichens. A land, for some of the year, of half light.

Someone is crouching by the gravelly shore. Over a bone. Old whalebone brittle, cellular. Tasugat is feeling it, stroking it, probing its porous tissues. He says that he is feeling for what is inside the bone. There is a "picture," an image, inside, and he wants it to emerge.

Snow and darkness are closing in. Around the cabin of the cooperative stores there is a pool of yellow light. A woman is going into the stores wearing kamik (snow shoes) and parka. Five feet tall: glossy black plaits and yellow skin. A woman of the Inuit [1] whose ancestors have probably lived in this area for the last 4,000 years. The co-op is steamy warm inside. One part of the shop is set out like a modest art gallery. This settlement on Baffin Island is an important centre of whalebone carving. Whales are no longer hunted by the Inuit, of course, and much of the whalebone that is carved is centuries old. On the shelves are four particularly powerful sculptures.

One is a sculpture of a figure doing a drum dance.[2] Reaching up in ecstasy. Stretched into the other world to bring healing to the people, perhaps, or to implore Sedna, the goddess of the sea, to provide animals for the hunt. The shaman going on a journey?

Next, whale vertebrae fuse into a face with hands or fish flippers at its sides.[3] In the back of the head another tiny face. A spirit figure, tupilak? One of those small evil spirits, often part human and part animal, brought to life by soul robbers through the chanting of magic words? Strange surfacings from the dark regions of the mind.

Then, another whalebone sculpture: a kneeling figure, gazing upwards, defiant, beseeching or terrorfilled. It is hard to know which.[4]

The fourth sculpture is in soapstone,[5] an Eskimo crouching over a seal hole waiting to kill.[6] Waiting for the sound of the seal's breathing. Listening.

Outside the co-op, the cold is brutal. Noahkudluk's dogs are tied up outside his cabin; they howl into the winter.

QUALAUTIK AND GRIEVING

Eesimailyee's dancing figure referred to above holds a qualautik which means "drum" in inuktitut.[7] He is performing a drum dance, a traditional Eskimo art form.

The traditional drum was flat, made from the skin of a walrus or the stomach lining of a whale stretched over a circular frame made out of the ribs of a seal or a walrus. In more recent years, wood has been available for drum frames. Drum dancing, at least in the eastern arctic and Baffin, would usually be the occasion of shamanistic trance. The participants would cover their costumes with amulets - eyes, beaks, claws of ravens - as a protection against evil spirits. With all these dangling from their costumes the people would produce a rattling sound in their throats as they writhed to the beat of the drum. The drummer held the instrument in one hand by a small handle attached to the frame. He stood with his legs apart and knees slightly bent, swaying from side to side as he beat the rim, rather than the skin of the drum, with a short stick of bone. As the rhythm took hold, the drummer fell into a trance. Luke Arna'naaq writes:

> "Traditional drum dances were sometimes called in order to ask a shaman to do something, for example, to find where caribou were located.... When men who had gone for store-bought supplies were long overdue, people would call upon the shaman during the drum dance to find out where the men were."[8]

Magic, the art of influencing and controlling, is intended through the gyrating and the writhing of the drum dance. All is for magic: the raven's claw, the rattling in the throat, the piercing scream. Fearful magic; and behind magic is a protest that the present world is alien and frightening. Grieving that this is so. Magic is part of the dream at the beginning of the process of creating. Magic is invoked because there is dissatisfaction with things as they are. It is invoked to dissolve this world and create a new one. This magic is, perhaps, powerless; but it is the dream that is powerful and all significant, and which offers some insight into Inuit creativity.

The dream is of the possibility of a different world. It is nourished by a sense of incompleteness, by dissatisfaction, by grieving and protest, by fear and pity. The dance is created and it pleads with the spirits and powers of the living cosmos. It is as though the Eskimo drum signifies the beginning of the art process or creativity. In the beginning of art is the dream. It is the dream of the possibility of a new way of being, of a different world.

SANANGUAQ AND CONNECTING

Are there other clues to the nature of Inuit creativity? What are some of the ingredients, for example, of the artistic experience of the sculptor? Note that what is being examined is the artistic or creative experience and process, not aesthetic appreciation or critical discrimination. There is a marvellous piece of sculpture by Pauta of Cape Dorset [9] of an Eskimo sculptor listening to the image inside the stone speaking its shape. This recalls Tasugat's comment noted above. The artist's task is to bring to form the picture, the spirit, in the bone; the sculptor carves a likeness of what is inside the material, allows the image to emerge. Sculptures are sananguaq (sana = making, nguak = likeness) things made or carved, realities created; images brought to form and life, freed from bone and stone.

Kenojuak, a great Baffin artist, was once asked what the inuktitut word for "art" was and she answered: "There is no word for art." [10] There is no word for "art", or for "to create", or for "beauty" in the inuktitut. Sananguaq is the word which signifies "artistic process," creativity. One important element of this process, I am suggesting, is the experience of "connecting". The Eskimo sculptor works in partnership with the material at a deep level of connectedness. The experience of creativity as "waiting on", as gift, appears to be very marked amongst the Inuit. Perhaps, in part, this is because of their persisting primal perception of nature as animistic. The material with which the sculptor is working has its own life and rhythms and these have to be engaged in. Waiting on the material, contemplating it, is an aspect in the artistic or creative process.

Victor Papanek gives a picture of an Eskimo working, exploring his material with his hand, turning it this way and that (the Inuit work omnidirectionally, fully in the round), and asking the material "What do you want to become?" [11] When the sculptor feels the form emerging from the bone, it has to be allowed to fulfil itself.

EVOKING

An important component of the Eskimo art process is beginning to emerge, that of evoking. Sananguaq is, in effect, the process of evoking what is in the depths of creation into new form and being. Inuit sculpture is evoked rather than conceived. The focus is on the reality that emerges, on the integrity of the reality, the energy, that is communicated, opened up and released. It is interesting, of course, that traditionally the Eskimo sees sculpture as process, act, ritual [12] - a process of, as it were, giving permission for another world to break in to this one. Sometimes, as I observed Eskimo sculptors at work and talked to them, I had the feeling that they were begetting sculptures rather than making them - allowing them to be.

Much current western art seems to involve an attempt to produce an object which causes mystification - not mystery. The focus is on the artist's intention and, to a lesser extent, on the receiver's reaction. A load of bricks is delivered to the Tate Gallery so that we can examine the artist's intention. So what? Stuart Brisley picks up a derelict suitcase in Camden and sets it up in a gallery, greasy trousers, underpants and all. We are certainly mystified - nauseated would be more accurate - as he turns out rubbish gathered on waste land.

Take the photographic images of Andres Serrano shown in London.[13] One image,"Piss Christ", is of a crucifix which has been soaked in a tank of urine. "What a marvellous colour urine is,"Coleridge once wrote. Does Serrano's image get beyond that? Is it an attempt at banal sensationalism? Like a Bach prelude played on an electronic synthesizer it hardly grabs at the guts (as worthwhile art should?).

Or wander around a construction by Damien Hurst.[14] His "Acquired Inability to Escape" consists of glass and steel containing an office table and chair: a reflection on being stuck, on impotence. This sort of art remains very much within the rational, conceptualizing processes of the mind; it conforms to a remarkable extent to society's dominant assumptions and expectations - despite frequent loud insistence on its being a "protest" - of irony and disillusionment.

The Inuit artistic process is far closer to the making of pots by the aboriginal Kogi of Columbia. "A clay pot is, of course, the earth itself.... A pot is not thought of as being man-made, but as being granted to the potter."[15]

Kogi "art" is that which has been evoked, given, and which is not for decoration or for sale. It has no meaning which is literal, specific or representational - only import or presence, and power. Inuit sculpture has this, too, despite being on a very small scale... But there are strangers coming up the beach from the arctic sea...

KABLUNAIT
Heavy eyebrows come on the scene. In inuktitut, kablunait means "the people with the heavy eyebrows" white men, in other words. With them come water tanks and electricity but, also conflict, and severe pressures on sananguaq..... Inside Pauloosie's wooden cabin his snow house has been recently abandoned the living room is hot. The television is on. A jigsaw is on the floor. There is the smell of bread baking. His wife is making bannocks following a Scottish recipe handed down through her family over many years.[16] Raw seal meat will probably be eaten with the bannocks. Visual stimulation is coming from crime films, from Mickey Mouse, and from kitsch calendars and biscuit tin pictures.Constructed realities are imposed by television screens - why bother to wait on meaning and interpret, when interpretation comes ready made? Why sit outside in minus 20C of cold, waiting for a chisel to release an image when images are crossing the blue screen at a rate of twelve a minute? Why travel over ice floes to attend to a seal hole when there are fish fingers in the store?

Heavy eyebrows have brought the values of new popular culture and mass media. Values, it often seems, revolving around competition, achievement and status symbols - the antithesis of the traditional values of a hunting and sharing society.

Heavy eyebrows have brought art as object, product, commodity. Art to capture the market. [17] "Yes, dear, that would look very nice in the sitting room. The grey colour will match the blue curtains very well. It will be a marvellous topic of conversation when we have people in." They have brought the sort of art that stands on a plinth: museum art. Interestingly, no traditional Eskimo sculpture has any base for standing on. It was not meant for display purposes but for use, for passing from hand to hand, for touching; then, it would be dropped, or tossed into the sea.

What is the response of Inuit creativity when it is caught up in the interface between cultures? The way ahead is going to demand discernment and a high sense of their own worth if the Inuit are not going to give in to souvenirism, nostalgia and the values of the market place. It is hoped that Inuit sculpture can remain linked to tradition,[18] to the profundity of accumulated intuitive perception and to the mythic, symbolic regions of the psyche. But, at the same time, whilst the left hand feels the way ahead and explores the material with the chisel, the right hand has to wield the mallet and complete the job. That hand must remain deft and must try out the new devices and possibilities which come when one culture reaches beyond its old bounds and creatively meets another. There must be exchange, dialogue and interrogation. Alienation or retreat from a foreign culture, or from the world of technology, solves nothing, leads nowhere.

It is worth remembering, however, that any genuinely creative art does not criticize one set of values or ideology by presenting an alternative set. Rather, the art which has a critical, subversive, prophetic role, is that which communicates mystery. Such art causes a clash between "ananonymous, soulless, immobile and paralysing ('entropic') power, and the life, humanity, being and its mystery." [19]

Significance for Education, with Particular Reference to Religious Education.

Drum dancing and sculpting whalebone somewhere near the North Pole - can these really have anything to do with education in the United Kingdom? Can they in any sense provide a model for creativity in education - for any pedagogical context, but perhaps, particularly, for religious education? If so, how? Why? By creativity or artistic process in this context is meant a quality of education, and not phenomena such as paintings, visual aids and artefacts, nor even necessarily, certain times set apart for "art".

Artistic process is most richly imaged as the patterns of a dance, a configuration of steps and movements. Some of these steps, I suggest, reflect the Inuit experience of artistic process: of grieving, connecting, evoking. These steps of the dance could just as well be named: disturbance of equilibrium, connectionmaking, attentive waiting or receptivity.

Disturbance of Equilibrium

The drum beats out the dream. The drumming tries to defeat the gap between what is and what might be: It expresses dissatisfaction. It disturbs; and through the disturbance comes the dance.

Humankind - and that includes young people in education and religious education classes in schools - needs to articulate dissatisfaction; to recognise and acknowledge the sense of incompleteness, absurdity, uncertainty; to apprehend and express the cruel gap between what is and what appears to be impossibility; to protest against the harshness of life. We need to protest (as Wallace Stevens says) against "the fatal dominant X": against the dominant consumption values of the modern world; against the world's pain and woundedness. We need to interrogate rather than cause alienation.

"The ruddy temper, the hammer
Of red and blue, the hard sound -
Steel against intimation - the sharp flash,
The vital, arrogant, fatal, dominant X."[20]

Dissatisfaction can find release in grieving through art forms as teaching and learning overflow into these and release them through the curve of the body, through the gesture in mime, the papier-mâché mask; through the tensions and resolutions,the balances and imbalances, rhythms and broken fragments of the dance.

MAKING CONNECTIONS

Disturbance of equilibrium needs a context of relationship if it is not to end in sheer anxiety. Thus, back to Tasugat's searching the bone, Pauta's sculptor listening to the stone..... Somewhere deep within Inuit creativity is the experience of connectedness. The Eskimo feel acutely that they are an integral part of their landscape; they are part of the cosmos. They are participators in life's mysteries. Noahkudluk's arms and legs are the rocks the earth, he told me.[21]

If there is to be real creativity in education in the context of religious education, various connections - five at least, I reckon - must be made.

Firstly, teacher and student must connect. They are partners in exploring. (Easy to pretend that this is so when it just is not!) This requires a real mutuality of participation and exposure; a willingness on behalf of the teacher to share her/his processes of thinking and responding; willingness to make space for the innerness of the students. There must be the desire to acknowledge its mystery: to respond to one enigma - story, parable, metaphor, whatever - with another enigma, rather than with analysis or explanation. To sustain metaphor, in other words.

Secondly, the teacher, alongside other teachers, needs to connect with the fashioning of a living metaphysic, a consensual mythos; to have a vital engagement with values and ideals which excite, and which, put before students, excite them too. In other words, which nourish the creative capacities by affirming that we are involved in absurdity, but also in discovering and making sense of it.

Thirdly, there has to be connection with the materials of the artistic process; with silence, words, body, movement, stillness, sound, wood, clay, flesh, line, paint...

Fourthly, there must be awareness that our community is the cosmos not the nation, race or faith group. (Taken seriously, what a difference this should make to curriculum.) And, at the root of connection with the cosmos is sensuality - sheer celebration of the gifts of the sense of touch, of sight, of smell, of hearing and of matter, of direct contact with the planet. Perhaps, if nothing more, religious education can awaken the senses. It can allow space in which to celebrate the texture of skin, of birch bark, cathedral sandstone, mosque tile work; to celebrate the smell of turned earth, of a stone rolled away, of the Sikh langar; the sight of an arti lamp in a dark shrine; of sunlight through a rose window; the sound of cloth rent, of birdsong; of church and temple bells. The world is rich and resonant with beauty.

I am suggesting that religious education has a fifth connection to make, also. Awareness of the connecting ecological self does not mean simply getting to know the patrolled, policed areas of being; it means finding openings, too, into the wild regions. A highly significant area for religious education and one to which Eskimo sculpture points, is that part of consciousness which handles what has been called "cosmic" faith. This has been called "the more intuitive, earth celebrating and participatory manner of experience",[22] The "metacosmic" faith systems on the other hand, are highly developed religions which provide more reflective and philosophically determined world views.[23] Part of connectedness is to be aware of the dialogue between metacosmic and cosmic, between the outer world of humanmade culture and technology, and the mysterious, shadowy, powerful, inner world. Somewhere in religious education there should be room to experience the ground of our innerness in the elements of the universe: in water, earth, air, fire; to reflect on the manifestation of these elements in sun, moon, stars, earth, sky, sea, rocks, trees and animals. Does religious education need to offer some routes back to the cosmic basis of our religions; to the cosmic symbolism which is found first in the elements? Do we need to rediscover our own paganism, that which we have brought with us from our country village (pagus), and not be ashamed of it? To get in touch with the elemental levels within us? With the strange mythic depths which are reflected in Inuit sculpture? It is difficult to assess the correlation between Inuit states of being and our own, but there seems to be value in connecting with the elemental world to find growing points into our own futures.

Within the process of creativity, the pagus, the "cosmic" level, finds equivalence in the brooding that goes on beneath the surface of consciousness - in, for example, dream, fantasy, twilight imaging. Can we allow space in religious education for this sort of brooding? For the half-light, the half-perceived?

RECEPTIVITY
In the Inuit experience of creativity, connecting engages evoking. What does this mean in terms of creativity as a quality of education, of religious education? Essentially, it means that education must make opportunities for letting the art process take over; letting the inner workings behind creativity take their course and unfold; letting the material be what it must be. It is to suggest that attentive waiting on meaning is a vital way of education. Simone Weil's "attente" is surprisingly relevant. "A way of waiting, when we are writing, for the right word to come of itself at the end of our pen, while we merely reject all inadequate words." That is how Weil puts it in "Reflections on the Right Use of School Studies". [24]

This gets to the heart of the Eskimo artistic process - receptivity. Waiting for the begetting, the disclosure, the fresh perception of what is really there, "as form in sculpture is the prisoner of the hard rock..." [25] And when the form stirs, emerges, it is perceptible form, not clear conceptual form, that comes.

To emphasize attentive waiting and receptivity is to put the emphasis on those components of creativity which complement the rational discursive elements in education. The rational discursive elements are not being denigrated. Religious education must encourage clarity and depth of informed thinking. But, it is to insist that the artistic process in a pedagogical context is not a way of decking out the conceptual. It is to emphasize the operation of the whole mind, the imagining which integrates the various operations.

This appeal is to the whole mind, and to the imagination which affects behaviour. The suppression of our dreams and of grieving tends to close down part of the brain; it stops understanding or paying attention. "That is why abstract analyses have so little effect on our behaviour. They merely provoke counterarguments, which oppose them in the same kind of language." [26] This is the effect, too, of the adversarial model of teaching, and hence the earlier advocacy of a partnership model.

CREATIVITY AND PROPHECY

Ted Hughes narrates a marvellous Sufi story. The Master had first told his "students" a story that, properly understood would open up their minds and hearts to the next phase of their training. One student was baffled and asked what the story meant.

> "The Master then asked him: 'If you had selected an especially fine peach at a fruit stall, and had paid for it and if the peachseller were then to peel your peach, and eat it in front of your eyes, before handing you the skin and the stone, what would you think?'" [27]

Is that what the artistic process is? I am arguing that part of its relevance is that it deals in firsthand interpretation, constantly renewed ways of attending to meaning, ongoing hermeneutic.

It allows the convergence of meaning and application.[28] In other words, there is a strong argument that creativity as grieving, connecting, attending, is ethical practice. I have argued elsewhere on these lines: that ethics is not primarily concerned with decisions and dilemmas as isolated events, but that these are to be set within a framework of vision (the work of the imagination) against which we can orientate ourselves and develop "character": behaviour, attitudes.[29] It is such vision which the imagination nourishes, and which nourishes grieving and yearning, the realization that life might be otherwise than it is. So creativity can support the moral impulse, even if it cannot define it, and the growth of the critical consciousness. Interestingly, Ciaran McKeown, a civil rights leader in Belfast in the 1960s, made a similar point in the Belfast News Letter (28.2.92): it is vision, creativity, commitment to "the daily immediacy of divinity in our midst, to the work of spiritual growth" which will bring about not airyfairy thinking, but a genuinely reconciled community in Northern Ireland. Indeed, creativity is, at its most authentic, critical, but critical in the sense of being interrogatory. The artistic process interrogates on the level of metaphor. It sustains and acknowledges inner plurality (utterly basic if there is to be genuine outer plurality). It avoids merely presenting an alternative ideology, and so falling into Havel's entropic power, or into selfperpetuating abstract analyses. In other words, it interrogates from outside the received framework or system, and frames its questions within a bigger context. In this way criticism, is not "diminished into the prose world" [30] and it can become prophecy.

Prophecy in the Judaic-Christian tradition - neglected, redolent of disturbed dust, of scorched stones and dried-up figs, but, in fact, still full of relevance, vitality and excitement. It is about living in symbols and images; poetry and story. It is about dissatisfaction, waiting. As well as defining a dimension of creativity, prophecy can provide themes which in the context of religious education can engage the artistic process.

Such themes are those of waiting; listening; breath,wind;wilderness; city; discerning; imagery; the fool and the clown; shaping; voluntary simplicity; the still, small voice; justice; political action; the life of Moses.... They are themes which move us from one way of perception, action, experience, to another. They initiate movement: they open the imagination to new possibilities against a broad perspective and vision. They do not merely protest. They bring us to the heart of prophecy: the birthing of alternative perception, and the willingness to wait on tomorrow as unknown future instead of consructing it as a shrine to the past.[34] Creativity becomes prophetic when it prepares us for a discontinuous future; when it escapes solipsism and mere self expression (so often, as we have seen, dominant in modern art), and relates to a wider context - that of the cosmos, the planet.

The planet - and it is the planet we should be thinking of, not the economy or the nation - needs challengers, prophets, healers and peace-makers. It does not need more successful people. It needs people who have the qualities of the proposed model: the ability to grieve, to connect, to receive.

RAWNESS AND IGNORANCE

For a moment let us move back to the raw arctic. On the way, we will call in at Times Square, New York. A few years ago, there was in the square a vast crucifixion in flashing lights: the Roman soldier offered the sponge to Jesus but out of Jesus' mouth flicked the words "Not unless it's Sarson's."[32] A contrast, in many ways, to those four sculptures in the co-op stores. Perhaps there is wit in Times Square, and some interrogation, too. But hardly the mystery and presence of the sculptures. It is these sculptures which have given us insight into the Eskimo experience of sananguaq. And it is sananguaq expanded by a look at traditional drum dancing and within the context of kablunait culture, which provides the prototype of the proposed model for artistic process or creativity. And this is a model which, although presented in a linear way here, should be seen (danced, would be better) as a total image.

Perhaps it all sounds fairly cosy and easy. It is not. The authentic artistic experience is as raw as the arctic. Painful. Touching the rawness of life. It is struggle and intensity of grieving. It is passion. Once again, it must not be confused with aesthetic experience or the work of the critic. Artistic process at its most vibrant is the prophetic "bubbling" of the Hebrew *nebi'im*; it is powerful, visionary, elemental, sometimes demonic, the imagination raw to the wind.

Creativity in a pedogogical setting can give only a momentary glimpse into such depths. But at least it can provide an opening into profound experiences of ourselves and of the cosmos as absurd and incomplete; of ourselves as part of an emergent creation or reality. And what is reality?

The Eskimo experience it as waiting, allowing what is there to take shape and become. The artistic process diminishes our sense of reality as we think it is. We are left waiting for a new truth to emerge. What comes to us is recognition of the fleeting, fragmentary, and plural nature of truth as we perceive it. As we live more keenly as artists, experiencing the artistic process, we are more able to adjust our received models of the world and let them open out. We are better prepared for making new metaphors and new futures. We wait, receptive, and aware of our ignorance. It is when we know ignorance, when creativity becomes attention, that one day, in the still wintery arctic, we pick out a scrawny cry - "a bird's cry, at daylight or before/in the early March wind...."[33] A cry, haunting, persistent and mysterious. Whatever this cry signifies, it throws into relief the power of the imagination to reach out to new possibilities through drum and whalebone: through, dreaming and grieving; through connecting which is compassion; and through waiting.

REFERENCES

1. Inuit is the plural of inuk meaning "human being". It is the term used to designate themselves by members of the Inuit Circumpolar Conference, an organization established in 19 by Eskimos from Greenland, Canada and Alaska. "Eskimo" comes from an Indian word meaning "raw meat eater" and was first used by the French in the seventeenth century and then by the British. It is assumed that "Eskimo" conveys disrespect but many Eskimos find this amusing. I was told: "We are Eskimos. We eat our meat raw".

2. Eesimailyee, Lazarussi, *Shaman Dancing*

3. Nakashuk, Tasugat, *Whalebone Spirit*

4. Nakashuk, Salasie, *Kneeling Man*

5. Soft stone traditionally used for carving oil lamps, qullisak, and the stone is known by that name. Many related but harder stones are used in carving and are sometimes loosely referred to as "soapstone."

6. Title and name of artist unavailable.

7. Inuktitut. This is the Inuit language. Eskimos of the eastern arctic have had a written language only since the end of last century. Syllabic writing was based on the syllabic system invented about 1839 for the Cree Indians.

8. Arna'naaq, (1987) p.9.

9. Swinton, (1972) p.40.

10. Swinton, (1972).

11. Papanek, (1991) p.11.

12. It is of course, difficult to say which Inuit artists still base their work on traditional Eskimo values and insights as opposed to western / Canadian - European values.

My conversations with a number of these artists indicate that traditional values and insights are still alive.

13. Saatchi Collection, London, 1991/92.

14. Exhibition, *Installation* at Institute of Contemporary Arts, London, 1992.

15. Ereira, (1992) p.157.

16. Many Eskimos in the eastern arctic feel strong connections with Scotland. Certainly in the past, they felt closer to Scotland than to Canada. This is because of Scottish whaling connections going back to the 17th Century but at their height in the early 19th century until the 1880s by which time the bowhead whale had been hunted almost to extinction.

17. This is not to denigrate the work of James Houston who in the late 1940s/1950s encouraged the Eskimos to start carving for world markets. His work cannot be entirely dismissed as the encouraging of vulgar values and souven irism. It can be argued that the good artists were stim ulated by Houston's work to take up carving and to have confidence in their own skills and insights, and not simply to produce what the kablunait liked. This was at a time when Eskimo art was almost dead.

18. To the earlier Dorset and Thule cultures. '

19. Havel, (1987) p.1.

20. Stevens, (1954) p.2 "The Motive for Metaphor".

21. This and other comments are all records of conversations which I had with the Eskimos.

22. Pieris, (1988).

23. Ibid.

24. Weil, (1951) p.73.

25. Thomas, (1978) p.41.

26. Hughes, (1992) p.22.

27. Hughes, (1992) p.22.

28. A point made with reference to David Tracy, *The Analogical Imagination: Christian Theology and the Culture of Pluralism* (SCM 1981) in Weber, p.84.

29. Lealman, (1983) p.54.

30. Brueggemann, (1982) p.54.

31. cf. Heschel, (1962) and Brueggemann, (1978) develop this.

32. Toynbee, (1981) p.43.

33. Stevens, (1954) p.534 "Not Ideas About the Thing but the Thing Itself".

Arna'naaq, Luke (1987): "Drumbeats of the Past" in *Isumasi* vol.1 no.1, Inuit Cultural Institute, Eskimo Point.

Brueggemann, Walter (1978): *The Prophetic Imagination*, Fortress Press.

Brueggemann, Walter (1982): *The Creative Word: Canon as a Model for Biblical Education* Fortress Press.

Ereira, Alan (1992): *The Heart of the World*, Jonathan Cape.

Havel, Vaclav (1987): *Living in Truth*, Faber and Faber.

Heschel, Abraham (1962): *The Prophets*, Harper Colophon.

Hughes, Ted (1992): "The Interpretation of Parables" in *Times Educational Supplement*, 20 March.

Lealman, Brenda (1983): "The Last Step of Reason?" in *Journal of Moral Education* vol.12 no.2.

Papanek, Victor (1991): "Who are the Best Designers?" in *Resurgence* no.145 p.11.

Pieris, Aloysius (1988): *An Asian Theology of Liberation*, T and T Clark.

Stevens, Wallace (1954): *Collected Poems*, Faber and Faber.

Swinton, George (1972): *Sculpture of the Eskimo* McClelland and Stewart, Toronto.

Thomas, R. S. (1978): *Frequencies*, MacMillan.

Toynbee, Philip (1981): *Part of a Journey: An Autobiographical Journal, 1977-79*, Collins.

Weber, Derek (1991): *Discerning Images: The Media and Theological Education*, University of Edinburgh.

Weil, Simone (1959): *Waiting on God*, Fontana.

Brenda Lealman is a Fellow in the Religious Studies Department at Westhill College, Birmingham. Formerly a national Religious Education adviser to the Christian Education Movement, and co-director of a research project into spirituality, she is a widely-travelled freelance writer and teacher. An influential writer and editor within the field of Religious Education, as well as a published poet, she has held an exhibition of photographic work and was recently awarded the *Resurgence* prize for writing.

Religions, the Arts and the Spiritual

INTRODUCTION

———

Richard Yeomans suggests distinctions between the sacred, the religious and the spiritual in art. Such distinctions are not premature specifications designed to circumvent argument. They are rather a preliminary sketch of suggestions whose provisional function is to make possible all the subtleties of relatedness and distinction that the author will wish to draw. Yeomans' categories allow for the inter-penetration of one by another. Consider Yeomans' suggestion that religious art embodies, 'elements of narrative and didacticism, as well as spiritual meanings and values'. On the one hand religious art may serve the narrative didacticism of a specific religious tradition; but it may also connect with the spiritual dimension - either 'transcendental values on a grand scale' or, 'more personal and intimate feelings and beliefs which simply affirm and give meaning to our humanity'. A little more speculatively - it depends on historical demonstration and often upon specific rules within religious traditions - it may be said that religious art provides the short-list from which certain candidate offerings may provide the substance of sacred art. Parallel exercises could focus on the notions of sacred and spiritual art to the same effect - a continuum of relatedness and an inter-penetration of distinguishable values. All of this has impor-tance for what I think may be the cumulative thesis of this book - that the spiritual is a universal human concern clearly related to the arts, to religion, and to our specification of the sacred. It may well be a significant development in education if we can conceive of the functions, range and form of arts education in the light of such a thesis.

When contributors discuss the inter-relatedness of religions, the arts and the spiritual, they are sensitive to different cultural and religious contexts. It is interesting that when Yeomans chooses a title for his work on the specific tradition of Islam, he emphasises the abstract expression of *spiritual* values. This suggests a radical Islamic concern to integrate personal, social and spiritual values into religious observance. Brenda Watson's discussion of the Christian case necessarily makes rather more of the diversity attributable to social and historical circumstances. Here too there has been a tradition suspicious of the arts as worldy and sensual, a desire to submit artistic subject matter and form to the adjudication of religious values; but she points to a distinctive situation in the West, where the relatively more relaxed hand of religious authority seems to have left us with an open question as to the hierarchy of spiritual values, and a relative autonomy on the part of the arts as their vehicle. It is this situation that Brenda Watson tackles in outlining a Christian theology of the arts. As a theology grounded in the revelatory impulses of both art and religion, it respects both the diversity of western approaches to the spiritual quest and the profound influence of Christian symbols in western culture. Her argument discloses a further element in the dynamics of art, religion and spirituality - the intriguing question as to whether bad art can serve religion. The reader may best be referred to the author's argument on this - with the comment only that the dynamics of spirituality have something to do with accommodating human diversity to a hierarchy of values.

It has been suggested that the spiritual is a universal human concern. The two final contributions focus on the arts without any developed or formal reference to religion. Thus while Phil Ellis and Norman Gibson occupy the space that opened up in western cultural history for the arts as autonomous, they stand fully wthin a broad understanding of the spiritual. Phil Ellis gives substantive form to notions of creativity by applying them to the specific opportunities of new music technology. He 'earths' the notion of creativity in a particular educational context. Norman Gibson offers what is at the same time a description of the art process and a way of understanding its making of meaning. His chapter occupies an important place in what is possibly the implicit or emergent thesis of the book as a whole. Putting together an original and basically secular language for the pursuit of meaning he, no less than other contributors, is intrigued by imagined possibilities and new understandings of the world. Let us leave it as secular, and leave it to the reader to decide whether art and religion may not be allies in a fundamental concern. The matter is debatable, and the autonomy of different spiritual paths may be a condition of their distinctive insights. But one crude mistake must be avoided. It does not follow that because a writer chooses to explore alternatively religious or secular frameworks of language and understanding, he or she lives only within one or the other. It may be a condition of our place in history that the educated person is alive to both.

RICHARD YEOMANS

RELIGIOUS ART AND SPIRITUAL ART: SPIRITUAL VALUES AND EARLY MODERNIST PAINTING

Distinguishing between the related ideas of sacred, religious and spiritual art, the author develops the meaning of the last category with reference to the others. At this stage he considers function, subject matter and form as possible defining factors of the different categories. Noting self-expression as a concern in post-Renaissance art, he proceeds via Ruskin and the Romantics to suggest that early modern art is (in its pursuit of meaning arising from mankind's placement in the world) a spiritual art. In the context of this quest, religious insights continued to influence artists whose quest was essentially spiritual in character. Examining case and counter-case in defence of the spirituality of early modern art, the author attends particularly to the impact of the theosophical movement on (among others) Kandinsky, Klee and Mondrian.

Before addressing the specific issue of spiritual values in early modern art, it is necessary to raise a few questions on the nature of religious art and spirituality in general, because some of the most potent expressions of spirituality in modern art fall outside the accepted religious domain. We frequently describe art as sacred, religious or spiritual, interchanging these words in a rather loose and vague way, and although it is not within the scope of this essay to arrive at any firm definitions, it is at least worth raising a few exploratory questions. I would tentatively and briefly begin by suggesting that sacred art, religious art and spiritual art differ in their respective emphasis and parameters. Concepts of sacred art involve a special degree and status of sanctity which are usually intimately bound up with tradition, devotion and acts of worship. Religious art occupies a more generic category embodying elements of narrative and didacticism, as well as spiritual meanings and values; while spiritual art covers a much broader spectrum of human feeling and is not necessarily conditioned or bound by any religious creed. A spiritual art may be concerned with transcendental values on a grand scale, but it can also involve more personal and intimate feelings and beliefs which simply affirm and give meaning to our humanity. What I have to say about modern art falls into this latter category and concerns spirituality rather than religion, but the two realms are not always separable as the following discussion will demonstrate.

ART AND SPIRITUALITY

On the surface, it seems a straightforward matter to describe the character of a religious art, discussing and comparing, for example, such features as the figurative symbolism of Christianity with the abstract art of Islam, or the exuberance of Hindu temple sculpture with the contemplative serenity of a Ghupta Buddha. However, describing the character of a religious art does not always address the question of what makes a religious art religious, or what defines the spiritual within that sphere. In discussing religious art, the first question arises as to how broad our terms should be in describing an art as Christian, Islamic, Hindu or Buddhist? Should the discussion be confined only to those categories of religious usage which cover sacred buildings, devotional images and religious artifacts, or can a prevailing religion define and encompass a wider cultural output? If so, should we not be more precise about what is the product of religion and what is the outcome of a culture? For example, in discussing the Muslim world, where the art is distinguished by its singular visual unity and coherence, and where the faith makes no rigid distinction between the religious and secular domains, questions are raised as to what is essentially Islamic in Islamic art, and whether there is a need to distinguish between the sacred and secular realms. Can one, for instance, reasonably describe a secular building, such as the Alhambra palace, constructed for the delight and indulgence of the Nasrid princes of Granada, as truly Islamic?

It is arguable that in a theocentric society, the Alhambra palace and other secular buildings and objects can express something of a definitive religious attitude and culture, and therefore religious function does not necessarily determine a religious art. Conversely works of art which have a formally religious role can be spiritually bankrupt and quite irreligious in their expression. Even within a sanctified tradition, religious subject matter is not a guarantee of a genuinely sacred art, as religious themes can be treated in a profane way. In the Catholic world of the sixteenth-century, the sensual treatment of sacred images preoccupied the proceedings of the Council of Trent where many clergy spoke of their alarm at the conceits and self-indulgence of a number of Renaissance artists, whose unedifying, licentious treatment of Christian scripture had led to the use of classical or 'pagan' nudities which could incite impure and lustful thoughts.[1] The orgiastic treatment of some religious subjects during the Renaissance did produce some profane works, but sensuality does not necessarily render an art decadent or profane, because even explicit eroticism in the context of some Hindu temple sculpture, can be harnessed to serve some of the most sacred spiritual concepts. In Renaissance art the classical nude may have inspired many a voluptuous Susanna or Saint Sebastian, but the same idealised classical sources for Michelangelo, expressed a Neoplatonic vision of the divine which, energised by his art and vision, could produce the spiritual profundity of the Sistine Chapel ceiling.

If it is not function or subject matter which defines a spiritual art, then is it, as Titus Burckhardt suggests, *form*? Burckhardt argues that it is the form of a sacred art laid down and transmitted by tradition which bestows its sanctity rather than personal expression.[2] There is little doubt that much of this argument holds good, as some of the most awesome and powerful expressions of religious values, such as those conveyed by the ancient Egyptians and the Byzantines, have afforded little scope for personal interpretation, and are contained within strict orthodox traditions. However, Burckhardt is principally concerned with the more circumscribed concept of sacred art, which is most intimately concerned with acts of devotion and worship and embodies a special sanctity and reverence more appropriately expressed in priestly, liturgical and formal structures. In this sense he is entitled to insist on tradition bound forms of expression, but within this argument there is also the question of how rigidly tradition is observed, because even the most rigid Egyptian and Byzantine canon acknowledges the need for the human spirit to breathe, and the necessity for form to be animated if it is to convey spiritual life and meaning. Burckhardt is generally uncompromising in his view that no sacred art can flourish outside a religious tradition and states that the modern insistence on self-expression is incompatible with a truly sacred art. He argues that with the abandonment of tradition, sacred art cannot exist in the modern Western world, and while acknowledging that works of genius have been produced, the twentieth-century is, by his reckoning, spiritually barren.

If one accepts a wider understanding of spirituality and questions Burckhardt's somewhat narrow and purist position, then we must reconsider the possibility that spirituality may reside in self-expression and the individuality of the artist. During the Renaissance we see a dramatic shift of emphasis, in which art is humanised, and moral and spiritual authority lies, not so much in the canons of form and tradition, but in the spiritual and expressive integrity of the individual artist. Such a point was made by Michelangelo with reference to Fra Angelico, an artist of great moral stature and purity of spirit, who exemplified those Christian virtues which John Ruskin, in the nineteenth-century, insisted were prerequisites for great art. Ruskin argued that the noblest art sprang from a religious source, and that only virtuous people were capable of creating art of beauty and spiritual authority. If we accept Ruskin's view that the spiritual authority of a work of art rests on the moral stature of the artist, we have to question what is meant by this moral authority, and whether it is necessary for the artist to furnish a personal example, as it is clearly evident that few artists are paragons of virtue, and that some who have led the most degenerate of lives, like Verlaine, have often given us the noblest and profoundest spiritual insights. Ruskin equated spiritual authority, to a great extent, with Christian morality, but moral strength in art, has little to do with morality and more to do with personal courage, conviction, originality and vision, which are qualities least likely to precipitate those actions which most conform to conventional Christian codes of conduct. Morality is not the same as spirituality, and the spiritual quest of the individual artist involves a personal, and often heroic journey, on paths beyond the bounds of conventional morality and religion. Spirituality does reside in the individual but it is a devolved spirituality independent of morality and the edifice of organised religion.

The art of the last two hundred years in the West has shown an increased secularisation of the arts, with a coexistent revelation that spiritual values can permeate a much broader human front in areas previously unthinkable within the traditional religious domain. When Ruskin asserted the essential moral purpose of art, he did in some measure, like many other Romantics, identify the life enhancing capacity of art to nourish, uplift and sustain the spirit independently of religion. The Romantics endorsed the essential spiritual role of art and suggested new areas of experience within which the human spirit might gain sustenance. They revived Longinus' notion of the sublime, expressed as "the echo of a noble mind"[3] and, like Samuel Palmer, identified a spiritual, pantheistic potency in landscape, which put humanity in a new relationship with the created world. Kant describes how the awesome and terrible aspects of nature and her moods can uplift and 'raise the energies of the soul above their accustomed height.'[4] Such sublime ideas and images furnish the content of many of Turner's paintings, and it was John Ruskin who championed Turner's art, but Ruskin's concern was less with landscape's sublime aspect, and more with the simple conviction that the artist, through his dedicated observation and celebration of nature, could convey something of the sacred order of the natural world and God's providence, love, and divine purpose in it.

The Romantics established the foundations of a free spiritual art, the values of which were to be sustained throughout the nineteenth and well into the twentieth-century, despite the onset of Realism and Impressionism, which in many ways represent a digression from the nineteenth-century's spiritual path. When Gustave Courbet stated that he would never paint an angel until he saw one, he challenged the prevailing idealism of Romanticism and Neoclassicism and established an earthbound attitude which spearheaded the subsequent factual and documentary nature of Realism and Impressionism. In the Impressionist world the artist became a *flaneur*, a detached observer of life, and the purpose of the artist was to represent dispassionately the tangible, material world of the rural and urban landscape with an objectivity analogous to the camera. Despite its secular disposition and objective rigours, Impressionism, with its freshness of vision celebrating the joy and pleasures of our earthbound world, paradoxically proves that the sacred and the divine can be revealed in everyday life and attitudes. Nevertheless, Impressionism was regarded by many as expressing the nineteenth-century quest for scientific truth, and it is in reaction to this perceived rationalism, materialism and positivism, that we observe a more emphatic assertion of spiritual values in the form of Symbolism and Expressionism. It is these two movements which account for the spiritual foundation of much early modernism and abstraction, for despite Titus Burckhardt's views, the twentieth-century has not been spiritually barren, and has been capable of expressing spiritual values equal to any other epoch.

Spirituality and Early Modernism

Throughout the latter part of the nineteenth-century we can observe the resistance to scientific rationalism in the growing interest in spiritualism, occultism, and the increased number of strange and diverse spiritual cults, some of which were to become, like La Rose + Croix, closely allied with the Symbolist movement. The Symbolist reaction against Impressionism, and writers like Emile Zola, can be seen by contrasting Impressionist subject matter, with its emphasis on the mundane world, with that advocated by the Order of the Rose + Croix, which included such themes as Catholic dogma, mysticism, oriental theogonies, allegory and the sublime nude.[5] Subjects like these, as well as occultism, Satanism, alchemy, hermeticism, Neoplatonism and neo-Catholicism, formed the esoteric interests cultivated within fashionable Symbolist circles, because they furnished a kind of exclusivity, that seemed to offer the key to the revival of a new sacred art. In some instances, Satanism and decadence formed a part of the cultural ammunition against conventional codes of bourgeois morality, which were regarded as synonymous with the prevailing material order. So it was that some of those who were most committed to a spiritual revival in art, paradoxically, represented the antithesis of Ruskin's artistic role model.

A group of French Symbolists who congregated around Gauguin, was called the Nabis (a Hebrew word for prophet). In their attempt to revive sacred art, they looked to older mediaeval iconic traditions, and interpreted religious themes within the Breton land-scape, in similar vein to Samual Palmer's brotherhood of 'Ancients', who earlier in the century had sought a vision of Canaan in the landscape around Shoreham in Kent. Paul Gauguin felt that art had to penetrate beneath the surface of Impressionism's coloured shadows, and seek its revival in primitivism and barbarism, finding inspiration among those cultures and people who were perceived as closer to nature, and whose lives were still governed by mysterious spiritual forces. Something of this superstition and magic, which he encountered in Tahitian society, is expressed in the atmosphere of the painting 'The Spirit of the Dead Watches', in which a Tahitian girl lies naked on a bed in abject terror and dread of the vigilant spectre in her presence. For him, Western art had been emasculated by the weight of its own history and culture, and he sought rejuvenation in the art of other cultures which he felt contained more spiritual force and embodied more directly and energetically the creative power of the artist.

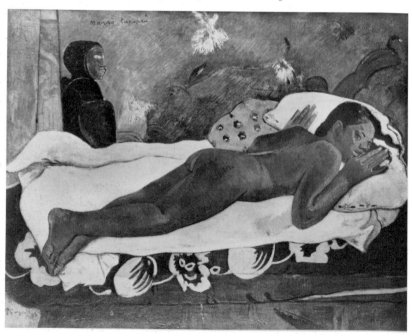

'The spirit of the Dead Watches' by Paul Gauguin.

Gauguin blamed the study of nature for the ills of Western art and in a letter to his old friend Shuffenecker he says:

> 'Some advice: do not paint too much after nature. Art is an abstraction; derive this abstraction while dreaming before it, and think more of the creation which will result than of nature. Creating like our Divine Master is the only way of rising toward God.' [6]

Such an idea might have been blasphemous to Ruskin's ears, but it ties in with new perceptions of art's relationship with the natural world, in which the artist, rather than copying nature, creates metaphors and correspondences, looking beneath the surface, and making parallel structures based on an understanding of nature's processes and manner of operation. To some extent it echoes a Goethean view, subsequently developed by Paul Klee, that the artist is of nature, and one with nature, who, rather than copying its material surface, follows its processes, in such a way that nature is reborn within the creative act on the canvas.

Gauguin's friend Shuffenecker was a member of the Theosophical Society, which of all the spiritual movements of the latter part of the nineteenth century, was the most influential on a number of key pioneering artists in both the visual arts and music. The Society was founded by Helena Blavatsky and Henry Steel Olcott in New York in 1875 and subsequently moved to India where it came under the influence of Eastern mystical traditions. It was a movement which drew from several philosophical and mystical traditions, including Plato, Pythagoras, the Gnostic teachers, Neoplatonism, the Indian Vedas, Sufism, Taoism and Buddhism. The Theosophists believed all religious traditions contained an outer and inner teaching, or exoteric and esoteric path, and were united in one common spiritual ground. It claimed a hidden order of adepts and initiates who were leading and directing the evolution of humanity towards a new spiritual era. These particular notions, and the ultimate belief in the world teacher, in the person of Khrishnamurti, became the dominant concern of the society under the subsequent leadership of Annie Besant, and was the cause of a breakaway faction led by Rudolf Steiner who became the Society's most influential intellectual focus in Europe. Like Helena Blavatsky, Steiner had embarked on a long spiritual journey, but whereas Blavatsky's quest had been rooted in occultism, Steiner's was more rigorously nurtured in natural science and philosophy. He had set out to reconcile science and religion and sought a non-mechanistic explanation of the natural world, seeking a new science of organic nature, which had begun with his monumental task of editing Goethe's scientific writings. He studied Darwin and Haeckel believing that it was essential that theology should come to terms with evolutionary theory. His philosophical studies of Kant, Fichte, Schiller, and his close association with Neitzsche, gave him the formidable intellectual power which he brought to the Theosophical Society. Steiner's philosophical, intellectual and religious background was Christian, and while he respected the mystical traditions of the East and shared the ecumenical beliefs of the Theosophical Society, he could not deny the unique nature of Christ or the Christian revelation. For him the notion of Khrishnamurti as a reincarnation of Christ was an absurdity, and he was suspicious of some of the occult beliefs of the Society, and for these reasons he left the Theosophical Society and founded the Anthroposophical Society in Berlin where a number of extremely influential modern artists encountered his teaching.

Wassily Kandinsky, one of the founders of abstract art, and one of the most influential artists of the twentieth-century was one figure, who, like Steiner, sought to reconcile aspects of modern scientific thought with the spiritual realm. Having studied within the Symbolist and Expressionist climate of Munich, he encountered the Theosophical Society, and its influence is manifest in his book 'Concerning the Spiritual in Art' written in 1912. In this book, Kandinsky warns of the 'nightmare of materialism' the 'tyranny of materialist philosophy' and attacks nineteenth-century positivism and those who 'only recognise those things which can be weighed and measured'. [7] He ridicules those scientists who hold claim to infallible principles, pointing out that science is constantly turning over all the old certainties, and that the advances in particle physics were opening up new perceptions of the material and immaterial world. In the course of the book he mentions the Theosophical Society and the shared belief that the world was entering a new spiritual era. Kandinsky lists those artists and movements he considered to be leading the spiritual revolution, including Maeterlink, Wagner, Debussy, and the Symbolist painters, Böcklin, Rossetti and Segantini, as well as the atom scientists. Particle physics had attracted a great deal of interest among Theosophical circles because it appeared to be a science which pointed towards the dissolution of matter and suggested an incorporeal existence which appeared to give scientific backing and credence to Theosophical notions of coarse and fine matter. It lent support to the monist position in many circles which maintained that there was only one substance, and that body, mind and spirit were merely manifestations of courser and finer matter.

In terms of painting, Kandinsky suggests that the material world was represented by naturalism, and the spiritual world was expressed either through Symbolism, where representation was the vehicle for conveying inner meanings, or abstraction which was the purist way of rendering spiritual values. This new spiritual order was to be initiated by those artists who turned away from naturalism, and as well as the Symbolists, Kandinsky draws attention to Matisse and Picasso: one who 'endeavours to produce the divine' (Matisse), and Picasso, 'who has achieved the logical destruction of matter.' This relinquishing of the material world had, for Kandinsky, been most successfully achieved in music which is the most abstract of the arts , acting 'directly on the human soul', and it is towards the abstract and spiritual domain of music that Kandinsky believed all the progressive arts to be advancing. Kandinsky endorsed Walter Pater's view that 'all art constantly aspires to the condition of music', but painting could only reach proximity with music when it had purged itself of representation and assumed abstract form. For Kandinsky, abstract painting was the purest visual expression of the spiritual realm, being emphatically a manifestation of spirit rather than matter.

The character of his writing in *Concerning the Spiritual in Art*, is essentially visionary, and much of the book is concerned with colour analysis which is grounded, not in perceptual psychology or optics, but in metaphysics and colour mysticism similar to Theosophist notions of the 'seven planes of nature'. According to this theory the seven planes rise in ascending order, from coarse matter on the lower physical plane to the higher mental and astral planes which can be only apprehended by initiates. In his Theosophical work 'Man Visible and Invisible', Charles Leadbetter describes how colour operates in a similar way, and that in the 'higher octaves' there are luminous and more delicate colours which are beyond normal perception. It was believed that the higher mental and astral aspects of a person could be recognised by a clairvoyant observer in the form of a cloud, or aura, and that the colour of the aura revealed thoughts, character and feelings. These colours represented numerous mental and emotional states including anger, hatred, love, pride and sensuality, but on the higher plane of intellect and spirituality, Leadbetter claimed that they assumed an aspect of 'living iridescent light.'[8] In the book *Thought Forms*, Annie Besant and Charles Leadbetter produce pictures of these various mental and emotional states which bear a striking resemblance to some of the abstract forms in Kandinsky's paintings and it is reasonable to assume their influence on Kandinsky, as his notebooks are annotated with references to this and other Theosophical publications. Beyond this, the influence of Theosophical literature is more to do with the attitude and metaphysical framework it established, as Kandinsky's colour mysticism is essentially his own, rather than any direct application of Theosophical colour theory. Theosophy enriched an existing spiritual dimension in his art, as Kandinsky had for some years been drawn to Christian iconography, taking inspiration from Russian iconic sources and Bavarian religious glass-paintings, and many of his early abstract paintings deal with themes like resurrection and last judgement. These paintings of circa 1913, demonstrate and express something of a heroic and majestic surge of freedom, in which references to the world of appearances have finally been shed, and Kandinsky has allowed his spirit and imagination free reign in dreaming up his abstract apocalyptic visions.

'Study for Composition 7 (sketch number 3)' by Wassily Kandinsky

Kandinsky was one of the leaders of the Blauer Reiter group of Expressionist artists in Munich and a close associate of the painter Franz Marc. Marc's writing and painting is imbued with spiritual values which are both in line with contemporary Theosophist notions of the new spiritual era, as well as older pantheistic Romantic traditions. In one of the Blauer Reiter manifestos he suggests that artists should 'create in their work symbols for their age, which will go on the alters of the coming spiritual religion', and in his own work he states that 'I am trying to intensify my ability to sense the organic rhythm that beats in all things, to develop a pantheistic sympathy for the trembling and flow of blood in nature, in trees, in animals, in the air...'[9] In Marc's paintings the natural world is charged with a spiritual energy in which animals and landscape occupy a single fluid continuum of light, colour, space and matter which are dynamically and rhythmically integrated.

'Animal Fates' by Franz Marc

This was much in line with Paul Klee's thinking, where he states that one can draw conclusions about the inner structure of an object from its exterior appearance and through communion with nature, where the artist achieves a synthesis between his 'outer sight' and his 'inner vision'. [10] In searching for this inner understanding the artist reveals the unseen truth and thus, rather than reproducing the visible, the artist 'makes visible.'[11] Dialogue with nature is a constant theme in Klee's writing, where the natural world is seen to be in a constant state of flux, change and becoming, and where the work of art is described as an animated extension and expression of nature's essential dynamics. As Klee states in his essay *Creative Credo*, 'all becoming is based on movement', and movement is the necessary condition for the production of a work of art. [12] For Klee, the internal movements which determine the microcosmic form, are just one fragmentary expression of a cosmic rhythmic order. Such ideas were expressed in his pedagogic writings, where Klee whimsically describes how a man pacing the deck of a ship generates his own movement, which is relative to the movement of the ship, the sea currents, tides, rotation of the earth, its orbit and the courses of the planets. In all Klee's writing movement is implicit in the genesis of form, and nature, like the artist, is seen as essentially creative and self-developing. Klee's understanding of these forces operating in nature find their echo in Steiner's perception of the balance of nature and the bio-dynamic methods of agriculture which he advocated. Although not a Theosophist, Klee was very interested in Steiner's theories, and was also thoroughly acquainted with those influences on Steiner, including Goethe and Ernst Heinrich Haeckel, whose revelations of the microscopic world had some influence on Klee's thinking and pictorial imagery. It is within the dynamic laws of matter and energy, and within the natural world, where the spirit and actions of the artist is one with the plants, animals, and wider cosmic forces that Klee's thinking takes on its metaphysical and pantheistic aspect.

'Cosmic Flora' by Paul Klee

In their search for a hidden order of reality behind the world of appearances, the Blauer Reiter artists are joined by another Theosophist and pioneer of abstraction, Piet Mondrian. Mondrian was a member of the Dutch Theosophical Society and a close associate of Dr M H J Shoenmaeker, a former priest who had turned to mathematics and written two distinguished and influential books outlining his mystical philosophy of the mathematical structure of the universe. Something of Shoenmaeker's mystical order of reality can be seen in Mondrian's ascetic rectilinear works, which represented a slow and gradual simplification and abstraction of the natural world, until he shed all traces of representation and constructed absolute symbols, pared down to the austerities of vertical and horizontal lines, and the three primary colours and tones. These abstractions expressed a form of Theosophic dualism in the union, balance and resolution of opposites projected in terms of vertical and horizontal lines, plus and minus signs, which themselves represent dualist notions of male and female, nature and spirit, inward and outward, as well as the transformation from the individual and subjective plane to the universal and transcendental. Mondrian's art represents a search for laws deduced from the natural world which express universal values, and his paintings are visual metaphors signifying the essential unity and harmony of creation.

'Pier and Ocean' by Piet Mondrian

These restful and serene paintings, which have no focus or 'subject' to engage or distract the mind, function like icons, as objects for contemplation and meditation, or as Mondrian states:

> 'Art - although an end in itself - like religion, is the means through which we can know the universal and contemplate it is plastic form.' [13]

In another extract from Mondrian's writing he states that 'as the spiritual merged with the secular, it became more and more apparent that the spiritual did not dwell in religious subject matter exclusively; otherwise with the decline of religious subjects, all spirituality would have gone out of art..'[14] Mondrian goes on to argue that with the annihilation of subject matter itself, abstraction was the ultimate expression of both the spiritual and the natural order.

Gauguin, Kandinsky, Marc, Klee and Mondrian are but a sample of painters exemplifying a spiritual dimension in their work, and the choice of these is due to their links with the Theosophical Society, but they represent just a fraction of those artists in the twentieth-century engaged in similar pursuits, and some might argue that all artistic endeavour is some form of spiritual quest. Spiritual values are by no means the exclusive domain of abstract art, and the twentieth-century has unleashed a bewildering diversity of creative activity encompassing many artists, like Jacob Epstein, Stanley Spencer and Marc Chagall, who have reinterpreted established religious themes, as well as others, like Pablo Picasso and Francis Bacon, who claim no religious affiliation but have, nevertheless, produced paintings of profound spiritual power. Abstract art has changed and developed over the century, periodically reasserting the spiritual values of the pioneers, but perhaps its last great upsurge was in post-war America where it found its most heroic expression, in the works of Mark Rothko, Jackson Pollock, Franz Kline, Willem De Kooning, Adolf Gottlieb and Barnett Newman, who reintroduced a sublime art which expressed a new transcendental spiritual consciousness with a radiant and explosive force on an unprecedented vastness of scale. In his essay 'The Sublime is Now', Barnett Newman discusses how the modern age is striving towards a new sublimity, and for him, the challenge of the modern world is to 'reassert the desire for the exalted' unencumbered with the weight of the past, and the onus of new spiritual art and revelation lies within us where 'instead of making cathedrals out of Christ, man or life, we are making it out of ourselves, out of our own feelings.' [15]

REFERENCES

1. Blunt (1964) p.118

2. Burckhardt (1976) p.8

3. Alloway (1975) p.33

4. Kant (1951) p.100

5. Lucie-Smith (1972 p.111

6. Chipp (1968) p.60

7. Kandinsky (1977) p.11

8. Kandinsky (1977) p.32

9. Leadbetter (1959) p.18

10. Klee (1919)

11. Klee (1920) p.18

12. Klee (1920) p.76

13. Dube (1990) p.125

14. Jaffe (1970) p.63

15. Chipp (1968) p.553

BIBLIOGRAPHY

Alloway, L. (1975)   *Topics in American Art Since 1945* Norton & Co. Besant and Leadbetter (1961) *Thought Forms* Adyar

Blunt, A (1964)	*Artistic Theory in Italy 1450 - 1600* Oxford University Press.
Burckhardt, T. (1976)	*Sacred Art in East and West* Perennial Books
Chipp, H. (1968)	*Theories of Modern Art* University of California Press.
Dube, W-D (1990)	*The Expressionists* Thames & Hudson.
Jaffe, H (1970)	*De Stijl* Thames & Hudson.
Kandinsky, W (1977)	*Concerning the Spiritual in Art* Dover.
Kant, E (1951)	*Critique of Judgement* Hafner
Klee, P. (1919)	*Ways of Nature Study* Bauhaus Press Weimar-Munich.
Klee, P. (1920)	Creative Credo' *Tribune der Kunst und Zeit, Berlin.* Published in *The Thinking Eye* Lund Humphries (1961).
Leadbetter, C (1959)	*Man Visible and Invisible; Examples of Different Types of Men Seen by Neans of Trained Clairvoyance* Adyar.
Lucy-Smith, E (1972)	*Symbolist Art* Thames & Hudson.

Richard Yeomans is a practising painter and art historian, and a Lecturer in the Department of Arts Education at the University of Warwick. He has held many one-man exhibitions of paintings and drawings, and participated in group exhibitions in London, the Midlands and North of England. He has travelled widely in the Middle East, and has a particular interest in the arts and culture of Islam, and has lectured widely on this topic. As an art historian he specialises in nineteenth and twentieth century painting, and his research interests are in post-war movements in British art and design education.

RICHARD YEOMANS

ISLAM: THE ABSTRACT EXPRESSSION OF SPIRITUAL VALUES

The visual arts may reach beyond theology and philosophy to manifest the most complex responses of religious values, thoughts and feelings. Whereas Catholicism has cautiously sanctioned an iconic and symbolic art in teaching the articles of faith, Islamic law has affirmed Muslim spiritual values through an art of deliberately formal abstraction. It discountenances idolatry and the representation of living beings in the religious domain. That Islam affirms the unity and indivisibility of the faith is evidenced in the spiritual geometry of calligraphy and illumination as well as in the architecture and social placement of the mosque. Case by historical case, the author explains how architectural features of the congregational mosque have supported the practice of the faith and have (as an abstract visual continuum in space) affirmed spiritual values.

In dealing with the expression of metaphysical truths and values, the language of theology is often inadequate to match the magnitude and complexity of the concepts and feelings involved. In the world of Islam, particularly within the Sufi tradition, it is the language of poetry, rather than theology or philosophy which communicates some of the most profound religious thoughts and feelings. Beyond that, certain spiritual values are ineffable, and as Wittgenstein stated, "There are, indeed, things that cannot be put into words. They *make themselves manifest*. They are what is mystical."[1] It is on this ineffable plane that the visual arts come into their own, and it is only through vision amd imagination that those higher spiritual perceptions, which are beyond the limits of language, can be made manifest.

This is true of all the religious arts, but what is remarkable about the art of Islam is that it expresses notions of the sacred and divine in a uniquely abstract visual language. The arts of Christianity, Hinduism and Buddhism have evolved a complex symbol system which is figurative in character, and contains a rich and varied iconography, including devotional objects which serve as icons for veneration and meditation, as well as complex illustrative programmes with powerful narrative and mythological content. It is a visual symbol system which, in one sense is unambiguous, and can be easily understood and *read*. Like the written word, there is a specificity in what the religious symbols signify, and their clarity and meaning have been regulated and enshrined in tradition laid down by religious authority. In Islamic art, the visual meaning cannot be read in a singular symbolic sense, as it expresses notions of the divine essentially through its *form*, in terms of abstract order and the totality of its spatial dimension, rather than through any iconic, literary, narrative or mythological content. As Titus Burckhardt points out, Islam rejects devotional images, and the Muslim artist is not concerned with a focused objectivation of the sacred, but with expressing transcendental notions of divine law and unity.[2] Before discussing the nature of this expression of divine meaning and purpose, it is necessary to look at the reasons why Islam has taken a different path from many other world religions, and perhaps, by way of introduction, it is useful to compare Christian and Muslim perceptions of the visual arts.

The contrast between Islamic and Christian theological attitudes towards the arts can best be seen in two documentary sources; one Christian decree emanating from the Council of Trent, and one Muslim legal document of the thirteenth-century. Following the iconoclasm which accompanied the Reformation in Northern Europe, the Catholic Church decided to review its attitude towards the visual arts, not simply as a Counter-Reformationary measure, but also in the light of the major Humanist revolution which had occurred in the arts during the Renaissance period. It was a question of not only clarifying the function and role of the visual arts, but also defining what constituted sacred or profane interpretations of religious dogma. In contrast to the visual austerity of the Northern Protestant churches, the Catholic Church decided:

> 'That the images of Christ, of the Virgin Mother of God, and of the other Saints, are to be had and retained, particularly in churches, and that due honour and veneration are given them; not that any divinity, or virtue is believed to be in them on account of which they are worshipped....but because the honour which is shown them is referred to the prototypes which those images represent....And the bishops shall carefully teach this: that by means of the stories of the mysteries of our Redemption, portrayed by paintings or other representations, the people are instructed and confirmed in the habit of remembering, and continually revolving in mind the articles of faith.'[3]

The Roman Catholic Church endorsed the devotional and didactic role of art and the Baroque art which followed the Council of Trent assumed a dynamic propagandist form which was designed to stir the religious veneration and imagination of the faithful.

For Islam, like Judaism, it is religious law which has traditionally provided the backbone of the faith, and it is to legal, rather than theological sources that one must look for an Islamic judgement on art. A thirteenth-century legist, Nawawi, summed up in some detail the Islamic view as follows:

> 'The learned authorities of our school [*Shafe'i*] and others, hold that the painting of a picture of any living thing is strictly forbidden and is one of the great sins, because it is threatened with the above grievous punishment as mentioned in

Traditions, whether it is intended for common domestic use or not. So the making of it is forbidden under every circumstance, *because it implies a likeness to the creative activity of God*....On the other hand, the painting of a tree or of camel saddles and other things that have no life are not forbidden.'[4]

For such a view to reach canonical form, the matter would have to be decided through the rigorous application of Islamic law, founded on revelation and reason, and on four main principles:

1. God's word revealed to Muhammad in the Qur'an.
2. The Traditions of the Prophet [Hadith].
3. Analogical reasoning [Qiyas].
4. Learned consensus [Ijma].

Needless to say, the *Qur'an* is the primary source of Islamic law, but its precepts and injunctions are of a broad and general nature, and more precise rules on certain matters need to be supplemented by those detailed accounts of the sayings and actions of the Prophet found in *Hadith* literature. If neither the *Qur'an* nor *Hadith* contain precise guidelines on such matters as art, then what is lacking in revealed sources, must be augmented and developed by the exercise of analogical reasoning, carried out by the learned religious authorities [the *Ulama*], and their consensus provides the basis of Islamic law.

The *Qur'an* itself has little to say about art as such, although it is uncompromising about idolatry as revealed in the following verses:

'O Believers, wine and arrowsmithing, idols and divining arrows are an abomination, some of Satan's work; so avoid it; haply you will prosper.' (sura 5.92)

'Tell of Abraham, who said to Aza, his father: "Will you worship idols as your gods? Surely you and your people are in palpable error."' (sura 6.74)

Muhammad's teaching was uncompromising in his assertion of pure monotheism, and a significant part of his early ministry was to eradicate polytheist idolatry and cleanse the Meccan sanctuary of idols. From the outset, Islam expressed a Semitic antipathy towards graven images, and this is ritually enshrined to this day in the stoning of the idols at Mina as a part of the annual pilgrimage rites. Apart from idolatry, there is nothing in the *Qur'an* referring to images, but one passage is frequently invoked regarding the nature of creativity, and this relates to one of the miracles of Jesus, in which God gave permission for Jesus to animate a bird fashioned from clay.

'He will say: "I bring you a sign from your Lord. From clay I will make for you the likeness of a bird. I shall breathe into it and, by Allah's leave, it shall become a living bird. By Allah's leave I shall give sight to the blind man, heal the leper and raise the dead to life."' (sura 3.43)

This passage, which reflects similar stories found in such apocryphal sources as the Gospel of Saint Thomas, suggests that only by God's will can matter be animated, and therefore only God creates and man should not be seen to usurp God's sole creative prerogative. However, questions of idolatry are always contentious and open to interpretation; as the Catholic Church decreed at the Council of Trent, devotional images should be revered on account of the prototypes they signify and not as objects to be worshipped in themselves. Figurative images do not necessarily imply idolatry and few artists would claim to invest themselves with Godly powers in their creative endeavours.

For further clarification of the position of art, the Muslim lawyer would seek further information in *Hadith* sources, where there are several unambiguous statements comparing the painter to the murderer of a prophet and condemning him to Hell on the Day of Judgement. However, as Sir Thomas Arnold points out, some of the iconoclastic attitudes expressed in *Hadith* may be explained as interpolations by Muhammad's followers and successors. By contrast, Muhammad himself is generally seen to be more ambivalent in some accounts where, for instance, he orders the destruction of paintings in the Ka'ba, but insists on one picture of the Virgin and Child being preserved.[5] There is one account of Muhammad discussing with his wives the church paintings of Abyssinia, and he was tolerant of pictures woven into certain household furnishings. However, two significant *Hadith* are emphatic where they consider the presence of images in the religious domain.

'Umar said, "We do not enter your churches on account of the statues on which are figures."'

'Anas said, "A'ishah had a figured curtain of red wool, with which she covered a side of her apartment the Prophet (peace and blessings of Allah be upon him) said: "Remove from us thy curtain, for its figures come before me in my prayers."'[6]

Muslim lawyers, weighing the evidence of the *Qur'an* and *Hadith* were bound to conclude that figurative art in the religious domain was unacceptable, but it took some time for such a view to crystalise, and when it did, it may ultimately have been prompted as much by political, as well as legal concerns.

By the early eighth century, Islam as a conquering power, needed to establish its own independent visual language and identity which could rival the Byzantine splendour of Christianity, and make Islam's triumph visually manifest. The earliest Muslim monuments, the Dome of the Rock (692) and the Great Mosque at Damascus (715) are monumental assertions of Islam's presence, and were built conscious of the need to rival Christendom's great churches. When Muqaddasi asked his uncle why the Caliph al-Walid had spared no expense in building the Great mosque at Damascus, his uncle replied.

'Verily al-Walid was right, and he was prompted to a worthy work. For he beheld Syria to be a country that had long been occupied by the Christians, and he noted there the beautiful churches still belonging to them, so enchantingly fair, and so renowned for their splendour, as are the Church of the Holy Sepulchre, and the Churches of Lydda and Edessa. So he sought to build for the Muslims a mosque that should be unique and a wonder to the world. And in like manner is it not evident that Abd al-Malik, seeing the greatness of the martyrium of the Holy Sepulchre and its magnificence was moved lest it should dazzle the minds of the Muslims and hence erected above the Rock the Dome which is now seen there.'[7]

The task of Islam was not so much to match Christian splendour but to assert its own independent identity, and just as the Catholic Church rejected Protestant iconoclasm for political reasons, so the Muslim world turned its back on those devotional icons and paintings which so defined the ethos and character of Christian art and worship. Islam had its own liturgy and unique revelation in the form of the *Qur'an*, and from the outset it was the word and the book which dominated Muslim thinking and worship. Islam had no need of pictures; as the Prophet stated, they were a distraction.

In Islam it is the word which is manifest in iconic form, and it is calligraphy which assumes the highest place in Islamic art. Calligraphy was encouraged at all levels of society from the sultan down, and the act of writing a *Qur'an* was in itself an act of religious piety and merit. Calligraphy is ubiquitous in the Muslim world, being manifest not only in the art of the book, but also on buildings, mosque lamps, carpets, embroideries, pottery, ivories, metalwork and coinage. From Spain to Indonesia it is a constant and unifying factor in Islamic art. The first revelation of the *Qur'an* commands recitation of the word and teaching by the pen.

'Recite in the name of your Lord, the Creator, who created man from clots of blood! Recite! Your Lord is the Most Bountiful One, who by the pen has taught mankind the things they did not know.' (sura 96)

The esteem in which calligraphy is held is expressed in a fourteenth-century encyclopedic work entitled *Nafa'is al-funun* by the author Muhammad ibn al-Amuli.

'The art of writing is an honourable one and a soul nourishing accomplishment; as a manual attainment it is always elegant, and enjoys general approval; it is respected in every land; it rises to eminence and wins the confidence of every class; being always to be held in high rank and dignity....The Prophet (peace be upon him) said: "Beauty of handwriting is incumbent upon you, for it is one of the keys of daily bread." A wise man said; "Writing is a spiritual geometry, wrought by a material instrument."'[8]

This notion of spiritual geometry lies at the very heart of Islamic art where it finds its most perfect expression in calligraphy and illumination. Those ineffable feelings of God's divine presence and purpose in the unity and harmony of his creation; that awareness of wholeness and infinitude manifest in the observable natural world and in those patterns and rhythms which govern it, assume iconic form in the dynamic and radiant geometry of Mamluk and Mongol illumination. It is a geometry which is at once boundless and contained, and forms the network in which those other fundamental aspects of Islamic art, calligraphy and arabesque, become enmeshed. These qualities are best exemplified by the frontispiece of a Mamluk *Qur'an* in the British Library which was written by Muhammad ibn al Wahid and illuminated by Muhammad ibn Mubadir and 'Abd Allah al-Badri in 1304 for the sultan Rukn ad-Din Baybars [Fig 1].

The structure of the design is based on a series of interlocking circles which hold the rectangle containing the eight pointed stellar panel. The geometry holds a resolution of static and dynamic forces, and this dichotomy is in turn echoed in the tension between the underlying geometry and the rhythmic arabesque it supports, as well as the contrast between the flourish of the cursive *Thuluth* calligraphy in the centre, and the static, monumental, hieratic *Kufic* script in the headings.

If illuminated manuscripts make visually manifest some of the highest abstract ideas of unity, totality, and universality, then architecture augments this on a wider visual and spatial plane. But these ideas of unity and totality are not confined simply to the

Fig.1 Mamluk Qur'an written by Muhammad ibn al-Wahid, 1304. (British Library)

abstract organisation of geometry and space, as architecture is a socially based art and also reflects in a concrete and practical way ideas of universality in terms of the social and religious constitution of the Muslim community. Unity and indivisibility is a defining characteristic of Islam, which is all-embracing and recognises no hard and fast separation between the religious and secular life. This integration between the secular and religious domain was manifest from the outset in Medina where the Prophet's ministry was not simply concerned with spiritual issues, but with the political leadership of the community and all the practical day to day matters of government. This is reflected in the daily activity of the mosque in which the Prophet would not just lead the prayers and preach, but would also teach, administer to the needs of the poor, act as law-giver and adjudicator, as well as plan battle campaigns and secure the economic well-being of the community. This wide spectrum of activity centred on the mosque, has broadly determined the subsequent development of religious building programmes throughout the Muslim world.

It is reflected and sustained in such institutions as the Turkish mosque complex, or *Kulliya* (a word meaning 'totality' or 'universality'). Suleyman the Magnificent's *Kulliya* in Istanbul is like a self sufficient city within a city, containing the mosque, several *madrassas* (theological colleges), an advanced law school, a *Qur'an* school, a hospital and asylum, soup kitchen, hospice, baths, shops and mausoleum. That the commercial and religious life of the community can harmoniously co-exist, is demonstrated by the fact that in most traditional Muslim cities the mosque is situated in the heart of the commercial centre. At Edirne, in Western Turkey, Sinan's great masterpiece, the *Kulliya* built for sultan Selim, structurally incorporates a covered bazaar which makes a financial contribution to its upkeep, and on a smaller scale Sinan constructed another architectural gem, the Rustem Pasha mosque, above the tinsmith's bazaar in Istanbul. In many instances, architectural cohesion is strengthened by the structural integration of the auxiliary buildings into the main body of the mosque. It is a common feature in many parts of the Muslim world to see the mosque, *madrassa*, hospital, and mausoleum combined in one architectural unity, as witnessed by the Qalaun and Sultan Hassan complexes in Cairo, thus asserting the paramount position of the mosque as the centre for the spiritual, intellectual and physical needs of the community. Only the political and military centres of power became separated in their citadels from the wider Muslim community.

If architecture expresses ideas of universality, totality and unity, in its functional aspect, then the same notions also determine its form and explain the abstract visual continuum which underlies all the Islamic arts. Islamic architecture is, in many respects, the most definitive architecture in formal terms, being distinguished by its rigorous organisation of abstract space. What it presents is architecture at its purest, with little to detract attention from that pure architectural disposition of mass, space and proportion. When the Prophet complained that those embroidered figures on A'isha's curtain distracted him from his prayers, he was to establish an attitude towards prayer and meditation which was to have a lasting impact on the environment of worship. There are no distracting pictures, and the spatial domain of the mosque is uncluttered by seating, furniture, tombs and monuments, and all those other accretions which have tended to fill Christian churches over the centuries. Prayer is arranged in horizontal rows facing the *mihrab*, or prayer niche, which is set in the *quibla* wall facing Mecca. The *mihrab* from where the *imam* leads the prayers, flanked by the *mimbar* (pulpit), provides the only focal point of the mosque interior, and it is usually around the *mihrab* where we encounter elaboration in design, in the form of Qur'anic inscriptions, tiling, and occasional flanking stained glass windows. The whole architectural purpose is to render the space, and other formal and decorative elements, conducive to concentrated prayer and meditation.

Within the essential unity of Islamic architecture there is regional diversity, and architectural space is expressed in many ways. The earliest congregational mosques followed the pattern established by the Prophet's mosque in Medina, which was a simple enclosed courtyard with two sheltered areas at each end constructed from palm trunks and palm fronds. The arrangement of a courtyard adjacent to the prayer hall, provided the most common ground plan of the early mosques, because, not only did it follow the pattern established by the Prophet, but it also proved to be an adaptable and flexible plan allowing for extension as the Muslim population grew. With the gradual conversion to Islam of the indigenous populations under Muslim rule, it became a simple matter to extend the bays of the prayer hall to accommodate larger numbers. This can be seen extensively at the great Mosque at Cordoba where 'Abd ar-Rahman 1, Hisham 1, 'Abd ar-Rahman 11, 'Abd ar-Rahman 111, al-Hakim 11 and al-Mansur each made their additions to the mosque and attempted, to some degree, to outshine their predecessors. Here the prayer hall is of the hypostyle type (hall of columns), with the extraordinary innovation, within an enclosed space, of raising the roof height by means of doubling the arch by placing one on top of the other in similar vein to a Roman aquaduct. Unlike the Roman aquaduct, the interstices between these arches have not been filled in with solid masonry, so that the double spring of the arches has a unique lightness of form resembling spreading palm fronds. The rhythmic power of these double arches, which become further complicated with the elaboration of a third intersecting arch in al-Hakim's section, is quite extraordinary, and the vast scale of the building, throwing the perimeter walls into the shadows, creates a feeling of boundless space occupied by a living palm grove of columns. [Fig.2]

Fig.2 The Great Mosque at Cordoba.

The spatial disposition of Ottoman architecture, like its Byzantine predecessor, is based on complex permutations of the dome. From the outset, when Byzantine centralised and basilican plans formed the basis of the Dome of the Rock in Jerusalem and the Great Mosque in Damascus, Islam has absorbed indigenous architectural styles and transformed and remodelled them to its own purposes. When the Turks conquered Constantinople in 1453 they, like Abd al-Malik and al-Walid in their time, had to make their mark and proclaim Islam's triumph by evolving an architectural form which could compete with the magnificence of Justian's great cathedral, the Hagia Sophia, and all the other beautiful churches in the ancient capital. Fortunately for Suleyman the Magnificent, he had the assistance of Sinan, an architect of extraordinary genius, who, almost single handedly created classical Ottoman architecture, and transformed Constantinople into one of the architectural wonders of the Muslim world. Early Ottoman architecture, which had absorbed many Seljuk features, began to evolve into a new style, incorporating the dome structures of Byzantium, and Sinan, taking his cue from the Hagia Sophia, extended these features to new heights of dignity and maturity. Suleyman's great mosque in Istanbul, has a dome arrangement similar to the Hagia Sophia, with a central dome supported by two half domes, which are further buttressed by a cluster of smaller domes and apses which carry the thrust of the central structure in a broad parabolic sweep to ground level.

Sinan regarded Suleyman's mosque as a work of maturity, but the mosque he built for Selim at Edirne is a masterpiece in structural and spatial organisation. Based on a centralised plan, the great dome crowns a vast cubic space surmounting an octagon of supporting piers, with half domes squaring the circle in the corners. The organisation and geometric perfection of the larger spaces, with their rosette dome clusters, is echoed and accompanied by the floriate and arabesque patterns of the Iznik tiling, which add colour to the whole. Within this environment of space and colour, the mind is unfocused and cleansed, rendering it susceptible to meditation and prayer. [Fig4]

Fig.3 The Mosque of Sultan Selim at Edirne.

The squaring of the circle, by which means a circular dome can be placed over a square plan, was solved by Byzantine architects who evolved the use of the squinch and pendentive.[9] In the Muslim world, the geometry of the squinch has taken on an extraordinary complexity with the development of the honeycomb and stalactite formations of *muqarnas*, which, like calligraphy and arabesque, become a distinctive feature of Islamic art.[Fig.4]

Fig.4 Muqqarnas from the Masjid-i-Shar at Isfahan.

These crystaline forms occupy *mihrab* niches, portals and domes, and suggest, at times, some of the celestial and cosmic visions described in the *Qur'an* and Islamic poetry. In the secular setting of the Alhambra palace in Granada, the dome of the Hall of the

Albencerrajes presents us with a nebulous structure of infinite crystaline complexity constructed on an eight pointed star.[Fig.5]

It is a celestial dome suspended over sixteen windows which admit the transforming light, as the sun and moon move their positions throughout the day and night. In its constantly changing aspect, it is an exquisite abstract expression of the cosmos, acting like a visual metaphor for those apocalyptic passages in the *Qur'an* referring to the scattering of the stars and heavens:

> 'When the sun is darkened, When the stars fall and disperse... ....I swear by the turning stars, Which move swiftly and hide themselves away, and by the night as it comes darkening on, and by the dawn as it starts to breath....'
> (sura 81)

Fig.5 The hall of the Albercerrajas in the Alhambra at Grenada.

The religious and secular domains in Islam intertwine, and the inscriptions in the Alhambra contain both *Qur'anic* texts and passages from poetry. There are many inscriptions from the work of the fourteenth-century poet Ibn Zamrak, and it may be his work, as well as that of the eleventh-century Jewish poet, ibn Gabirol, which may more precisely explain the iconographic context of the dome in the Hall of the Albencerrajes. The following passage is from ibn Gabirol:

> 'The dome is like the Palanquin of Soloman hung above the glories of the chambers,
> that rotates in its gyre, shining like opals and saphire and pearls;
> this it is in the daytime, while at dusk it looks like the sky whose stars form constellations.'[10]

These sublime and transcendental ideas are expressed in an imagery in which poetry and abstract architectural form are one, and this essential harmony and correspondence between one art form and another, is also fundamental to all the other arts. There is a constant visual interplay and continuum which unites all the Islamic arts, and in the mosque, it is the enfolding totality of these diverse art forms, which creates the environment into which the individual is absorbed and surrendered to contemplation. To some extent, this totality and unity has been explained only in the formal terms of geometry, arabesque and calligraphy, but one other paramount factor, which also defines something of the common ground of Islamic art, is colour. Islamic art cannot be represented by the cold linearities of geometry alone, as colour is the animating factor in much Islamic art, breathing warmth and life into the paradisal, floral intricacies of the arabesque. Colour, as an autonomous entity, has been liberated in the Muslim world and allowed an expressive function unparalleled in any other world art. It is the crowning glory of much Islamic art, accounting for the sensuous luxury of Islamic textiles; particularly carpets, embroidery and costume, as well as the exquisiteness of miniatures, stained glass, mosaic and tiles. The floor plan of the Iranian mosque is softened and enlivened by the rich resonance of coloured carpet patterns, in which floral arabesque, medallion and cartouche forms, are frequently repeated and mirrored in the limpid, jewel-like colour of the overarching dome.[Fig.6]

In the Masjid-i-Shah in Isfahan, the ceramic tiles adorn both the exterior and interior of the mosque and *madrassa*, and the iridescent colour almost dematerialises the elegant proportioning of the mass, and transfigures the geometry and arabesque into an ethereal weightlessness, expressing something of that essential Persian lyricism and mysticism which has its parallels in the finely wrought religious poetry of Rumi, Hafiz, Sadi and Attar.[Fig.7]

Fig.6 The Dome of the Masjid-i-Shah.

Fig.7 The Masjid-i-Shah.

This building, more than most, represents the perfect synthesis of all those concepts of unity and transcendentalism in Islamic art and religion, manifesting all those ineffable thoughts and feelings on an imaginative plane which is uniquely the domain of the visual arts.

REFERENCES

1. Wittgenstein (1961) p.151.

2. Burckhardt (1967) p.106.

3. Blunt (1962) p.108.

4. Arnold (1965) p.9.

5. Arnold (1965) p.7.

6. Muhammad Ali pp. 74, 127.

7. Grabar (1973) p.64.

8. *Op cit* Arnold. p.2.

9. According to the Penguin Dictionary of Architecture: 'SQUINCH. An arch or system of concentrically wider and gradually projecting arches, placed diagonally at the internal angles of towers to fit a polygonal or round superstructure on to a square plan.' ' PENDENTIVE. A concave Spandrel leading from the angle of two walls to the base of a circular dome. It is one of the means by which a circular dome is supported over a square or polygonal compartment.'

10. Grabar (1978) p.148.

BIBLIOGRAPHY

Arnold, T. (1965)   *Painting in Islam* New York, Dover.

Blunt, A. (1962)   *Artistic Theory in Italy 1450 - 1600* Oxford University Press

Burckhardt, T. (1967)   *Sacred Art in East and West* London, Perrenial Books.

Burckhardt, T. (1976)   *Art of Islam* London, World of Islam Publishing Company.

Grabar, G. (1973)   *The Formation of Islamic Art* New Haven & London, Yale University Press.

Muhammad Ali,(1978)   *A Manual of Hadith* Lahore, The Ahmadiyya Ajuman Ishaat Islam Lahore.

Wittgenstein, L. (1961) *Tractatus Logico-Philosophicus* Routledge

BRENDA WATSON

THE ARTS AS A
DIMENSION OF RELIGION

The author's initial approach is to look from religions towards the arts. Religious priorities, while traditionally attributing a range of subordinate roles to the arts, have shown ambivalence towards the arts' seductive power, and have sometimes preferred certain styles and art forms above others. The question arises as to whether bad art can serve religion. From her comments on this, the author proceeds to another approach, developing her defence of the view that the arts may be inherently religious. The arts of a culture certainly share in the religious concern to make meaning and bring order out of chaos; and they may have deep reference to the culture's religiously established symbolic order. Such considerations lead the author to outline a Christian theology of the arts, and finally to suggest a strategy for religious education that might do reciprocal justice to both religion and the arts.

The title of this chapter is deliberately ambiguous. Like optical illusions in which the same picture can be seen in quite different ways, so the arts as a dimension of religion can be approached from two distinct angles. The focus can be either on the arts, and whether or not a religious significance can be seen lurking there, or on religion to see what explicit role the arts have with regard to it. This chapter needs to explore how far the two approaches can be brought into harmony. I shall begin with the second.

RELIGIOUS ATTITUDES TO THE ARTS

All religions rely heavily on the arts. Endless examples can be given of the expression of religious belief in story, verse, painting, sculpture, architecture, embroidery, drama, dance, music, the making of religious artifacts, the artistry of religious ritual, stained glass, culinary arts, cultivation of gardens, calligraphy, book illustration, mosaics, and so forth. There can be at least five reasons for this impressive use of the arts:

- The natural expression of delight, of a sense of awe and wonder, of involvement in something greater than oneself which gives joy, of wanting to give glory to God.

- A means of inspiring people, communicating insight and building up religious community by creating an environment conducive to deepening religious devotion.

- A two-fold educative function, for the arts are effective as carriers of messages and also provide means of reinforcing learning through participation in what is to be learned.

- A control function both as an outlet for emotions which might otherwise prove wayward or damaging, and as a means of manipulating people in such a way as to promote a particular response.

- A status symbol - the arts can advertise the power and glory of the religion responsible for their patronage - they can foster religious imperialism.

The last two uses of the arts are not inherently religious, and from a religious point of view indicate abuse: the purpose of the arts is to express praise, devotion, dedication to God and not human ambition. Nor should responsibility for evoking community spirit be a question of manipulative social control, but of promoting genuine personal creative involvement. Of the three other points, religious people can easily fall into a trap with regard to the third: namely, of seeing the arts as primarily audio-visual aids or suitable "follow-up" material in teaching. When this happens the arts lose their own integrity and autonomy as worthwhile in themselves.

The first two reasons for religious expression through the arts do normally treat the latter with respect. There is good reason for this because all religions discern a close link between the divine and this world of time and space. Thus within the three semitic religions of Judaism, Christianity and Islam, the doctrine of creation teaches that human beings are made in God's image and this validates the artistic impulse to create as God has created. Perception of this relationship inspires artistic awareness which shows itself in creative expressions at every level from the simplest to the most sublime.

RELIGIOUS MISTRUST OF THE ARTS
Yet this positive and welcoming attitude to the arts taken seriously in their own right is often believed to present certain dangers. This accounts for a certain ambivalence towards the arts which is present in most religions at different times and with different intensity and usually towards some manifestations of artistic taste and not others. The temptations which can beset genuine religious respect for the arts include their power of distraction and seducement from the main purpose of religion. In particular Islam shares with Judaism serious suspicion of representative art. The fear is that such representation may easily become idolatry when forms become more compelling than that for which the forms stand. In response to this Judaism has placed far greater emphasis on verbal expression than on the visual, whilst Islam has produced master-pieces in architecture, geometric design, calligraphy and other visual forms which avoid figurative representation of objects in the natural world or of human beings.

Within other religions there has been more ambivalence. The same kind of anxiety was present in early Buddhism which turned its back on the riotous proliferation of images of the India of the sixth century BCE. Subsequent development within Buddhism however enabled for example the wonderful sculpture and painting of the Ajanta cave temples in India. Within Christianity the ambiguity of religious attitudes to the arts can be clearly seen in for example the great iconoclastic controversy of the eighth century over the use of icons, the movement towards monastic and architectural simplicity associated especially with Bernard of Clairvaux in the twelfth century, the concerns of the Protestant reformers and subsequent Puritan groups, and the suspicion at various periods towards the use of instrumental music in churches.

Often these reservations with regard to the arts are lampooned by those who lack such inhibitions, yet in fact they probably present an essential aspect of the polarity needed for keeping both religion and the religious use of the arts healthy. Listening to sung evensong in an Anglican cathedral pinpoints the dilemma neatly for me. Incredibly beautiful, it seems to offer one of the most perfect images of heaven on earth which it is possible to find. Yet at the same time I am conscious that it is also very inadequate, and can even stand in the way of religious understanding. Its beauty is achieved through a certain exclusiveness: the worshipper has no way of participating other than by listening - which easily becomes passive when any outward form of expression is denied. Then there are problems, for many people today, associated with the tradition which enables the evensong to function: the exclusion of women, the affirmation of hierarchy as somehow God-given, the archaic nature of some of the language, and so forth. Besides all this, I am conscious of the tremendous ease with which one can worship the music and not God: the music can be so lovely that it is wholly absorbing, and God can become incidental to it.

RELIGIOUS PROSTITUTION OF THE ARTS

If religion has to its credit much of the finest artistic creations that the world has seen, there is another side. Religions have been responsible for much trash: what almost all artists might agree is sheer bad taste and insensitivity to artistic awareness. As one writer, Richard Griffiths, discussing religion and the arts recently put it, "I am tempted to agree with the disc jockey who, searching for a suitable title for a piece of Christian pop music, came up with: 'I found Jesus and lost my talent'."[1]

Yet if good art can obscure the divine for some people, it is important to reflect on the way that bad art can convey the divine for other people. Doggerel hymns and sentimental tunes can become the vehicle for deep religious insight and experience. What are we to say about this? St Paul wrote, "We have this treasure in earthen vessels that the glory may be of God and not of us."[2] There is a profound insight here for religious people: that the shoddiness of much of the audio-visual aids pressed into the service of religion does help at least some people towards a greater awareness of how completely inadequate are any forms of expression to encapsulate divine reality.

This does not mean that trash is desirable. In any interface between the arts and religion, this question needs to be taken seriously. Many people have turned away from religion because of its patronage of the banal, the sentimental and the superficial. Furthermore, whilst bad art can and often does convey deep religious insight to people, it can insidiously have a deadening effect upon religious as well as artistic sensibility. People brought up on a diet of poor verse and sentimental pictures will easily tend to see the essence of religion also in naive and unrealistic ways. The parallels between the arts and religion, if both are taken seriously, can indeed promote mutual flourishing. The Christian poet R.S.Thomas could write:

"the tree of poetry
that is eternally wearing
the green leaves of time."

Quoting this, Griffiths argues: "Christian art is not necessarily good art; but all good art, in my view, is implicitly Christian."[3] This raises the obvious question today: is it? We need to discuss both the nature of the arts, and what is meant by "Christian".

Are the Arts Inherently Religious?

On the surface of it, this would seem not to be the case. In the modern western world, most artists, poets, novelists, dramatists, skilled craftsmen, dancers, musicians and so forth are not religious people. Any links with religion appear tenuous and many are openly atheistic or agnostic. Even where religious art is admired, it is normally on grounds other than religious. Thus many of the giants of the past like Michelangelo and Leonardo da Vinci can be, and are, interpreted mostly as revealing humanist insight. They painted religious subjects because they lived at a time when society was still religious, but they approached them as artists not as religious believers. Even where a composer such as Haydn prefaced his non-religious quartets and symphonies with the words, *Ad majorem gloriam dei*, this is easily discounted today as just part of Haydn's psychological makeup: any link between great music and religious devotion is seen as quite arbitrary and explainable in relativist terms.

Not all voices in the arts world would agree with this easy dismissal of any organic link between the arts and religion. A notable example is that of the art critic Peter Fuller who died in 1991. He has drawn attention to the predicament facing modern art through its disassociation with the creative symbolism of religion. "Incorrigible atheist and aesthete that I am, I believe it to be a moot point whether art can ever thrive outside that sort of living, symbolic order, with deep tendrils in communal life which, it seems, a flourishing religion alone can provide." As an admirer of the superlative artistic achievement of the gothic cathedral, he acknowledges that this *could* not have happened (not just did not as an historical fact happen) without a deep commitment to certain aspects of Christian theology. "Unbelievers can enjoy the cathedrals but we could never have made them. ... Gothic architecture, in both its ornamental detail and its structural brilliance, is a material elaboration of Christian belief."[4] He asks what has taken its place now that Christianity is no longer in general currency in western society and its symbolism no longer shared. He questions whether talk about the "spiritual", or the "transcendent", as acceptable non-religious terms having no intrinsic relationship whatever with religion, can bear much weight. He speaks of "the fashionable appropriation of the language of the 'spiritual' to defend work of a numbing vacuity."[5] He might have quoted Archibald Macleish: "A world ends when its metaphor has died..."[6]

The search for overall meaning which makes sense of fragmented isolated meanings seems to be inseparable from the pursuit of the arts. The dilemma for Peter Fuller, as for the vast majority of his contemporaries in the modern world, is the crisis in faith. Alternatives to religion like post-modernism have not yet shown themselves to be sustainable. Post-modernism bears the stamp more of a reaction to metaphysical dogmatism, whether religious or scientific, than as a philosophy strong in its own right. That we do not invent the world is blindingly obvious to every artist who knows only too well how recalcitrant clay and wood and oil are - they have to be respected, cajoled, entered into, enticed into shape. The attitude required of the artist is in fact one more like adoring humility before the givenness of both matter and meaning than one of self-assertive inventiveness. The creative aspect is certainly to the fore in the arts, and it yields a sense of artistic fulfilment. Yet this mysterious quality itself - which is the real life-blood of the creative artist - is something to give us pause to think. It has to do with the unfolding of order - even, indeed especially, if we started off with chaos. Yet why should we be so deeply satisfied by order, design, meaning? Awareness that we live in a universe which displays such characteristics has been a prime inspiration to artists' achievement throughout the ages. The artist has to work long hours to create a tiny millimetre of the beauty discernible even in a single daisy. It is significant that Beethoven heard music in the trees, as did Elgar.

PARALLELS BETWEEN THE ARTS AND RELIGION

I believe that all this would appear obviously to have links with religion, except where, *on grounds other than artistic ones*, religion is seen as untrue or at any rate doubtful and often also as undesirable. There are several other considerations arising from the nature of the arts as arts which support a close relationship with religion.

(a) The arts revolve around the experience of awe and wonder. They point to a quality of life which is more than the mundane. Kandinsky, in his book concerning the spiritual in art, notes "Religion, in the sense of awe, is present in all true art."[7] The arts deal with a givenness which is perceived. As Keith Swannick noted:

> "The crucial concept here is not creative self-expression or social relevance, or technical skill, it is responsiveness. ... Aesthetic means to feel more powerfully, to perceive more clearly. Its opposite is anaesthetic."[8]

(b) The arts, like religion, seek the really real and not just the superficially so. They relate to knowledge. Jeremy Begbie expresses it like this:

> "The autonomy of art will best be safeguarded, I believe, not by wrenching it apart from knowledge, nor by equating it with conceptual or moral knowledge, but by seeing it as a distinctive, particular but quite genuine means of knowing the world."[9]

It is important we appreciate that the arts are not anti-intellectual. As Ken Robinson has pointed out[10], one reason for the importance of arts education is because of their own intellectual integrity. Children need to be helped to experience this so that they are liberated from imagining that only science provides a reliable route to knowledge. Indeed even scientific investigation requires the exercise of artistic ways of knowing, as many modern scientists acknowledge.

(c) The arts have an inherent concern for personal integrity which parallels the religious search for spirituality. Kandinsky wrote: "I value only those artists who really are artists, i.e., who consciously or unconsciously, in an entirely original form embody the expression of their inner life."[11] Fuller gives a devastating criticism of a modern German successful painter and the nub of it is, his painting "lacks even an echo of authentic expression".[12] Whether or not this is a fair comment on Baselitz, it certainly reflects what Fuller believes to be essential for real art. Such personal involvement however is not to be confused with purely emotional reactions or self-centredness. Great artists display engagement without entanglement. They give themselves wholeheartedly to their subject - authentically - yet without imposing themselves on the subject or doing violence to it.

(d) The arts express this inner life, as does religion, through external forms which have to be "read" aright, which have to be penetrated for their real essence. Kandinsky discusses the modern phenomenon of the connoisseur: "His eye does not probe the outer expression to arrive at the inner meaning."[13] Suzanne Langer wrote about artistic judgement in similar vein:

> "The worst enemy of artistic judgement is literal judgement, which is so much more obvious, practical and prompt that it is apt to pass its verdict before the curious eye has even taken in the entire form that meets it. Not blindness to 'significant form' but *blindedness* due to the glaring evidence of familiar things makes us miss artistic, mythical or sacred import."[14]

The distinction here between literal external copying and inwardly seeing the meaning of an artistic production is crucial.

(e) The purpose of the arts, as of religion, is a serious one, but yet it relates to a particular kind of satisfaction, of joy. Someone has said that "dedication is the difference between art and pastime". Certainly this involves treating the arts with seriousness, even though not pretentiously or with pomposity. Music for example should not be regarded as mere "aural perfume" or "mental wallpaper".[15] Yet the seriousness is balanced by a quality of playfulness, of sheer delight without concern for anything else. T.S.Eliot, discussing *Ash-Wednesday*, wanted to quote these lines of Byron:

> "Some have accused me of a strange design
> Against the creed and morals of this land,
> And trace it in this poem, every line...
> But the fact is that I have nothing planned
> Except perhaps to be a moment merry ..."[16]

(f) The arts cannot ignore the dark side of life as well as the pleasurable, the suffering as well as the happiness. Instead of pretending that that side is not there, they seek to transform it. Jeremy Begbie has noted, "The artist who passes lightly over the disorder of our world is in danger both of self-deception and utter irrelevance."[17]

The connection between joy and pain is perhaps something which needs to be discussed in connection with the word 'spiritual'. I recently heard a professional musician speak of the spiritual experience of music and of the private pain behind the creativity which posterity could enjoy so freely.(18) This has obvious links with religion, and especially with Christianity, to which I now turn.

Towards a Christian Theology of the Arts

As an example from the religious side of the interface between the arts and religion, let me take Christianity. Whether all good art is implicitly Christian art depends on the meaning we give to "Christian". If this is focussed on the distinctive doctrines of the incarnation, the trinity and the significance of the death and resurrection of Jesus, these feed back into a heightened awareness of the importance and validity of this world. They take more seriously, not less, all artistic endeavour.

Aspects of fundamental Christian belief indeed correspond to the six points just outlined relating to the arts. Thus, regarding the first, it was a Christian theologian, Rudolf Otto, who invented the term the "numinous" to denote the awe and wonder perceived as at the heart of Christianity as of religion in general. The second point is also reflected in Christianity's concern with what is the case - both as regards historical facticity and cosmic reality and significance. It is indeed the insistence on uniting the two which is the source of the "offence of particularity" which Christianity presents to many outside its orbit. For it revolves around the concept of revelation, claiming that it *does* matter that people have awareness of the nature of God and can respond knowingly. Relating to the third point concerning personal integrity, it can be plausibly argued that the very word "person" owes its development to its use within Christian theology. Christianity lays great stress on the freedom, responsibility and salvation of the individual person as well as of society.

With regard to the need to distinguish between external form and inner meaning, Christianity has always liberally used metaphor, imagery, parable and story to communicate its message. Its sacramental understanding of the significance of even the simplest objects and happenings - of "heaven in ordinarie" as George Herbert put it [19] - is supremely exemplified in the Eucharist. Christianity thus requires discernment at various levels from the purely external and literal to the most profound and mystical. Finally the fifth and sixth points concerning the element of delight and yet also of awareness of suffering are centrally reflected in Christianity. For it focuses on the notion of "gospel" - good news. Authentic Christian experience has a quality of lightness, peace and joy about it, however much its practitioners may sometimes suggest otherwise. "God deliver us from sullen saints" prayed St Teresa of Avila! Yet the cross and resurrection of Jesus is historically and theologically at the heart of Christianity.

The Transforming Quality of Christianity

Christians believe the essence of their "good news" is that order is imposed on disorder and meaning created out of tragedy: blind forces which dehumanize become placed within a structure and given purpose. The cross - besides its historical significance - thus becomes a powerful symbol which can be seen at the intersection of the world, uniting the divine and the human, the happiness and the pain of life, into a pattern as wide and deep as eternity itself. A painter such as Rouault has been able to communicate something of this theological understanding. Fuller notes how Rouault has been called "the painter of inwardness, of the supernatural light that glows in the profoundest depths". He speaks of:

"...the revelatory radiance of the stained glass above the high altar which gives his pictures of whores a dimension that is entirely absent from say, Bacon's existential butchery."[20]

This is the gospel of Calvary and Easter. Those receptive to its light can become transformed.

It is interesting that an atheist like Fuller is particularly concerned that Christianity seems to have lost its nerve. Referring to Edward Norman's Reith Lectures which argued that the "justification for Christianity lay not in its espousal of contemporaneous, philosophical, psychological or political beliefs, but rather in its soteriology and christology", Fuller goes on to comment:

> "Though I myself reject the Christian claims, I believe there is no other ground Christianity can stake out for itself. Indeed Norman's seems to me the only sort of Christian position with any degree of intellectual, spiritual or cultural credibility about it. I also feel that Christians who hold such views are far more likely to commission, or to create, vigorous, living, spiritual 'art' than those who, like us poor atheists, have lost all their redeeming illusions and are thrashing around in an all too human and depressingly material world."[21]

The problem of course is that, for so many people today, such Christian doctrines lack credibility and wear the character of illusion. The truth of such beliefs is up for challenge, whether from secularists or from other fellow religionists. Any interface between the arts and religion today must start here, otherwise the religious implications of the arts will not be recognised. The deeply controversial nature of the value and belief assumptions of our western secularised societies must be acknowledged, so that the issue becomes an open one instead of remaining hidden from the majority of people and from the majority of children. Arts education in schools needs to have dialogue with RE which openly states the disagreement and can therefore help all concerned to examine for themselves how valid the alternative positions are.

A MODEL FOR RELATING RE AND THE ARTS

Such a strategy in fact parallels the kind of approach needed within religious education to the teaching of world religions. We have to find a way of bringing the controversy up front - a way which is not destructive but affirming of people as they engage in a lifelong task of widening and deepening their perceptions and experience. Artistic creativity dies if a person imagines that near-perfection is already achieved and there we can rest. As an art teacher friend of mine commented on some much admired painting by one experienced person in an art class: "There's no future for her as an artist - she's come to the end of the line and has nothing fresh to say." Her work betrayed smug self-satisfaction and therefore lacked the depth of genuine artistry.

This attitude of constant developing and learning more, and being excited by new discoveries, is something which can and should accompany both arts education and multi-faith RE at every stage from infant to college level and throughout adulthood. It is one of the things we can be absolutely sure about, even though we cannot prove it, that there will always be immeasurably more to learn, and more wonder in store for us as reality unfolds itself before our exploring gaze. If trouble is taken to try really to get on the wavelength both of the arts and of religion, the possibility of a harmony can be envisaged. This can be up for debate in the laboratory as it were of a lifetime's experience. It should at least be made available to children, and from an early age, so that they can consider it with increasing maturity.

Two prominent models of RE today are the phenomenological and the experiential. Can they relate in depth to arts education? The phenomenological, as commonly understood, tends to undervalue the importance of inwardness. It tends to see symbolism from an external point of view and does not really help either religious people or artists to take on board the commitment aspect of both religion and the arts. The essence of both the arts and of religion tends to be marginalized. This has the effect therefore of devaluing both the arts and religion. Does the experiential model for religious education - the quest for pupils' spiritual development - fare better? It is radically centred on pupils' own inner perceptions and is therefore much more akin to arts education. It takes the experience of awe and wonder, and of the impossibility of adequately expressing mystery, seriously. Nevertheless it has weaknesses: it can for example belittle the value of tradition and the way in which the individual is part of a wider community which impinges itself necessarily on how 'inwardness' is expressed. It tends to be weak on the public aspect of knowledge - a 'true for me' approach can lead to a narcissistic escapism. It too therefore devalues the arts as well as religion in the end. What I think we need to argue for is a third model for religious education, one which I have elsewhere termed "essentialist".[22] This would put at the centre what is in fact central to religion, and in a way which allows what is central to the arts also to be respected. It would bear in mind that all education must be related to the central concerns of pupils, otherwise it fails as education. This emphasis on centredness can acknowledge the diversity of different traditions without fear, because they can become accommodated within a wider perspective only to the extent that it does justice to each one.

If the arts and religion are thought of as two separate triangles, the phenomenological approach model of RE tends to place these alongside each other, even though some overlap is discussed. The experiential model on the other hand tends to conflate them, not making it clear where one begins and the other ends, if indeed there is any distinction. Neither of these models therefore does justice to either religion or the arts. An essentialist model works on the basis of a constant growing into greater awareness. The two triangles become part of a third wider one which retains each of the original triangles in their wholeness. Such a model argues for a degree of transformation, change, development, but this is implicit in education anyway. Another way of expressing the same kind of model - and which also has the merit of taking into account the concept of the spiritual - would be to think of a triangular pyramid. If the arts triangle or the religious triangle is flat on the ground then it remains in isolation, but if it can be raised by means, we may suppose, of the spiritual insight that a person accumulates then it can create a third dimension. The analogy of the spiritual to that of a raising agency has resonances within all the major religions. In these ways the arts and religion can be seen to enhance, deepen, and challenge each other to their mutual benefit, and jointly add considerably to the potential of the curriculum as a whole.

REFERENCES

1. Griffiths (1992) p.9.
2. 2 Cor.4 v.7.
3. Griffiths (1992) p.9f.
4. Fuller (1990) p.189.
5. Fuller (1990) p.xviii.
6. Macleish quoted in Whittle (1966) p.6.
7. Kandinsky (1977) p.xvi
8. Swannick quoted in Green (1990)
9. Begbie (1992) p.23.
10. Robinson (1990) p.535.
11. Kandinsky (1977) p.vii
12. Fuller (1990) p.7.
13. Kandinsky (1977) p.49.
14. Langer (1951) p.264f.
15. Parrott (1985) p.9.
16. Byron quoted in Eliot (1933) p.30f.
17. Begbie (1992) p.75.
18. Bernard Blay of the McNaughton Quartet at a music course at Hitchin 1992.
19. Herbert quoted in Slee, N (1992)
20. Fuller (1990) p.45, 49.
21. Fuller (1990) p.192f.
22. See Watson (1993) pp.48-53.

BIBLIOGRAPHY

Begbie, J (1992)	"The Gospel, the Arts and our Culture" in *The Gospel and Contemporary Culture* ed. Montefiore H, London, Mowbray
Eliot, T.S (1933)	*The Use of Poetry and the Use of Criticism*, London, Faber & Faber
Fuller, P (1990)	*Images of God: The Consolations of Lost Illusions*, London, Hogarth Press

Green, R (1990)   "Let's Do Music in RE!" in *Resource*, Vol.12 No.2.

Griffiths, R (1992)   "Religion and the Arts: Baudelaire and R.S.Thomas" in *Theology* Vol.XCV No.763 Jan/Feb

Kandinsky, W (1977)   *Concerning the Spiritual in Art*, New York, Dover

Langer, S (1951)   *Philosophy in a New Key*, Harvard

Parrott, I (1985)   *A Musician's Credo*, Oxford, Farmington Trust

Robinson, K (1990)   "The Future of the Arts in Schools" in RSA Journal Vol CXXXVIII No.5408

Slee, N (1992)   "Heaven in Ordinarie: the Imagination, Spirituality and the Arts in Religious Education" in *Priorities in Religious Education*, edited Watson B, Lewes, Falmer

Watson, B (1993)   *The Effective Teaching of RE*, Harlow, Longman

Wittle, D (1966)   *Christianity and the Arts*, London, Mowbray

Brenda Watson is a former Director of the Farmington Institute for Christian Studies at Oxford, and is now a part-time academic consultant to the Farmington Trust. Independent consultancy gives her a wide range of contacts with teachers, clergy, parents and others. Her *Education and Belief* was published by Blackwell in 1987. Editor of *Priorities for Religious Education*, published by Falmer, she is now preparing a book for Longman's *Effective Teacher* series.

PHIL ELLIS

RESONANCES OF THE FUTURE - A CONTEMPLATIVE COMPUTER:

ASPECTS OF A SOUND EDUCATION

The essence of music does not lie in what can be written down or in rigid conceptions of tonality, melody and harmony deriving from the eighteenth century keyboard, but in the making of sounds that exist only in time. New music technology has re-emphasised the possibility for timbre, texture and dynamics to replace melody, harmony and rhythm as the dominant counters of creativity. The author discusses musical creativity as an exploration of experience, and as a making or doing of something that offers inner and spiritual fulfilment. While recognising the importance of tradition in music education, he urges a progressive liberation from concepts associated with older technologies, the liberation of technology itself from the rule-bound past, and a practical pupil-responsiveness to the creative challenges of the new. Against this background, the chapter explains the development and relevance of a new computer program called Designing Sound.

This chapter will examine an approach to the creative and aesthetic experience in music - one which engages with our inner needs, our spirituality. It will briefly place this in an historical and educational setting and describe a project which has harnessed the computer in support of this context.

The arts are in part concerned with creating and inventing, with making something which did not exist before. It could be said that this experience is important at all stages of personal development, from child to adult, from novice to expert. Laing observes that 'man creates in transcending himself in revealing himself' [1], and we are lacking in a whole personal dimension if we have no experience of being individually creative - we will certainly have no real language, even if we have been taught the vocabulary. Music is the most abstract of the arts, having its existence only in time. If we capture music in written form and reproduce this exactly as it appears on the printed page, it will sound unmusical and mechanical. The real music - its essence - lies in what cannot be written down, in the nuances of the performer(s) and of the performance, different every time yet recognisably 'the same' piece of music. Unwritten changes in speed (rubato) for example, or melodic inflections using microtones (moments of pathos in operatic arias, 'blues' notes in jazz, and so on) are often the most expressive moments of all.

For well over two hundred years Western music has focused almost exclusively on a limited number of ways of selecting, organising and notating sound, rather than on sound itself. These ways are commonly based on the seventeenth-century designed music keyboard, with a tonality established firmly around 1722 and Bach's *Well Tempered Clavier*. We have become so tied to the piano keyboard that we have fixed our tuning and sound structuring to an alarming degree; we have become almost trapped by this aspect of musical language.

Yet music has moved forward in many ways, particularly during the twentieth century. It has been said that Debussy was the first composer since Monteverdi to have had a real interest in sound. Prior to the early years of the century we can view melody as being linear and harmony as vertical, yet timbre can simultaneously be a combination of both these aspects of music. Ravel pointed out that it is possible to orchestrate in points of colour rather than in lines as the (musical) Romantics did. During this century it has become possible to make music which gives expression through a focus on timbre, texture and dynamics, replacing melody, harmony and rhythm as predominant elements.

Music and Technology

In 1932 the conductor Stokowski predicted a time when people would be able to create in sound, musically, 'directly into tone, not on paper'.[2] Technology as applied to music has only recently made this prediction a reality, first with the tape recorder, and more recently with a range of digital processing and sound-making devices.

The British composer Jonathan Harvey is one of a new generation of electroacoustic composers who are beginning to realise Stokowski's prediction. Harvey has explored technology and music in depth whilst retaining the spiritual dimension of creativity. He believes that technology enables us to search for and create the actual sound as it will be heard in performance, whereas more traditional methods of composing which were developed before the advent of technology forced us to search for the *notation* of sounds. This notation could lead to the realisation of the imagined sound and its effect only in performance. Harvey's musings on the 'interchange between reason and soul'[3] are particularly apposite, and he has likened the (electroacoustic) journey into the exploration and creation of sound to the inward journey of meditation. The application of computers to music allows 'the conception of new areas of work' (*Ibid*).

Xenakis and Stockhausen provide two more examples of contemporary composers who enthusiastically embrace technology in the furtherance of new music. Stockhausen believes in transforming personal experience into a medium 'that's more timeless, more spiritual'.[4] Just as a contemporary physicist needs to take new discoveries into account in order to do important work, so must the artist and musician. We should not 'fall into one aspect, but always meditate and enlarge consciousness.'[4]

Computers began life as 'computing machines', specifically designed to speed up mathematical calculations. The subsequent development of the programmable computer led to computers becoming general-purpose machines, useful in a number of contexts. Computer applications typically have to do with storing and retrieving information, and processing it in a variety of ways very quickly. But the computer in this general sense cannot generate information, only process it. To be useful in the context of the arts, computers must enable the new to be possible - there is little excitement merely in apeing the past. It is one thing for a machine to remove drudgery or repetitive (non-artistic) tasks; but to allow us to easily confront and become directly immersed in the medium of sound itself, and to encounter new and uncharted possibilities - then there is real excitement.

It is ironical that the more power and speed we have available in the computer, the more contemplative we need to be when working in the domain of sound, distinct from the *organisation* of sound. Bigger and faster does not necessarily equate with better. Another irony is that the increasing power and speed of computing enables us to delve ever more deeply into the effects of sound, and so become more aware of the aesthetic possibility of sound and silence - within stillness. This moves us closely towards Koestler's investigations in the area of creativity and mathematics, where non-verbal thinking seems to predominate, where 'we have to get away from speech to think clearly.'[5] If we can be immersed within sound and think immediately with sound itself, we can generate the space and stillness to explore, to resonate, and to develop our own creativity more directly.

Before the advent of twentieth century technology, in order to compose music we usually had to acquire technical skills. As we have already seen these skills were most often focused upon, and sometimes confined to, the piano-style music keyboard. The design of the keyboard, with its tones and semitones laid out to accommodate our fingers and thumbs has its own efficiencies, but also imposes severe limitations. Twentieth century music technology seems only now to be beginning to consider this straightjacket around modes of performing sounds, and indeed to a consideration of the very sounds themselves. We will return to the 'well-tempered' way of organising pitch in Western music later, but it seems that we are only slowly rediscovering that, for example, bell sounds and other 'clangorous' or 'non-harmonic' combinations have beauty, and a powerful musical potential. We may now be at the start of a renaissance as new technology presents us with possibilities for exploring uncharted seas of sound, and additional ways of organising and performing new musical structures of the mind.

Midi (musical instrument digital interface) has become a standard way of utilising the computer for the control, or the exchange, of information between digital electronic musical devices. Ironically, the popular thinking and design of this 'standard' seems to be rooted firmly in musical thinking from the past, and is only slowly being adapted to a more forward-looking direction. Manufacturing interests dictated the midi standard, and in this world finance rather than aesthetics is the dominant influence. These interests resulted in a rigid, metronomic, often severely constrained and mechanical patterning of sound - a feature of much of the commercial sector of the music business: music to entertain, or to distract the attention, rather than a focus on the abstract.

Education through Music

Until quite recently music in education has tended to concentrate on learning *about* the subject rather than providing opportunities for all pupils to be involved in practical and creative musical experiences. The style of education offered is crucial. We cannot learn to swim by sitting behind a desk, just as we, as very young children, do not learn first to speak, then to write, in a silent aural - or oral - world. In the 1580s Montaigne observed of education that 'the usual way is to bawl into a pupil's ears as if one were pouring water into a funnel, and the boy's business is simply to repeat what he is told.'[6] It is not progress to use contemporary technology, including the computer, as a substitute for 'bawling', however much 'information' might be available, and however attractively or distractingly it might be presented.

If we use computer programs which are musically rule-based, or tied to traditional forms of notation, we cannot fully function in the domain of sound. When we encounter situations in which the rules have yet to be determined, such programs cannot be used without proscribing true innovation. They resonate so powerfully with the past as to deny real exploration and subsequent creation of the future. Education certainly should include a concern with the past, our heritage and cultural roots, historical developments, and an understanding about what makes such music actually work. 'Theory is the lamp which sheds light on the petrified ideas of yesterday and of the more distant past', something which 'does not precede practice, but follows her.'[7] But education is also to do with leading people towards the future, of generating new knowledge, encouraging individual and original thinking, revealing new possibilities with unknown boundaries; and the excitement of the new, the undiscovered or uncharted - resonances of the future.

In a sound education, not only can we explore new realities with computers, we can also discover and create new worlds of sound. This we can subsequently explore and bring to life. In music it is often fruitful to combine new soundworlds with acoustic instruments. Instruments which are rooted firmly in the historical progression of musical thinking can be used in combination with those reflecting the technological progress and development of their time - the one can enrich the other. We can work from where we are in this century, and "move forward in both directions simultaneously".[8]

Recent developments in education have resulted in composing being accepted as a practical activity that all children should be engaged in from the first years of schooling through to GCSE and beyond. However, in this context composing should not be pastiche, nor seen as a vehicle for self-expression. It is an abstraction of emotional, possibly spiritual, life - at least once removed from the reality of the event itself, yet inescapably bound up with it, only in part Wordsworth's 'passion recollected in moments of tranquility'.

Langer clarifies this view, describing music as being a 'logical picture' of emotions, moods, tensions and resolutions; 'a source of insight, not a plea for sympathy'.[9] And she goes on to observe that in the same way as words can be used to describe events or situations we have not encountered, so we can through music encounter and explore areas of experience otherwise denied to us; an inner, or spiritual experience, which may enrich our everyday life. Clearly this has great potential in education and it may be possible through technology to enable more people to engage in these experiences.

CREATING NEW MUSIC

Many writers from a variety of backgrounds broadly identify creativity as a three-stage experience or process [Hargreaves (1986), Huntley (1970), Kandinsky (1914), Koestler (1978), Whitkin (1974), et al]. This process begins with exploration and experimentation; we then go through a stage of focusing, often experiencing periods of seeming inactivity whilst subconsciously we 'mull over' or reflect upon creative and expressive problems; and finally we realise our ideas, sometimes but by no means always accompanied with the 'blinding flash' or new insight.

We are still only beginning to learn how to engage all children in composing music, an activity in the west which has historically been confined to only a very few 'special' individuals. The composer Paul Hindemith gives us some guidelines which can further help define the ground for creativity in music. He suggests three considerations: the 'inherent qualities and possibilities of sound; the purposes the material has to serve; and our plain and reliable (musical) common sense'. He continues with a powerful argument in favour of freeing ourselves from traditional thinking and stylistic rigidity. His answer to teachers' perennial question of where to find (musical) material - how to compose - is to pick *any* sounds in our world which our ears can hear which may be 'useful in forming musical creations'.[10]

Indeed we do not have to look very far to find well-tried, successful alternatives to the traditional Western model of composing, and we can learn a great deal from the music of other cultures. Messiaen reveals many non-western influences in his work, as does John Tavener with his meditative, sometimes ritualistic music. Toru Takemitsu provides us with a wonderful combination, rather than synthesis, of two contrasting cultures. In some of his music traditional Japanese instruments with their distinct, sometimes micro-tonal tunings, happily coexist with the traditional Western symphony orchestra. He also uses alternatives to Western ideas regarding musical structure. Placing the emphasis on flow and progression rather than on a geometric or argumentative structuring of sound can lead us towards a more reflective, contemplative world, a world which is mirrored increasingly in twentieth century music. In Bali each village gamelan prides itself in having a slightly different tuning system from its neighbour, and people play around with tuning differences for their expressive qualities. In other words, the whole world can be viewed as a music box, and some examples of music technology enable us to create and explore other new worlds.

INVENTIVE EXPLORATION

Discovery and creation provide an excellent opportunity to exploit the internal digital manoeuvring of computers - where a reality can be constructed in a different and separate medium from the event itself - a medium which can be innocent and non-influential. This mirrors Laing's (1967) observation that our creative experience lies within ourselves, yet 'still beyond ourselves'. It is crucial that this 'beyond ourselves' happens in a neutral way, one which does not preclude alternative ways of thinking and expression, nor even suggest possible ways, yet very few computer music programs have been designed to be neutral.

In music the most common performance instrument to be linked to a computer is a 'piano-type' music keyboard. We have already observed that this is usually confined to the seventeenth-century keyboard design, with a tonality which was fixed around 1720. The use of this device most often predetermines not only pitch relationships and modes of performing, but also influences approaches to musical structure and expression. Much of the commercial exploitation of music technology has been based on the thinking which led to this very keyboard, and is apeing the past, rather than breaking new ground. Some of the sounds used today may be superficially of this century, but their organisation and intention is clearly belonging to an earlier time - another example of McLuhan's 'marching backwards into the future'.[11]

If we consider some other traditonal instruments of music, the human voice is the best instrument ever - it can be truly microtonal and incredibly timbral. The violin and cello can also produce microtonal and timbral music, but our conservatoire training is often exclusively concerned with diatonic tuning systems and a severely limited timbral palette. Voices and a number of acoustic instruments can often more easily be played in alternative tunings and timbres than the traditionally accepted 'correct' ways of notated music. It is possible that music of the twenty-first century may provide for the exploration of these neglected aspects of music and also lead to the invention of new ways of performing sound - just as new instruments have been invented alongside the technological innovations of the time throughout the history of music.

We all have the potential for receiving personal, spiritual experiences through the direct activity of creating expressively with sound. Children are particularly fascinated by computers and technology in general. Can these two factors be brought together successfully in the classroom to enrich the educational experience of children in the late twentieth century?

A MODEL FOR CONTEMPLATION

There are some preconditions which may enable anyone to be creative, to encounter an 'inner' experience through music, harnessing some of the new possibilities provided by technology. We have seen how an exclusive diet of Western music can be a two-edged sword; we need to rediscover music as sound, and musical structure as an 'open' rather than a closed form, with neither aspect relying on one (silent) form of notation. As a step towards reawakening a contemplation of sound in music we have worked towards producing a computer application called *Designing Sound* specifically for music in education.

Our starting points included:

• understanding that music is sound, not symbol;

• believing that all creativity, at whatever level, begins with exploration, and includes the joy of discovery;

• enabling (musical) performance instruments, in particular the 'piano-type' keyboard, to be malleable, not confined to any one tonality or sound style;

- providing a 'musical canvas' to enable the organisation of sound into expressive structures, not predetermined forms;

- giving people time to reflect on these explorations, to experiment with them and discover ways of applying the results;

- enabling these activities without the prerequisite of either a traditional musical training, or computer expertise.

We have arrived at three essential conditions:

- the freedom to explore and discover within the medium of sound;

- the ability to preserve, then refine the results of these explorations and discoveries;

- the imagination to respond to these new sounds by creating new structures for expression.

A NEW MUSICAL INSTRUMENT

A five-year research and development project based at the University of Warwick and funded by NCET (the National Council for Educational Technology) allowed us to examine some aspects of new technology, sound and music, and learning in schools. Initially a number of schools were invited to help develop and trial ideas for a new approach to using computers in the music classroom. Children in primary, secondary and special needs schools have all contributed to the subsequent development of *Designing Sound*, a computer program which has ease of access and 'friendliness' as one of its keynotes.

One of the most important interfaces between user and computer is the screen, (see example, Fig 1 below). The layout of screens for the program was developed by continually responding to the reactions of children and teachers involved in the project: the choice of colour; the vocabulary used; the size, shape and position of words on the screen; the size and position of the different boxes used throughout the program; and so on; the final form of the screens evolved very gradually.

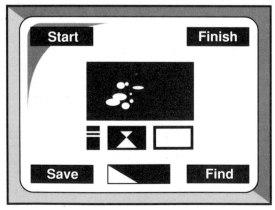

Fig. 1

During these early stages we progressively developed a model for the program. Subsequent analysis revealed that the divine proportion was present in many places in the layout of the individual screens used in the software (see Huntley, 1970). This had emerged partly by allowing children to influence the design where possible. When we discovered this relationship, these proportions were used as a formal reference point in the creation of screens used throughout *Designing Sound*. The ratio was not slavishly adhered to, but the rectangles and areas used in the different displays all reflect and reinforce the aesthetic qualities and properties of the ratio. It is no coincidence that the *Designing Sound* logo takes the form of a nautilus shell.

THE PROGRAM IN USE

The first stage of the software - *Exploring, Discovering* - allows the user simply to explore sound, rather like having a lump of 'musical clay' to turn into a whole variety of sound shapes, colours, textures, and so on. Access to this exploration is through the largest of the 'boxes' on the computer screen (see Fig 1 above). It is through exploring this box that many musical elements and characteristics can be encountered, and an almost infinite variety of timbre or sound quality is 'hidden' within the box.

A second stage allows these sounds to be further explored, developed and refined. Aspects of pitch, volume, articulation and different ways of playing (performing) can be experienced. The results of these explorations can be collected into groups with a specific use in mind, and saved to computer disc as *Sound Sets* - collections of new musical instruments.

 The third stage focuses on the organisation of sounds into an expressive aural design - a musical composition - and this is supported by the *Ensemble* part of the program. *Ensemble* enables instruments from a *Sound Set*, or 'preset' instruments from the keyboard or synthesizer, to be easily recorded and then played back. Up to eight different musical parts can be recorded progressively and cumulatively, each using a different instrument if required.

Having recorded a part, we can use the computer to find the musical effect of, for example: changing the speed of music without altering the pitch; inverting the recording, playing the music backwards and other musical techniques enjoyed by Bach and beyond! We can transpose any track up or down to the limits of the keyboard or synthesizer; we can turn any or all tracks into 'loops' of endlessly repeating patterns of sound, allowing us to explore elements of minimalist music as well as more traditional ostinato patterns and accompanying figures. At any stage of this process the work can be saved on computer disc, and retrieved and further developed at a later date. We can explore increasing complexity whilst preserving simplicity. We can all become musicians having visions.

This three-part structure (see Fig.2) reflects the models for supporting or developing creative and aesthetic experience already described.

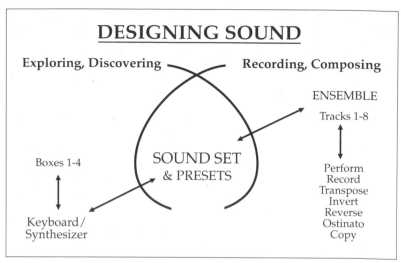

Fig.2

Barriers and Gateways to Innovation

One of the difficulties many people encounter when using computers is having to type accurately on the QWERTY keyboard. This aspect of computing has been kept to an absolute minimum in *Designing Sound* and is not needed at all for the basic functioning of the program. Although a computer 'mouse' is nowadays almost a standard way of running computer programs, we have found that a tracker ball, with its simple, more tactile mode of operation, allows even greater freedom when using the program to explore and control sound, in particular with younger children or people with special needs.

In the performing aspect of making music, synthesizers and keyboards traditionally only allow the 'piano-type' way of playing, but because of new technology we can now exploit a number of alternative ways. A variety of 'midi' wind instruments, percussion pads and other 'controllers' can be used to perform the instruments created with the computer and synthesizer. It is even possible to connect a 'Sound Beam' where the smallest physical movement can be used for musical exploration and performance. Moving an arm, lifting a finger, a slight nod of the head, all these movements can be transformed into musically expressive jestures, of ways of performing musical sounds.

The commercial nature of popular modern music often reflects the pacy, loud freneticism of late twentieth century society, mirroring a reality that is everywhere elsewhere. Much of this music seems to distract the listener, to encourage incessant almost thoughtless movement, rather than present an abstraction worthy of contemplation. This trend is becoming a dominant influence in some areas of our present society.

When first encountering *Designing Sound* most people invariably try to use the program too quickly. This observation holds true across the range of age and ability. At first people tend to scribble with the computer mouse rather than move it carefully or thoughtfully, and so allow no time for interaction or reflection with the sounds that are produced at this stage. Only after some experience of using the program do people tend to slow down and allow sufficient time for interactive contemplation to become possible. However, growing familiarity with using the program enables thoughtful, considered, contemplative modes of behaviour to be observed. These can lead to more focused, attentive and receptive states of mind. As the old Chinese saying tells us: 'there is nothing that cannot be achieved through inactivity'. *Designing Sound* can encourage contemplation in sound - there is no instant solution.

Unlike some other computer music programs *Designing Sound* will not do anything. It is a tool, like having a (very special) pencil or crayon. Very young children can scribble with this, whatever nationality they may be or language they may speak - and the Shakespeares, Picassos and Einsteins of this world use the same tool to make their marks - the implement itself does nothing! Using *Designing Sound* enables us to create sounds which have never been heard before, as well as more ordinary sounds - we can make the **information** of music itself in an environment where sound is the medium, not the notation, not the machine. *Designing Sound* aims to excite the musical imagination, to enable ideas to be explored and music to be constructed and performed in an open, non-prescriptive way, and in any style. What happens next it is up to the user - and the teacher.

Whitman describes music as being 'what happens when the instruments remind us'. If we move towards a reflective and open awareness, towards an experience of sound in stillness, we can perhaps move towards the reality we all carry within ourselves. From these resonances and reflections we can respond from the inside out. Rather than feel out of control, or under the control of external influences, we can explore the new and feel more in tune with ourselves and others. We can then allow time to enhance our inner resonances, enrich our inner experience in new ways; explore 'unity through diversity', and perhaps build an inner aural 'proportion of the divine' for ourselves.

REFERENCES

1. Laing, R.D. (1967) p.36.

2. Manning, P. (1987) p.11.

3. Harvey, J. (1986) pp.175-190.

4. Cott, J. (1974) p.71.

5. Koestler, A. (1979) p.150.

6. Montaigne (1958) p.54.

7. Kandinsky, W. (1977) p.12.

8. Ellis (1986)

9. Langer, S. (1967) p.222.

10. Hindemith, P. (1961) p.78.

11. McCluhan, M. (1967) p.75.

Chang, A.I.T. (1956)   *The Tao of Architecture*, New Jersey, Princeton University Press.

Cott, J. (1974)   *Stockhausen - Conversations with the Composer*, London, Pan Books Ltd.

Ellis, P. (1986)   *Da Capo*, British Journal of Music Education, Cambridge, Cambridge University Press.

Emmerson, S. (1986)   *The Language of Electroacoustic Music*, Basingstoke, Macmillan Press Ltd.

Hargreaves, D.J. (1986)   *The Developmental Psychology of Music*, Cambridge, Cambridge University Press.

Hardy, G.H. (1967)   *A Mathematician's Apology*, Cambridge, Cambridge University Press.

Harvey, J. (1986)   'The Mirror of Ambiguity', in *The Language of Electrocoustic Music*, Ed. S. Emmerson, Macmillan.

Herbert, R.L. ed. (1986)   *Modern Artists on Art*, New York, Prentice Hall.

Hesse, H. (1970)   *The Glass Bead Game*, trans. R. & C. Winston, London, Jonathan Cape.

Hindemith, P. (1961)   *A Composer's World*, New York, Anchor Books.

Huntley, H.E. (1970)   *The Divine Porportion*, New York, Dover Publications.

Huxley, A. (1947)   *The Perennial Philosophy*, London, Chatto & Windus.

Kandinsky, W. (1977)   *Concerning the Spiritual in Art*, New York, Dover Publications.

Koestler, A. (1979)   *Janus: A Summing Up*, London, Pan Books Ltd.

Koestler, A. (1989)   *The Act of Creation*, London, Penguin Group.

Laing, R.D. (1967)   *The Politics of Experience and the Bird of Paradise*, Harmondsworth, Penguin Books Ltd.

Lao Tzu (tr.1963)   *Tao Te Ching*, trans D.C.Lau, Harmondsworth, Penguin Books Ltd.

Langer, S. (1967)   *Philosophy in a New Key*, Cambridge Massachusetts, Harvard University Press.

McCluhan, M. (1967)   *The Medium is the Message*, Harmondsworth, Penguin Books Ltd.

McCluhan, M. (1967)   *Understanding Media*, London, Sphere Books Ltd.

Manning, P. (1987)   *Electronic and Computer Music*, Oxford, Oxford University Press.

Michie, D. & Johnston, R. (1985) *The Creative Computer*, Harmondsworth, Penguin Books Ltd.

Montaigne (tr.1958) 'On the Education of Children', in *Essays*, trans. J.M.Cohen, Harmondsworth, Penguin Books Ltd.

Storr, A. (1976) *The Dynamics of Creation*, Harmondsworth, Penguin Books Ltd.

Whitkin, R.W. (1974) *The Intelligence of Feeling*, London, Heinemann Educational Books.

Wilson, C. (1980) *The New Existentialism*, London, Wildwood House.

Phil Ellis is a Senior Lecturer in the Department of Arts Education at the University of Warwick. An original contributor to the Schools Council Music Project, his work is now centred on a National Curriculum development project - *Designing Sound* - which includes a new approach to technology in music education. His book of music projects across the curriculum, *Out of bounds*, was published in 1987.

NORMAN GIBSON

IMAGES AND ART:
INTERPRETATION AND MEANING

Marking a moment in time and space, we make and do things. With an urge to discover what is or may be the truth, we try to weave a textile of intuitive and conceptual understanding, asking questions towards a new understanding of our world. Through symbols we strive to reconcile 'Lebenswelt', which is the world of common experience and established meanings, to the more abstract and obscure 'Weltanschauung' of imagined possibilities. The author illustrates and explains this process with its hints of other possible worlds and its layers of perception. He explains how its tensions lie between 'correspondence' (some relation to established frames of meaning) and the 'coherence' of achieved perceptions; and he explains how the 'resonances' of our experience bear upon the reconciliation of the two.

A BEGINNING

Many years ago - an adult way, perhaps, of saying 'once upon a time' - medicines and pills were sold in bottles of blue jewel-like glass. When these strikingly coloured vessels began to disappear from chemists' shelves, I cannot say with any certainty, but during my childhood they were a common sight. One morning, the last of a summer vacation in Edinburgh shortly after my tenth birthday, I had the impulsive idea of tying one of those bottles - miniature blue - underneath a holly bush in my grandmother's garden, letting it hang from a hidden branch a few inches above the ground. No one else knew about this. The secrecy was of instinctive importance. The following summer, for the predictability of these holidays was part of this scheme-of-things, I had the subtle satisfaction of rediscovering the secret bottle. The string, unexpectedly, had turned a feeble grey colour; the bottle had retained its pristine gleam. Looking back with a more erudite eye, I can see that the string signalled decay while the bottle confirmed endurance. Entropy and perpetuity are symbolically held together now in a regenerated image.This small intuitive act is still crystal clear in my memory.

It expressed, I think, a childlike existential curiosity and set down a kind of time marker - physical evidence of continuity. The impulse represented, too, the placing of a semi-conscious trail mark in my mind as well as in the world. This was not a defined act of art but one, rather, of mental playfulness. Peter Berger sees play as a celebratory symbol of the "deathlessness of childhood" [1] - the antithesis, as it were, of 'memento mori'. Play is the imaginal radix, perhaps, of all creative endeavour. What that larger endeavour might be, though, cannot be held in a single definition; but somewhere in its deeper layers are concerns to make sense of time and space, to transform the void into a habitable world of people and locations, and to value given meaning as fertile ground for continuous renewal.

During his childhood, Carl Gustav Jung concealed, in a forbidden attic, a little wooden manikin and an oblong pebble from the Rhine. These had profound if inexplicable consequence for him at the time, and their memory was vividly reanimated decades later when he saw their significance in a new light - the light of his knowledge of soul-stones. He came to recognize the connection between the intuitive childhood act and a black stone figure carved in adulthood. This figure he called "Atmavictu" - the breath of life or the creative impulse. [2] The marker-image, or visual signifier, of time and space and events - and the miniature blue bottle was one such for me - appears as a generative symbol for intuitive and conceptual drives towards understanding. This can involve a subtle interplay between the iconic and the textual, and it is instructive to note that the roots of the word 'text' are to be found in the Latin 'texere' - to weave. The textiles of understanding are delicately woven from, and into, the acts of both showing and telling.

THE INTERROGATIVE IMPULSE

We may, quite fairly, expect art to be a source of pleasure or to be the object of admiration and contemplation; and, in some less easily articulated way, to be be concerned with reality and truth. And it is truth, according to John Russell, that is the primary concern of art:

> For hundreds of years, and on many matters of supreme importance, it had the edge over all other sources...it told us what we wanted to hear - that experience was not formless and illegible...

In the modern era, however, art has been perplexing and elusive, and Russell writes:

> ...we are quite right to be dismayed when art seems to shift its ground in ways that we find difficult to follow. And art has shifted its ground, and recoded its messages, and questioned its own nature, and reshaped the ordeal by initiation to which we are subjected before we can understand it completely. [3]

These are vexatious ideas. Is art to be true to something, true to itself - both or neither? What is the 'real' in its referents? The creative impulse, then, has an equally potent counterpart in what I conceive to be a perpetual interrogative impulse: that is, an urge towards meaning, illumination and truth. I shall want to return to these issues later. For the moment, it will suffice to remember Herbert Read's affirmation that art has to do with emotion, not the slack emotion of sentimentality but that, rather, of bracing encounter. This view resonates with what John Berger has to say about poetry:

> It's to do with an immense, cold, cold space - and in such space, somewhere quite small, something which is a little warm and indisputably human.[4]

One way of understanding this cold infinitude might be to see it in terms of as-yet-unrealized potential, the space between the actuality of 'warm' human experience and the possibility of alternative worlds. I take this to be partly what D.H.Lawrence meant by "fecund darkness".[5] Such worlds are elusive, and human instinct shifts uneasily between the known and the imaginable. The domain of everyday human affairs is familiar and secure - or relatively so - but it is this very margin of relativity that marks out the territory of the imagination. The philosopher, Hubert Dreyfus, discussing Heidegger's ideas about the human 'self', makes the point that "People are eager not to deviate from the norm". However, Dreyfus also affirms that Heidegger was concerned to show that "...out of this rather amorphous public us...autonomous individuals crystalise...".[6]

ELUSIVE WORLDS

There is, thus, a tension - sometimes creative, sometimes destructive - between our inhabited worlds, between the 'Lebenswelt' of common experience and the 'Weltanschauung' of philosophical and cultural concepts. The former implies 'a real world' - out there, recognizable and communicable. The latter suggests, to a degree at least, a more abstract and perhaps occluded world. Between them lie the acts of symbol making and, indeed, the creation of what Aldous Huxley called "vision-inducing treasures". Huxley was thinking particularly of the fabricated brilliance of certain kinds of artifacts and architecture which "...are capable, in suitable circumstances, of transporting the beholder's mind in the direction of its antipodes." [7] The antipodes of consciousness are the deep imaginal and, perhaps, spiritual territories of the human psyche.

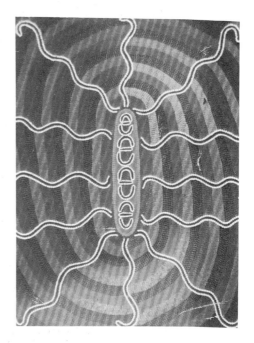

Taking this last idea further, I want to turn to images and forms in the visual arts and to look first at a contemporary aboriginal painting, 'Men's Business', by Paddy Carroll Tjungurrayi (Fig.1). At first sight, this is wholly non figural.

The surface is evenly overlaid with a restricted range of motifs - spots, lines and semi-circular markings. The purely

Fig.1 'Man's Business'
by Paddy Carroll Tjungurrayi

sensory display of this canvas might delight or satisfy the eye independently of cognition. But ancient spiritual knowledge, transformed by 20th century techniques and cultural influences, lies beneath the composition as its originating source. This map-like image refers both to life in the bush and to existence in the Dreamtime - the first quotidian, the second metaphysical. In other words, the painting holds in tension the two domains referred to earlier, the 'Lebenswelt' or world of ordinary human circumstances and the 'Weltanschauung' or realm of transcendent cultural knowledge.

I recall, too, a particular sculpture in Florence, the 13th Century 'Madonna col Bambino' by Arnolfo di Cambio, in which such interplay takes alternative form. The otherwise unitary stone of the carved Madonna is inlaid with eyes of quartz. The impression is one of enhanced realism and, simultaneously, one of extended preternaturalism. The shining quartz corresponds to our common perception of eyes but at another level, paradoxically, the expressive effect is one of detachment and other-worldliness. In this icon, anatomical depiction and transcendent symbolism are juxtaposed. Two dimensions of humanly construed reality coalesce in a single image.

Moving again to contemporary sources, we can see that Bridget Riley's paintings can have a distinctive physical effect on the retina (Fig.2).

Fig.2
The optical elements which she orchestrates are precise, considered, and alternately subtle or dramatic. Her paintings appear to shift between visual conundrum and

musical rhythm and, as Cyril Barrett notes, the "...assault on the eye can be quite painful...the eye is attacked and 'devoured' by the paintings." [8] Is there a cognitive aspect in Riley's works? Are they susceptible to understanding? Is the arresting surface the canvas, the retina or the receptive mind? Do they remain a purely sensory experience, or might they invoke complementary concepts? Are they, in other words, self contained and coherent, or must we look searchingly for correspondent perceptions in the physical realm?

LAYERS OF PERCEPTION

On these kinds of question, and the arts can generate such interrogative responses, I want to explore the somewhat metaphorical terms - transparency and opacity - in relation to a different spectrum of visual objects. Again, questions about and relationships between perception and conception are embedded themes. The act of seeing is a subtle one.

Plates are familiar articles in the everyday world. They are basic necessities and we have to produce them. We are not obliged, however, to make them beautifully or decoratively. Yet, as Ted Cohen points out "Art is the one thing we do precisely because we don't have to do it". But he goes on to affirm:

> Of course we do 'have to do it'. Our spirit requires it, and we know, deeply, that without doing it we will be less than human, less than we can be. [9]

Plates, then, are objects which have both functional and aesthetic character. A semantic difficulty appears here, however. At root, aesthetic refers to sensory perception, with the plain implication that all perceptible forms have aesthetic qualities. This would be to over-simplify the term. Aesthetic sensibility is a complex faculty; it involves discrimination beyond, though it is not dismissive of, personal sensitivity. It is a fusion of feeling and informed judgement.

Let us consider two rather different plates. The first is contemporary Egyptian. It is made of dark wood and has a dense, symmetrical pattern of inlaid ebony and mother-of-pearl. The configuration is entirely geometric. The eye seems to be arrested at the surface of the form and there is no hint of pictorial narrative, nor any evident requirement to look through the pattern, as it were, towards a referent or meaning-laden image. In this respect, the plate (Fig.3) is satisfyingly 'opaque'.

Fig.3

This is not to refute concerns with historical origins in design. Instead, it is an acknowledgement that there may be fundamental 'visual grammars' to which the human eye and brain are predisposed, and to which they may become finely tuned. The second plate, also contemporary, is Australian (Fig.4). Here the design is figurative and it relates schematically to an indigenous mammal - the echidna. The image has two forms of reference. The first assumes knowledge of spiny hedgehog-like creatures; the second is embedded in the conventions of ancient aboriginal art. This plate might be considered

Fig.4

'semi-transparent'. The eye is engaged by the linear pattern but also sees through it, to the referent or correspondent subject beyond. Similarly, in a painting of his wife by Cezanne(Fig.5), the 'subject' is unamibiguously or transparently portrayed - a seated woman in a patterned armchair. It might be argued that all other considerations are

Fig.5

matters of style and that Cezanne's principle intention was to create a frame through which the viewer comes face to face with the sitter or, at any rate, with her representation. Style, itself, if we follow Winckelmann's use of rhetorical theory to analyse classical sculpture, can be construed as a type of grammar. [10] If this is the case, then transparency implies deeper layers and these need to be 'read' by interpretative processes.

In the Cezanne, though, the nature of the picture - as painting - makes a further impact on the viewer's perceptions. The tactual quality of the paint, the interplay of colours and the rhythms of tone and mass create another plane of encounter.

This, too, invokes responses which are both affective and cognitive. There may be a poetic or musical quality in the sensory elements of the work that are virtually independent of the notional subject. Matters of technique, chemistry and period all impinge on the variant interpretative processes. In short, the medium itself becomes a hermeneutic stratum.

CREATIVITY AND REALITY

At this point, I want to return to earlier questions on truth and reality in art, and to consider how these might relate to what are known technically as correspondence and coherence theories. In his book, *Realism*, Damian Grant characterizes correspondence theory as scientific and coherence theory as poetic. Truth, according to the former, is "discovered by a process of knowing" and, with respect to the latter, "created by a process of making."

"The correspondence theory", Grant writes, "is empirical and epistemological."

> It involves a naive or common-sense realist belief in the reality of the external world...and supposes that we may come to know this world by observation and comparison. The truth it proposes is the truth that corresponds, approximates to the predicated reality, 'renders' it with fidelity and accuracy...the correspondence theory defers automatically to the fact, and requires that truth be verified by reference to it...it takes its confidence from the substantial agreement of the majority in its description of reality, which it therefore calls objective.

On coherence theory, Grant has this to say:

> ...on the other hand, the epistemological process is accelerated or elided by intuitive perception. Truth is not earned by the labour of documentation and analysis is but coined, a ready synthesis, and made current - as is any currency - by confidence, 'the confidence of truth'. Evidence is replaced by self-evidence.

He goes on to describe the correspondence view of reality as being "waylaid by truth", and the coherence perspective as the creation of reality "in the very act of perception." [11] Now, while all of this might seem a remote way of interrogating reality and, at first glance, at odds with our expectations and experiences of the visual arts, there are more familiar expressions of the same enquiring impulse. People ask of art: what is it about?, what does it mean?, or, what is it meant to be? These are essentially 'correspondence' questions indicating trust in an underlying reality to which the art-work refers. Alternatively, and implicitly recognizing embedded truth, we may hear the question: what is it? This is rather more of a 'coherence' question. It allows that art might be self-evidently real, that it might hold - as both signifier and signified - its own truth. Different art forms, however, make varying demands on the viewer and it might be, at times, that sculpture's greater physical presence - its inhabiting of common space, its tactility, weight and volume - reduces the referential burden on the viewer. If, for example, we examine the super-real 'Motorcycle', made entirely in wood by Yoshimura, it might appear that we are looking at a piece of 'verist' sculpture; a work which faithfully corresponds to our perceptions of normal or real world encounters.

But Yoshimura is not dealing with unamibiguous realism and he makes the point, "I'm not really reproducing the thing. I'm producing a ghost." [12] In 'accommodating' this sculpture, the compulsion towards visual recognition - knowing the artist's referent - is inescapable. Coming into contact with the same work by touch alone, however, might challenge our ability to put a name to our perceptions.

I should like to turn now, for a moment, to a different order of imagery - to the mirror. In a plain looking-glass, we have secure expectations that what we shall see there will be un-remarkable; a straightforward reflection of our predictable appearance. No 'image', it seems, could correspond more completely to our perceptions of the real world. We know too that convex mirrors will produce a dependable distortion and that the concave surface of a spoon, for example, will invert the 'picture'. The latter are examples of mediated reality to which we become readily, if only subconsciously, accustomed.

Magritte, however, in his painting entitled 'Not to be Reproduced', pushes our expectations of mirror images some distance beyond the boundaries of what we normally accommodate. In the painting - with his back to us - stands the figure of a man, evidently looking at his reflection in a mirror. In the glass, this figure is repeated, so that the subject appears to gaze at his own back view. The painting seems to address itself to the viewer's - and the painter's - physical presence in front of the picture. It is the viewer's (and painter's) image of the subject which is 'mirrored', not the subject's. In a strange way, the subject's view and identity remain hidden or uncertain. We are not privileged to share his perceptions with him. One way of interpreting this picture is to see it as visually parallel to the 'readerly' text. The painting anticipates variant, perhaps eccentric, and ultimately personal readings while, at the same time, presenting imagery in concrete, conventional and matter-of-fact style. The stability of real-world perception, in this evidently representational picture, is challenged by inventiveness and wit. I am reminded here of Kundera's affirmation:

> The art inspired by God's laughter does not by nature serve ideological certitudes, it contradicts them. Like Penelope, it undoes each night the tapestry that the theologians, philosophers, and learned men have woven the day before. [13]

Umberto Eco describes the mirror as "...a threshold-phenomonen marking the boundaries between the 'imaginary' and the 'symbolic'." The young child first perceives the mirror-image as reality, then simply as an image and finally as a personal image. "In this 'jubilant' acceptation of the image, the child reconstructs the still scattered fragments of his body as something outside himself...." [14] In the Magritte, the viewer has no reflected presence but that presence is, nonetheless, implied by the painter's play on our perceptual expectations. We come to learn how to 'use' mirrors but our learning is not solely nor immutably visual. Learning is, itself, a creative process.

RESONANCE

The idea that Modernism represented a clean break with the past and an attempt to start again with 'tabula rasa' might seem attractive at first glance. But it depends, first of all, on where one looks and, secondly, on how one sees. Beyond personal perception lies the wider territory of rhetoric, and it matters greatly how one chooses to listen to and interpret the persuasions and counter claims of critics, historians and educationists. Nonetheless, the modern era has generated a superabundance of art forms, manifestos and philosophies, and one result of this has been a temptation to run for cover and to take refuge in the putative security of former periods, on the assumption that in them lay more dependable expressions of truth and closer approximations to reality.

Reality mediated by art is not, however, unchanging, though art may subtly affirm continuity by way of creation: not 'creatio ex nihilo' nor the seeking of initial conditions - and the search for meaning does tend to become reductive in the direction of 'primitive' conditions - but a sensitive apprehension and expression of linking conditions. This seems as true for contemporary sciences as for contemporary arts.

What, then, is the nature of these linking conditions and how do they pertain to the arts and to education?

For a long time now, I have admired a particular artefact - the centre-board of a Peruvian raft, some 700 years old. There are some figural indications in this piece of crafted timber; small and highly formalized carvings which hint at mythical origins. But the design of the centre-board includes non pictorial elements too - distinctive red rectangles, a graceful inverted arc, and step-and-fret motifs on one side (Fig.6). The distribution of these forms is subtle and elegant, and the piece - as pure form - conveys a satisfying sense of asymmetrical equilibrium.

As with the aboriginal painting mentioned earlier, there is a possibility of coherent sensory response. 'Knowing', though, that this 'is' a raft centre-board and, moreover, that it comes from a particular historical community, cannot be discounted in the overall apprehension of its aesthetic character.

The name of the object is a potent cognitive signal - a distillation of its 'raison d'etre' in the world of human utilities. Seeing through the linguistic layer of its name, I can bring to mind the touch of a hand, the untying of a rope, perhaps, and the splash of the board's release into water. What I think this suggests, is a coalescence of tacit and cognitive responses to a particular artefact. The first is a sensory reaction, brought about in my case by a sculptor's eye 'reading' appreciatively the marks and forms of another's craft. The second is an imaginal interpretation of action and function in a distant epoch.

This is one example of what might be called resonance - between direct experience on one hand and remote human activity on the other, triggered and mediated by a crafted object. Here we have a visual equivalence to the "linguistic trinity" [15] - syntax, semantics and pragmatics, or structure, meaning and use. Resonance is the interplay of imaginative and intellectual responses to a single craftwork - in part to its coherent physical character and in part to its correspondent or referential value. This is not to suggest mental or neurological partition in any technical sense, but rather to recognize that shifts of focus take place in our fields of consciousness. These shifts suggest the linking, rather than initial, conditions of perception upon which human wisdom may be built.

Fig.7

A variation on this theory of resonance is evident in the painting shown (Fig.7). This was made by a ten year old child and produced in response to a reading of the Miller's Tale, from Rosen's book 'Children's Poetry'. [16] The painting offers a portrayal of the miller; but rather than follow faithfully the descriptive details in the poem, the child has painted an image rather more like a self-portrait by Van Gogh - a picture containing few of the visual details indicated by the text.

The work implies a kind of co-authorship, a relationship with the text that corresponds in some measure to it, while retaining a degree of original perception and interpretation in a coherently personal art-form. Resonance, in this instance, is a subtle reverberation between ideas rather than a direct 're-sounding' or faithful transcription.

Max Ernst advocated keeping one eye open and the other closed: the open eye remaining alert to the world of events and the closed eye maintaining contact with the inner life. [17] In his painting, 'The False Mirror', Magritte offers a potent visual equivalent to this. A vast eye is simultaneously seen and, it appears, seen through (Fig.8). In a way, this painting is almost emblematic of art. The eye suggests itself as a semi-transparent membrane, osmotically and ambiguously mediating sensation towards perceptiveness - and the reverse.

Fig.8

Relating to and transcending received meaning, and recognizing that there are no ultimately original or terminal positions from which to adjudge reality, are dimensions of consciousness which seem to converge in the enterprise and adventure of art - in both its making and its reception.

MEMORY AND RENEWAL

When I reflect on visits to Florence over the years, it is not only to such specific images as the Madonna and Child, discussed earlier, that my memory returns. The city itself - its streets and spaces, temperatures and atmospheres - is reanimated as a more wholly affective kind of physical experience. In German, this type of warm holistic reminiscence is known as 'Errinerung'. An alternative word for memory, 'Gedächtnis', connotes more instrumental or cognitive processes. Sometimes art is an evocation, sometimes a more analytic form of recall. At times our reaction is welcoming, contemplative, intuitive - an indwelling, or tacit form of understanding. By contrast, the encounter with art can evoke a need 'to know'; it demands an intellectual and analytic engagement. But this too is an affective response, for knowing is a source of deep satisfaction, achieved by interpretation. Here, the effort is not a solitary one for interpretation is founded upon exchange. Knowledge is communicable, not only in terms of art as a direct encounter but also in respect of its context - its location, purpose, style and construction. This knowledge is available to the receptive learner. It may not be final knowledge, but it is, in a real sense, objective.

Art, then, exists in an authentic community of understanding; and truth, according to Dietrich Bonhoeffer, can only exist in community. The community he had in mind, it cannot be doubted, was one which was capable of self scrutiny and renewal - "a world come of age".[18] Towards the end of Hitler's reign in Germany, Bonhoeffer was executed for having the courage of such convictions.

Growing and Being and Living with Paradox

I want to draw this essay to a close by considering two related images. Both are founded on the spiral, itself a powerful symbolic form. One is the double helix structure of DNA, the molecule of heredity. In the words of one of its discoverers, James Watson, "the structure was too pretty not to be true."[19] Paradoxically, the rather ramshackle demonstration model constructed in the laboratory was far from pretty. So perhaps attractiveness is as much to do with conceptual elegance as with visual sensibility. Seen schematically, the sugar-phosphate backbones with their hydrogen-bonded base pairs resemble a spiral staircase.

The second image is architectural; a double-spiral staircase inside St.Peter's in Rome. The two stairways coil slowly together in parallel. On ascent or descent, one can see those approaching from the opposite direction without ever coming face to face. Differing forms of knowledge seem, at times, to share this paradoxical kind of space. They come within sight of each other but never quite meet. Visual art may resonate with other aspects of expression and it may demonstrate exploratory tendencies which seem to have a good deal in common with other investigative processes. Nonetheless, it remains a largely independent and major 'grammar' of human intelligence, with all the richness and subtlety that intelligence implies.

Education also embodies the paradoxical. Etymologically, 'education' suggests contrasting paradigms: 'educare' purports training, upbringing and, by inference, the fitting of the individual to a given social setting; while 'educere', on the other hand, allows for a leading forth, a recognition and facilitation of individual potentiality. The first interpretation appears to lean towards the theory of correspondence: the individual is educated by reference to existing orders or cultures - and the young child seems to need and welcome this. The adult domain appears to be an explicit goal - an at least temporarily authorized version of reality to which to aspire. Jerome Bruner makes the point that:

...infants and young children from very early on appear, like adults, to be Naive Realists who believe that there is a world of objects 'out there' and that others are experiencing the same world that they are. And, indeed, whatever philosophical position we adults may eventually take, however constructionalist our epistemology may become, I think Naive Realism is everybody's working belief... [20]

The second interpretation shifts in the direction of coherence theory - celebrating the early conditions of infancy and having in prospect the full development of creative maturity. One soon sees the emergence of independent action in the growing child. In the visual arts, the shifts are complex. Infants demonstrate a virtual autonomy of pure form in their earliest and, perhaps, most pleasurable handling of materials. This appears to change, at least for a while, as children strive towards correspondent or representational imagery. But, here, correspondence has to do as much with art itself as with the referent world of sense perceptions. Art remains part of the child's 'working belief'. Coherent potency in the creative acts of art may return at a later stage, and it seems that it can ebb and flow in the experience of even the most mature practitioners - perhaps for the very reason that art tends to run against the mind's ingrained perceptions of functioning existence. We might hope for, at best, an educational experience which spirals optimistically. As Dag Hammarskjöld understood it, the principles and thoughts of his childhood formed the point of cyclical return in adult life; but this was, as Henry P. van Dusen writes, "...at a higher level." [21]

CODA

At the time of writing this essay, one of my students discovered in a dusty studio-cupboard an old box packed with glass medicine bottles. Among them lay a miniature blue one, identical to that of my childhood memory. Jung might have considered this to be one in these clusters of events which transform our perceptions of time and space. I have no personal theory to promote, but it pleases me to report the coincidence.

REFERENCES

1. Berger, P. (1969) p.75.

2. Jung, C.G. (1963) pp.34-36.

3. Russell, J. (1985) pp.13 and 14.

4. Berger, J. in a televised discussion 'Another Way of Telling', BBC, 28 May 1989.

5. Lawrence, D.H. (edn.1978) p.447.

6. Dreyfus, H. in Magee (Ed.) (1987) pp.266 and 267.

7. Huxley, A. (1961) p.93.

8. Barrett, C. (1971) p.112.

9. Cohen, T. (1990),p.18.

10. Potts, A. (1990), p.229.

11. Grant, D. (1985), p.9.

12. Yoshimura, F., cited by Kim Levin, 'The Ersatz Object', in Battcock, G. (1975) at p.102.

13. Kundera, M. (1988) p.160.

14. Eco, U. (1988), p.203.

15. Bruner, J. (1986) p.82.

16. Rosen, M. (1985) p.49.

17. Ernst, M. in a televised interview of 1961 shown on 'The Late Show', BBC, 21 February 1991.

18. Bosanquet, M. (1968), p.260.

19. Watson, J. (1968), p.210.

20. Bruner, J. (1983), p.74.

21. Van Dusen, H.P.(1967) p.49.

| BIBLIOGRAPHY |

Barrett, C (1971): *An Introduction to Optical Art*, London, Studio Vista.

Battcock, G (1975): *Super Realism: A Critical Anthology*, New York, Dutton.

Berger, P (1969): *A Rumour of Angels*, New York, Doubleday.

Bosanquet, M (1968): *Bonhoeffer True Patriot*, London, Mowbrays.

Bruner, J (1986): *Actual Minds, Possible Worlds*, Massachusetts, Harvard University Press.

Bruner, J (1983): *Child's Talk*, Oxford, Oxford University Press.

Cohen, T (1990): 'Clay for Contemplation', in *Crafts*, London, Crafts Council.

Eco, U (1988): *Semiotics and the Philosophy of Language*, Basingstoke, Macmillan.

Grant, D (1985): *Realism*, London, Methuen.

Huxley, A (1961): *The Doors of Perception and Heaven and Hell*, Harmondsworth, Penguin.

Jung, C.G (1963): *Memories, Dreams, Reflections*, London, Collins and Routledge & Kegan Paul.

Kundera, M (1988): *The Art of the Novel*, London, Faber and Faber.

Lawrence, D.H (edn.1978): *The Rainbow*, Harmondsworth, Penguin.

Magee, B (Ed) (1987): *The Great Philosophers*,London, BBC Books.

Potts, A (1990): 'The verbal and visual in Winckelmann's analysis of style', *Word and Image*, Vol.6, No.3, London, Taylor and Francis.

Rosen, M (1985): *Children's Poetry*, London, Kingfisher.

Russell, J (1985): *The Meaning of Modern Art*, London, Thames and Hudson.

Van Dusen, H.P (1967): *Dag Hammarskjöld, A Biographical Interpretation of 'Markings'*, London, Faber and Faber.

Watson, J (1968): *The Double Helix*, London, Weidenfeld and Nicolson.

Norman Gibson, Head of Arts, Design and Performance at the Manchester Metropolitan University, was formerly a Lecturer in the Department of Arts Education and Director of Studies for the MA in Art and Design Education at the University of Warwick. A sculptor and designer, he has shown work in many solo and national exhibitions, and has had extensive teaching experience within primary, secondary and higher education sectors. His ongoing research is concerned with visual-verbal interplay in creative activity and production.

RELIGIOUS EDUCATION AND THE PURSUIT OF MEANING

INTRODUCTION

Much of our effort in recent years has been to establish religious education in a plural context, as something meaningful to all our children amidst a plurality of religious traditions and conscientiously secular outlooks. Finding the same pluralism naturally reflected in school staffing, we have wanted to establish RE as a professional activity to which teachers of various personal persuasions could contribute conscientiously - in the same way as they might teach history, for example, while holding differing personal views on its meaning and philosophy. Nor should this be thought an unworthy or impossible goal - for the professional standpoint is one of goodwill, of respect for the concerns of others and for the whole society that education needs to serve. And indeed great progress has been made in this battle against the professional marginalisation of RE.

Nevertheless, there has been an unfortunate aspect of all this, one that looms large in current debates. It is that we are too often seen as talking in negative terms, or in terms that have leave a somewhat negative impression. This can be said of such excellent concerns as the avoidance of indoctrination, the need to be impartial, the need to be fair, and the need to be balanced in what we offer. They are worthy considerations, and by no means exclusively secular concerns. But in the context of developing the boundaries of RE, its content and its professional basis, it is not too surprising that some people have questioned the kind of concern for religion that may be implied. They have wondered whether we might not be trying to preserve our children from the life-changing force of religion and to offer instead a standard diet of cultivated agnosticism. They have suspected the deliberate evacuation of religion through an aggressively secularised understanding of education. Those of us who hope to see a workable consensus renewed in RE should, I think, wholeheartedly admit that religious education stands condemned if it amounts merely to multicultural information or a catalogue of external behaviour in rites, rituals and festivals. We should accept that suspicion will be more than justified wherever classroom activity amounts to mere descriptivism under the guise of objectivity. The nature of our problem now is to talk positively about the exploration of religious insights as the heritage of all our children.

If we now try to think of religious education against this background, we must say that it should offer knowledge and understanding. But this goal must be understood in a particular way, a way that is sensitive to the religious outlook. Somehow we must put to our young people the inspiration that moves religiously committed people, the ways in which they engage with the world, the passion that underlies their pursuit of holiness and truth. In essence the religious outlook is that knowledge and understanding have a conversive or life-transforming quality, and that in the end they yield pride of place to holiness. And though holiness often seems to embrace a supreme kind of wisdom, you do not have to be clever to be holy.

If religious education is to acknowledge the driving force of religion, we would do well to pay some attention to religion's ultimate emphasis on personal holiness as a concern transcending religious information, knowledge and understanding. Often appearing as a kind of spiritual giftedness, its recognition by others may be itself one of the spiritual gifts. It may be the case, I think, that parents have in mind some awareness of this when they demand something more from RE than mere information and cultivated tolerance. They do not want less than informed tolerance, but they want us to convey more than that because they know that religion itself amounts to more than that. Now, it is clearly a tall order to speak of holiness as a classroom pursuit; and I do not think that parents demand GCSEs in personal sanctity. Regarded as curriculum content in any formal sense it is too easily reduced to the bathos of 'moral example'. What we can and should do is to recognise that the kind of knowledge and understanding we deal with RE is not something entirely at arm's length from the learners. We should recognise that RE can and will change people in some way, and parents have rightly sensed something fundamental to religious concerns in expecting RE to offer the vision of transformation. This is not an illicit indoctrinatory concern. It is an educational concern. It asserts simply that all enlargement of awareness - be it secular or religious - changes people. How it may do so is a matter of personal experience in the context of individual lives.

Recently a splendid lead has been given by John Hammond, David Hay and their colleagues. They have been determined to put the experience of religion at centre stage.

> Religious education must perform two tasks if it is to face the question of the religious believer's intention squarely. First, it must honestly present religion for what it claims to be - the response of human beings to what they experience as the sacred. Secondly, religious educators must help pupils to open their personal awareness to those aspects of ordinary human experience which religious people take particularly seriously. It is important to note at this stage that both tasks, whilst they point directly at the sources of religious motivation for the believer, still leave open questions of the ultimate truth of religion. They are therefore educational rather than indoctrinatory in intention.[1]

Here too there is the long-standing concern about indoctrination, but no trace of religious self-effacement. Rather, the claim for widely and deeply felt personal experiences to be represented in education is a counterbalance to the institutionalised indoctrination of secularism.

Religious educators are sometimes accused of attempting to indoctrinate their pupils. But when religious education is correctly understood, it becomes clear that it is the reverse of indoctrination. What it does is to demonstrate that there is more than one perspective on reality. It enlarges, rather than diminishes freedom. [2]

As a commentary on this one might suggest that the freedom of which it speaks is a value inherent in the religious life no less than in the secular. Of their very nature, both education and religious faith deny blindly uninformed compulsion.

In this book, Brenda Wall refers briefly to seeking something more than the projects and activities of experiential learning described by John Hammond, David Hay and their colleagues. I do not think she does so in any opposition to the programme of those writers. It is rather that she moves on to reconsider the organisational context of religious education and to suggest other creative approaches. For Brenda Wall the way forward lies in placing religious education among the creative arts and in using art methods for the personal and shared exploration of world faiths. Her suggestions stand here alongside those of John Alcock and Robert Green in the fields of drama and music respectively. Together, all three are committed to the shared spiritual dynamics of religious education and the arts, and sensitive to the dynamics of education as a force for human development. On the other hand the possibilities arising with John Alcock and Robert Green do not ostensiby or necessarily demand the curriculum framework suggested by Brenda Wall. Readers will doubtless form their own conclusions about suitable or possible frameworks. In primary schools, where the flow of the timetable may allow more latitude and continuity of activities, organisational questions do not perhaps arise with the same force as they do in secondary schools. But in either case, it may be possible through a variety of organisational forms to take the opportunities of applying cross-curricular insights.

CONCLUSION

Perhaps the dominant concern should be to speak positively of religious education as a creative force. Parents have wanted for their children the opportunity to take religious belief seriously. Clive Erricker offers a new and distinctive way for us to think about this. Clearly sympathetic to the the earlier argument of Steve Attridge, he takes up the suggestion that people move from and towards alternative mythic structures in understanding themselves and the world. His point is not to say that religion is fictitious. It is to say first that when we try to take hold of religious insights and ideas we build them into a story about our own lives. Corresponding to the iconic, symbolic and metaphorical activity of the artist, the scope of this educational conversiveness is nothing less than a constant re-orientation of ourselves. He uses this to discuss what we do in RE and to discuss our responsibility as teachers. He suggests that the teacher will recognise some responsibility not just for informational transactions but for the imagery of life that is offered in classrooms. Sensitive to the pastoral obligation that runs alongside all teaching, he uses examples drawn from medicine and psycho-therapy to illustrate the potential depth and seriousness of of the issues.

Clive Erricker's view of the teacher's reponsibility offers an implicit standard of an essentially pastoral kind - a standard perhaps of mental health and personal well-being. Alongside this it will be important to consider the suggestions of Robert Jackson. He too is concerned with the approach of teacher and pupil to 'otherness', but he approaches the question from a different direction. Dissatisfied with the notion of 'empathy' as it has been understood in the tradition of phenomenology, he outlines another approach drawn from the social sciences. Readers will judge for themselves whether (or to what extent) the approaches of Jackson and Erricker may be opposed. The editor chooses provisionally to think that they are complementary strands in a continuing dialogue about the impact of RE and how to secure and understand it. Erricker's concern for the subjective impact of RE does not mean pure subjectivism in the treatment of religions; and while Jackson is concerned for a proper objectivity in our approach to the religions, he no less insists on an artistic element in the processes of understanding. Brenda Watson's "essentialist" model for RE (in the previous section) is another distinctive contribution to our understanding of the issues that arise here.

References

1. John Hammond, David Hay *et al.*, *New Methods in RE Teaching: An Experiential Approach*, Oliver and Boyd, 1990, ch.2, p.11.

2. *ibid* ch.3, p.15.

CLIVE ERRICKER

THE ICONIC QUALITY OF THE MIND

Through metaphor we generate meaning and order reality for ourselves in pursuit of mental and spiritual health. Personally or socially established metaphors are the icons of received meaning. The author investigates metaphorical processes, illustrating their impact on personal well-being. Educational and religious institutions bear a particular responsibility for the metaphorical reality they create; and we need to see education not as the uniform imposition of discrete world-views (a confrontation between subject and object) but as a continously intersubjective dialogue. The heart of this will be a mutual sympathy, a respect for persons who participate as we do in the quest for effective metaphorical structuring. Bringing all this together in terms of a personal story, the author demonstrates the inadequacies of a Cartesian objectification of knowledge in the area of the humanities.

'Language is a window on the mind' (Chomsky)

'Truth is a mobile marching army of metaphors,
metonymies and anthropomorphisms' (Nietzsche)

This chapter is about metaphor and its importance in establishing meaning in our lives. It explores how metaphor is conveyed in images. It examines how this iconic quality of metaphor represents a characteristic quality of the mind that enables us to construct the stories by which we live. It then asks how far particular metaphors and the way in which they are constructed, contribute to or detract from our well-being. It concludes by suggesting that developing communication between and reflecting upon the plurality of our metaphorical perceptions is one of the primary educational tasks that we must address.

METAPHOR AND ICON

Technically, the term metaphor usually refers to a figurative use of language. Similarly, the term myth is applied to a story that has no historical foundation. In these cases metaphor and myth are understood as decorative. By this I mean they don't add to what is known, rather they embellish what we know already or allow us to fantasize or imagine beyond that knowledge. It is in this sense that we understand them to 'paint a picture'. The presupposition of such an understanding is that this already depends upon a literal use of language that acts as the foundation for our knowledge. It assumes that we have the facts already. Icon and metaphor are inter-related terms in that Icon functions in the visual field in a similar way to the use of metaphor in language. Neither offers us a literalistic representation. Both act as signifiers which translate the literal facts of our lives into mythology and so bring it alive. In this article I wish to explore a different understanding of the terms icon and metaphor than the decorative. I wish to suggest that both refer to a way of expressing knowledge that cannot be communicated in a literal manner, visually or in language. There is a mental-imaging that is vital to the ordering of our psychological reality and which cannot otherwise be accounted for. Metaphor actually generates meaning. It constructs a landscape in which we have a place. It does so by ordering things such that they gain significance in relation to our sense of self. Just as a shrine groups objects of significance into an inter-related whole that is understood in a way that is not simply dependent on the literal shape of the objects or their individuality so metaphor constructs the landscape of our minds.

METAPHOR, PERCEPTION AND WELL-BEING

Susan Sontag quotes Aristotle as giving the most succinct definition of metaphor.[1] She states that metaphor 'consists in giving the thing a name that belongs to something else.'[2] Sontag goes on to interpret this statement by explaining: 'Saying a thing is or is like something it-is-not is a mental operation as old as philosophy and poetry and the spawning ground of most kinds of understanding... Of course one cannot think without metaphors. But that doesn't mean there aren't some metaphors we might well abstain from or try to retire'.[3]

Sontag, in her investigation of metaphor related to illness, exposes that metaphor itself has the power to generate well-being or disease influencing the physical condition of the person and the way it is understood. Her experience of having cancer confronted her not only with the disease itself but the metaphoric use of the word. Having cancer was to be cancerous and so to be set aside from society by being tainted, incurable, under the sentence of death. Here was an example of how people can become dehumanised, less than they are, not scarred by the effect of the physical condition but by the effect of the metaphorical use of the word being associated with that physical condition. A person with cancer does not have a contagious disease but metaphorically speaking that person is cancerous and the presence of that condition suggests that we are all at risk. As a consequence, the sufferers are seen as deformed (metaphorically) and disabled by the application of the metaphor to themselves. He or she understands herself differently as a consequence of the metaphor rather than just the disease.

Sontag quotes Nietzsche who puts it very simply:

'Thinking about illness! - To calm the imagination of the invalid, so that at least he should not, as hitherto, have to suffer more from thinking about his illness than from the illness itself - that I think, would be something! It would be a great deal!'[4]

Substitute 'person' for invalid and 'condition' or 'situation' for illness and we see that Sontag's observations say important things about the metaphorical realities we construct in educational and religious frames of reference. The institutions of religion and education that exist bear a responsibility for the metaphorical reality that they create. When Nietzsche speaks of calming the imagination it cannot be done by doing away with metaphor. The understanding of our human condition depends upon metaphorical enterprise, but which metaphors should we retire and which should we seek to develop and sustain? As a first step toward answering this question let's look at the operation of metaphor in more detail.

Returning to Aristotle's definition, the point about giving something a name that belongs to something else is that we use the literal world to explore and define the non-literal. This is a complex endeavour. The literal world is one of entities available to our senses. In a scientific sense we have tended to regard it as an ordered world separate from our own subjectivity; but this is a very neat and orderly fiction if it suggests that we can encounter the literal world of itself and on its own. The psychology of advertising provides us with everyday examples of the fallacy of such thinking. When we buy detergent, cigarettes or beer we come into relation with ready-made metaphors, and off the shelf myths at the same time as the literal thing itself. The metaphorical reality arises immediately in the perception of the object and the way in which it is contextualised. It isn't that we see the literal world first and then place metaphor upon it. They come together in the act of perception. What is seen is both object and icon at the same time. That is, it is already invested with significance and so possesses an iconic quality, however slight or marginal, by our coming into relation with it. The acts of naming and classifying constitute a recognition of this ordering and signifying process. In order to see this most clearly we have to step out of our usual perception of things and be confronted with another.

All understanding is based upon perception, and from this arises classification. Everything is *seen* within the context of perceptual constructs or hermeneutical frameworks. Foucault suggests that: 'in fact there is no similitude and no distinction, even for the fully untrained perception, that is not the result of a precise operation and of the application of a preliminary criteria... The fundamental codes of a culture establish for every man the empirical orders with which he will be dealing and in which he will be at home.'[5] The implication of this is that we do not establish a fresh perception of the world for ourselves as individuals but work from a culturally inherited one. The environment exists for us as a process of consciousness in which we are involved and within which our sense of identity is formed. The basis of this process is the construction of metaphor and metaphor is our means of conversing with ourselves and others as to the way in which order arises out of the inherently unordered thusness of the world.

An observation by the anthropologist Sheila Kitsinger provids us with a visually significant image to work within. In this passage Kitsinger refers to a condition known as 'Kayak-angst' suffered by Eskimos and relates it to the institutionalised experience of women in childbirth.

> 'A condition known as kayak-angst has been described among Eskimos. When the Eskimo hunter is out alone on a calm sea paddling or sitting quietly, there develops a lowering in the level of consciousness brought on by the absence of external reference points at a time when the hunter is engaged in simple repetitive movements or sitting motionless and staring at the sea. He gets confused and dizzy - and even the psychologists who were studying this found that they were disturbed in exactly the same way when they tried to do it, too.

> This condition may arouse vivid memories in some women who have been alone in a hospital labour ward for any length of time, lying with nothing to see both the ceiling and a tiled wall, sometimes with a light shining in their faces. It is important to create points of reference, therefore, in case this sort of stress should occur and threaten a women's equilibrium. Familiar objects, the presence of her husband or a midwife or doctor she already knows and likes are important.'[6]

This example of disorientation experienced by Eskimos and childbearing women alike, illustrates our need for an environment in which we can place ourselves or, to put it more forcefully, identify our place. But it is clear that it is not simply a physical knowing where we are that is necessary but a reminder of who we are, identifying ourselves through our relationship with our environment. It is this sense of being reminded, a continuous and persistent reconstructing or remembering that is the most revealing aspect of Kitsinger's observations. It is evident that the landscape in which we literally find ourselves is not the only environment that we inhabit. There is also a concomitant landscape of the mind. Mental images (evoked by association with the literal but also informed by memory) provide the framework for our reconstruction of the world.

Significantly, whereas the Eskimo experiences his angst-ridden condition as an occupational hazard, the childbirthing woman experiences it due to professional ineptitude. However such criticism cannot be offered at the level of whether the individual nurse or doctor carried out their duties well but rather at the level of what, conceptually speaking, the institution understands its function to be. Clinically everything may go well and yet the total experience of giving birth may still be traumatic. The reason for this apparent contradiction is that institutionally there is no consideration of the underlying metaphorical reality upon which the individual's well-being depends.

This trauma is, at least, localised in space and time for those in childbirth but the neurologist Oliver Sacks generalises and deepens the intensity of this experience in relation to the role that those professionally involved in medicine, religion and, I suggest, education play in human society.[7] In speaking of the role of medicine in the world today he observes that in his experience as a doctor, those who identify themselves as being ill often are not suffering from an everyday complaint but entertain the idea of another sort of medicine that will restore their health and wholeness to them and rectify their sense of what is lost and must be found. This sense, he suggests, is in fact a metaphysical one and modern medicine, for all its rational sense, is unable to provide a remedy.

What Sacks points to is the need for an holistic awareness of the appropriate role of institutions in society whether they are concerned with medicine, religion or education. When we consider this in an educational context we realize the problem of identifying our professional responsibility. Above all, we are responsible for contributing to the fundamental well-being of the child which means engaging with his or her metaphorical reality and working with it in an holistic manner. Bruno Bettleheim summarises this task well when he states:

> 'Today, as in times past, the most important and also the most difficult task in raising a child is helping him to find meaning in life. Many growth experiences are needed to achieve this. The child, as he develops, must learn step by step to understand himself better; with this he becomes more able to understand others, and eventually can relate to them in ways which are mutually satisfying and meaningful'.[8]

This construction of our personal myth is a sensitive business. How are we to be responsible for the well-being of our pupils in this respect and what characterises an authentic educational model that takes account of the need for children to determine their own metaphorical reality?

SEEING AND SUBJECTIVITY

The first step is to acknowledge that whatever paradigm we adopt will itself be metaphorically grounded. Diana Eck illustrates this well by recalling a memorable episode in Hindu mythology:

> 'the great God Siva and the goddess Parvati are sporting in their high Himalayan home when Parvati, in play, covers Siva's eyes with her hands. The whole universe is suddenly plunged into darkness. When Siva's eyes are closed, there is no light anywhere, except the fire of Siva's third eye, which threatens destruction. The all-seeing gods are said never to close their eyes, and from the near-disaster of Siva and Parvati's play, it is clearly a good thing that they don't, for the well-being of the world is dependent on the open eyes of the Lord'.[9]

The open eyes of Siva being necessary for the well-being of the world introduces us to the metaphor of *seeing*. As long as the lord sees us, we are well: the world is ordered and its progression, in contradistinction to its destruction, is maintained. The alternative is chaos. That chaos refers to our individual, internal psychic order as well as that of the social and physical word. It is consciousness itself that is disordered in the Hindu view. Not only is that which is seen disordered but the seer himself. Eck affirms the iconic quality of metaphor with reference to this story and especially the quality of *darsan*, the 'seeing' of the divine image which she calls the single, most common and significant element of Hindu worship. I wish to work from the concept of *darsan* as conceived within the Hindu tradition to an analogous but more broadly based use of the metaphor of 'seeing' in an educational context. Eck goes on to communicate the power and importance of seeing in the Hindu tradition by saying 'in the Hindu view, not only must the gods keep their eyes open, but so must we'.[10] The key feature of Eck's analysis is that *darsan* results in not only being seen by the divine but in the conferring of the blessing of becoming a seer by going through that experience. She extrapolates from this that 'as

142

teachers and students of a culture as visually orientated as that of India we too must become *seers*'.[11]

In looking at Hindu images of the Gods we are advised by Eck to read them as visual texts requiring discussion, interpretation and re-reading. The significance of re-reading is that what we see ceases to become simply illustration and achieves its own subjectivity such that 'what catches the eye may change our minds'. How is this to occur? If that which is seen is recognised as having its own subjectivity then seeing also involves the sense of being seen. In the Hindu context this involves the seer in receiving, in return, 'a sacred perception, which is the ability to truly see the divine image'.[12] By means of this grace the devotee experiences a transformation in perception that removes the ego from the centre of his or her iconic world.

So, according to Eck; 'seeing, after all, is an imaginative, constructive activity, an act of making'. In fact seeing here refers to an act of metaphorical awareness in which the organic intersubjectivity of our being in the world is holistically realised.

We can translate this analysis into the educational sphere. The significant issue is the valuing of the individual in relation to others. It isn't the case that one becomes valued by taking on the particular perception of others, but that, in an intersubjective awareness, both the similarities and differences of view are valued positively as a process of communication. However, the outcome of such communication should not be seen as a uniformity of view in terms of the models of reality or mental landscapes used by those who identify themselves as belonging within different cultural, ideological and religious traditions. Rather it is the provision of a paradigm that provides the possibility of communication and that allows us to take steps toward a shared sense of *being together*. An acceptance of inter-subjectivity. Oliver Sacks provides us with an interesting example of how such an idea might be exemplified in relation to the concept of well-being by analysing the visions of Hildegard, the 12th century Christian mystic. Hildegard suffered from migraine, and was the recipient of visions. Sacks quotes one of her visions with commentary as follows:

'One such vision, illustrated by a figure of stars falling and being quenched in the ocean signifies for her "The Fall of Angels":

I saw a great star most splendid and beautiful, and with it an exceeding multitude of falling stars which with the star followed southwards... And suddenly they were all annihilated, being turned into black coals... and cast into the abyss so that I could see them no more.

Such is Hildegard's allegorical interpretation. Our literal interpretation would be that she experienced a shower of phosphenes in transit across the visual field, their passage being succeeded by a negative scotoma.'

Sacks concluded that:

'Invested with this sense of ecstasy, burning with profound theophorus and philosophical significance, Hildegard's visions were instrumental in directing her towards a life of holiness and mysticism. They provide a unique example of the manner in which a physiological event, banal, hateful or meaningless to the vast majority of people, can become, in a privileged consciousness, the substrata of a supreme ecstatic inspiration'.[13]

Hildegard's metaphorical reality gave meaning to the effects of an unfortunate medical condition and turned what would otherwise have been solely a matter of clinical enquiry into the condition of a deluded patient into the celebration of a 'privileged consciousness'. She was both a migraine sufferer and a visionary and the two could not be separated. The basis of Hildegard's visions was her belief that they were a communication with God. She states:

> 'During these five seconds I live a whole human existence, and for that I would give my whole life and not think that I was paying too dearly...'[14]

If we were to treat her as having a deranged mind due to her medical condition we should be dismissing the importance of what her metaphorical reality has to offer, yet that would clearly be the conclusion we must come to on a purely medical basis. Such a judgment would be tantamount to treating Hildegard as a sufferer of a complaint and objectifying her in the same way as Sontag spoke of herself with cancer. If we allow ourselves to enter into an inter-subjective relationship with Hildegard, in the same way as her metaphorical reality allowed her to enter into such a relationship with God, we arrive at a much richer perception of her worth as an individual and thereby enrich ourselves without, in the process, taking on her metaphorical perception. This is the process of education. It is not a matter of distinguishing between religious and non-religious world views nor of determining the ultimate worth of any metaphorical reality but arriving at an appreciation of the metaphorical realities that we all hold and distinguishing between those which on the basis of an inter-subjective paradigm nourish well-being and those which, by contrast, in operating only with a subject-object paradigm can endanger the health of individuals and collectivities. Briefly put, one of the significant aims of education should be to enable such an exchange of vision.

THE SUBJECT-OBJECT AND THE INTER-SUBJECTIVE PARADIGMS

The subject-object paradigm has eroded our well-being because it has become the pervasive epistemological model. In 'Viewpoints: Metaphor and Monsters - Children's Storytelling', John Pickering and Steve Attridge contrast Cartesian and Vichian perspectives on learning.

> 'The Cartesian perspective is the dominant Western model which emphasises reason over against intuition and the capacity for precise language and distinct thought as being evidence of a rational soul...'[15]

> 'The literal, the logical and the rational were considered to be the core of human intelligence rather than the poetic, the emotional and the intuitive. metaphor belonging as it clearly does to the latter category, becomes under this view, a decorative covering laid atop of a more fundamental rational linguistic base'.[16]

> 'Vico, contrastingly, emphasised the capacity to bring nominal order to experience through metaphorical indentification... needs and emotions are now placed at the heart of the human mind, rather than being seen as distortions of an essentially rational core. Language becomes the rational clothing of a metaphorical body'[17]

The two important distinctions that follow from identifying the Vichian perspective are 'the centrality of metaphor in cognition and the necessary interconnectedness of emotion and cognition'.[18]

These observations illustrate the impoverishment of only working with the Cartesian model. On its own it offers a limited construct within which to identify our world and our place in it. Effectively, we recognize a world that is devoid of our own subjectivity and in which we identify other subjects objectively. This paradigm determines that we objectify others, so treating them as objects as a perceptual rule. It appears to work in a highly effective way in mathematical and scientific thinking when the basis of how things are belongs to the realm of 'fact'. But then we realise the concept itself belongs to that paradigm. So long as 'fact' is the bed-rock of knowledge cognition has to operate in a subject-object manner with the myth of true objectivity being the guiding vision. Once this paradigm becomes pervasive, the study of history, language, religion and what we might call the humanities are all identified as areas of enquiry on this same basis, and their worth will be judged according to their 'epistemological yield' when viewed in the context of this paradigm. The elision of the terms 'fact', 'truth' and 'knowledge' that we constantly experience with children and students is due to the way we have confused these paradigms intellectually and educationally. We have not identified the paradigm we are using, where it has come from and its value for the task we are undertaking. Nor have we analysed the way in which our conceptual terms are within the framework determined by operating according to a particular paradigm.

The significant shift that occurs when metaphor is seen as central to cognition is, in Samuel Levin's terms that 'what is metaphoric is not language but the world'. In other words we construct the world from our own metaphoric cognition. It is easy to see the dangers of going down this road, but educationally we have barred the gate and psychologically shut ourselves out with all the concommitant effects in terms of the skills of perception, communication and reflective awareness that this entails.

'Well-being' is a conceptual term that depends upon an intersubjective educational paradigm for its meaning and as with all educational goals it is value laden. The question is not whether it is something we should ask children to consider, but whether, in response to the expression of their own needs already identified, we decide it is our educational responsibility to assist and guide them.

An example of how young children work with simple metaphoric models that take account of well-being was provided by my own seven year old daughter, Polly. She spoke of two friends whose parents had separated and now lived in streets adjacent to one another. The children stay with their father at the weekend and their mother during the week. In one sense they could be said to have two homes. However, Polly's perception of this was that they are 'passed' from one parent to the other, She was insistent on the use of this word. In her own experience it is connected to 'passing to and fro', 'pass it on', 'pass the parcel' and so on. The force of this term lay in the recognition that her friends had become 'objectified', passed back and forth between the parents and that this was a sad state of affairs. It was not good for them. They had no home.

We can see this 'objectification' occurring in the observations of Sontag and Sacks, and discern its effects. Both Sontag and Sacks speak of illness as an 'objectified state' in which the patient is treated literally, as a physical object with no subjectivity or metaphysical reality. Kitsinger's image of the birthing mother as patient focuses this perception of the person as patient to be dealt with. If we were to apply such a perception to Hildegard we could only speak of the way in which a migraine sufferer had retreated into a private and imaginary world rather than of the rich metaphoric vision that sustained her.

Apparent in all of these cases is that whilst we grow within the context of metaphoric realities already established within cultures and traditions, educationally these constructs must be understood as organic. They are not simply passed on to a child, but that which a child grows up within the context of, and enters into. This dialectical process depends on inter-subjective communication. We can recognise in all this much of what we do to children that does not contribute to their development and well-being. We can recognise also the ignorance with which we often pursue the art of religious education.

Learning starts by avoiding the objectification of children and the mythologies of others that we introduce them to. This has a direct effect on curriculum planning, concepts of knowledge, teaching styles, models of learning, classroom organisation and values in education. Fundamentally, what we are concerned with here is summed up in Wittgenstein's aphorism that 'the world of the happy man is a different one from that of the unhappy man'[19] and the force of my argument is that this is the primary educational distinction we must work with in helping children to construct their own enabling metaphors.

References

1. Sontag, S (1991) p.91.

2. Aristotle: Poetics (1457b).

3. Sontag, S (1991) p.91.

4. Sontag, S (1991) p.99.

5. Foucault, M (1970)

6. Kitsinger, S (1987) p.184-5.

7. Sacks, O (1982) p.27.

8. Bettleheim, B (1989) p.3.

9. Eck, D (1981) p.1.

10. Eck, D (1981) p.1.

11. Eck, D (1981) p.5.

12. Eck, D (1981) p.6.

13. Sacks, O (1985) p.161-2.

14. Sacks, O (1985) p.162.

15. Pickering, J and Attridge, S (1990) p.416.

16.   Pickering, J and Attridge, S (1990) p.437.

17.   Pickering, J and Attridge, S (1990) p.438.

18.   Pickering, J and Attridge, S (1990) p.437.

19.   Wittgenstein, L (1971) p.72.

BIBLIOGRAPHY

Bettleheim, , B (1989):   *The Uses of Enchantment: The Meaning and Importance of Fairy Tales*, New York, Random House.

Eck, D (1981):   *Darsan, Seeing the Divine Image in India*, Chambersburg, Anima.

Foucault, M (1970):   *The Order of Things*, London, Tavistock Publications.

Kitsinger, S (1987):   *The Experience of Childbirth*, Harmondsworth, Penguin.

Pickering, J And Attridge, S (1990): 'Viewpoints: Metaphor and Monsters - Children's Storytelling', in *Research in the Teaching of English*.

Sacks, O (1982)·   *Awakenings*, London, Picador.

Sacks, O (1985):   *The Man Who Mistook his Wife for a Hat*, London, Duckworth.

Sontag, S (1991):   *Illness as Metaphor and Aids and its Metaphors*, London, Penguin.

Wittgenstein, L (1971):   *Tractatus Logico-philosophicus*, London, Routledge and Kegan Paul.

Clive Erricker is now a freelance writer and lecturer teaching at the West Sussex Institute of Higher Education. Until recently a Lecturer in the Department of Arts Education and Deputy Director of the Religious Education and Community Project at the University of Warwick, he is the author of numerous influential publications in the field of Religious Education. As a member of the Shap Working Party on World Religions in Education, he is currently editing a book on the teaching of World Religions for Heinemann.

ROBERT JACKSON

RELIGIOUS EDUCATION AND THE ARTS OF INTERPRETATION

Religious education calls for appreciation of world-views that frequently lie outside the experience of children. This challenge has been seen in terms of phenomenology's temporary suspension of personal judgements and the development of empathy. Critical of notions widely used in phenomenology, the author finds a more productive and reliable approach in the 'interpretive' anthropology of Clifford Geertz, whose work is cited to demonstrate the artistry of ethnography, and to illustrate the operation of 'experience near' and 'experience distant' concepts towards a balanced understanding of otherness. Referring to curriculum materials arising from The Religious Education and Community Project *(which reflect the project's ethnographic methodology) the author concludes with some observations on religious education's approach to 'otherness'.*

Whatever else religious education may be about, it has to include some element of understanding the world views of others. Indeed the Education Reform Act of 1988, in identifying Christianity and the other principal religions practised in Britain as areas of study, requires that it should (clause 8 [3]). Yet most children in English and Welsh schools (to confine the discussion to those who fall under the terms of the ERA) are from backgrounds in which organised religion is outside the family's regular experience. Whatever material from religious traditions is presented, it will for such children have a sense of strangeness or 'otherness' about it. Its discourse will include concepts and a vocabulary and grammar which may not be fully commensurable with their own. That discourse may describe experiences which are outside those of most young people. Similarly children from one religious background may be unfamiliar with the concepts and practices of other religious traditions.

In the 1960s religious educators were introduced to phenomenology as an approach or method to help the pupil to enter the experience of religious believers and practitioners.

According to the influential *Schools Council Working Paper 36*, the phenomenological approach:

> ...sees the aim of religious education as the promotion of understanding. It uses the tools of scholarship in order to enter into an empathic relationship with individuals and groups.[1]

The idea was to help students to suspend temporarily their own judgements and to 'enter' empathetically the faith or tradition of people from different religious backgrounds in order to gain an insider's understanding of a religion. The phenomenological method has been attacked unfairly for devaluing 'the vital ingredients of faith, belief and practice' and for being inherently relativistic and unconcerned with issues of truth.[2] I have responded to these criticisms elsewhere, along the lines that they may be valid as objections to some poor textbooks and teaching materials, but that they do not apply to the phenomenological approach as such.[3] This is not to say that this method is not flawed in other ways.

The main problems with phenomenology as a theoretical underpinning and method for religious education are two fold. First of all there is a presupposition that there are essences which are universal in human consciousness. In the work of many phenomenologists of religion this assumption is expressed in terms of essences (*eideia*) which are held to be universal in human religious experience. Apart from being ironic that a method which claims to be presuppositionless should itself be based on a presupposition, it is the nature of that presupposition that gives us pause.

Much recent work in philosophy, the social sciences, cultural criticism and literary theory would question the existence of universal 'essences' common to widely varying ways of life and which can be exposed through the application of a method. Wittgenstein and others have drawn attention to the matter of broad context in assessing the meaning of terminology within a language. Wittgenstein's contention is that for a large number of cases in which the word 'meaning' is employed, the meaning of a word is its use within the language of the particular 'form of life', (we might say 'mode of discourse' or even 'world view') in which it is found.[4] This view does not imply that there is *no* commonality in human nature, but it cautions us against looking for a variety of universal essences embedded in the consciousness of people, carrying a common meaning regardless of the culture or world view in which they are set, and which can be uncovered methodologically. Rather people from different cultural settings or ways of life use language in particular ways which expose the meaning of words within it. The 'grammar' of language use has to be grasped before the meaning of the terms becomes evident. To posit 'essences' corresponding to one's own (or one's own 'culturally familiar') use of a term like 'religion' or 'the numinous', and especially of a slippery concept like 'spirituality', and then to go hunting for its direct equivalent in another way of life is to make (to borrow Ryle's term) a 'category mistake'.

The problem does not end here, for we do not only have to be cautious of our own and our contemporaries' tendencies in this direction. Earlier examples of culture contact have resulted in the projection of terms, assumptions and structures from one world view on to those of others, structures that have subsequently become embedded in literature and language and which have tended to be accepted as received truth or common sense. This is not just a matter of inadvertent misunderstanding, but results from an unequal power relationship. In periods of colonial expansion the on-going imbalance of power has permitted politically and technologically stronger cultures or groups to *define* weaker groups.

Edward Said traces the modern origins of this 'Orientalism' to the seventeenth century with its classical expression in the nineteenth and early twentieth centuries.[5] Its tendencies include paternalism - with Western writers speaking on behalf of a silent Orient, reconstituting its decayed or forgotten 'truth', and knowing more than its mere natives ever can - and the abstraction of stereotypes such as the eternal and unchanging East, the sexually insatiable Arab, corrupt despotism and mystical authority. Said's examples are almost entirely from the Arab Middle East, but his principles apply just as well, for example, to the 'structuring' of Hinduism in the eighteenth and nineteenth centuries by the British (and to a lesser extent by other Europeans) in India.

The term 'Hinduism' is Western and was probably first used in print not by an Indian, but by a British Orientalist in 1808.[6] The concept to which it refers, was expressed as 'Hindoo', 'Gentoo' or 'Hindu' religion by British writers in the eighteenth century. This was conceived as a 'golden age', monotheistic Vedic religion (with Sanskrit paralleling classical Greek and Latin) which was contrasted with modern, debased, polytheistic superstition. In effect the British Orientalists determined a Hindu renaissance which they saw as a 'type' of the European one. And they did this (with a few exceptions such as H H Wilson) with very little direct experience and grasp of the living Hindu tradition. Their construction, together with the evaluations and interpretations of Anglicists and of nineteenth century (mainly Protestant) missionaries, determined the perception of 'Hinduism' as a 'religion' with a particular history and content (and with some unsavoury modern practices) found in the Agreed Syllabuses for Religious Instruction of the 1950s and beyond and whose legacy still detectable in some school books on Hinduism.[7] Some deconstruction is needed, therefore, by students embarking on a study of 'Hinduism'. The conclusion of this brief discussion is that any cross-cultural search for religious or spiritual 'essences' is philosophically dubious and lacks a grasp of historical influences on the building of concepts. Otto's contention, for example, that the 'numinous' is a unique... 'category of value' and a mental state 'perfectly *sui generis* and irreducible to any other', cannot be regarded as an axiom.[8]

The second problem with phenomenology is the great store it sets on the use of empathy as a means to understanding another's world. First you bracket out your presuppositions and then you empathise. The earlier discussion should have revealed how unrealistic the first of these endeavours must be. For the eminent phenomenologist of religion, Gerardus van der Leeuw 'bracketing' or *epoché* depends on an attitude of warmth, 'spontaneously warm, self denying devotion' towards the phenomenon.[9] Leaving aside van der Leeuw's specific claim, it should be clear from the discussion above that even a step in the direction of epoché requires at least some skill and knowledge. Pragmatically, you can try to be aware of at least some of your presuppositions and to hang on to that awareness (as we have seen that might require some historical study as well as philosophical skill), but no more. The inquirer, with his or her assumptions, questions and concerns peeking through, is still there.

Next we come to empathy (*einfühlung*) itself. In van der Leeuw's words empathy is 'transposing oneself into the object or re-experiencing it'.[10] The metaphor of transposition reveals van der Leeuw's intense interest in music and he compares empathy with religious phenomena with one's experience of music:

> We give ourselves over to a melody by way of empathy, we discuss its elements not as a quantifiably measurable series of vibrations of the air nor as expressions of a certain idea, but as a phenomenon, as it were as 'tonal ideas'...[11]

What van der Leeuw does not discuss is his own close familiarity with the grammar of the European high-culture music to which he is referring and its role in his ability to empathise with and to interpret examples of it. One wonders what he would have made of a Balinese *gamelan* orchestra, the sounds of the South Indian *nagaswara* or an alto saxophone solo by Charlie Parker. This is not to say that any of these might not have 'spoken' to him or touched him emotionally but to suggest that he would likely have made some very serious errors of interpretation had he relied on empathy alone to make sense of them. There is also no intention of implying that the capacity of *sensitivity* which is associated with empathy is not an important ingredient in grasping another's way of life. I would contend that sensitivity is a necessary but not a sufficient condition for understanding. Maybe one's capacity for empathy develops *after* grasping the 'grammar' of someone else's discourse.

Phenomenology, at least in its classical form, fails to provide the tools to interpret the world views of others with the minimum of distortion. Fortunately there are other disciplines and methods which are of considerable help. In the context of the study of living 'religions' ethnography is particularly fertile ground, especially since much of its recent work accommodates insights from other fields in the social sciences and from work in the arts. Historically, ethnography (and social or cultural anthropology more widely) has faced issues of interpretation familiar to religious educators. The image of the anthropologist E B Tylor imposing an evolutionary structure (from animism to polytheism to monotheism) on to the history of religion[12] is mirrored by some approaches to the 'Old Testament' in 1950s and 1960s Agreed Syllabuses, and even in school books sometimes still found in use in schools. A title like *From Fear to Faith* gives the picture.

At the other extreme, accounts written entirely by insiders (which, in combination with other sources, have an important part to play in religious education) sometimes take for granted as 'normal' or ignore as 'common sense' key symbols and institutions which might awaken a sense of understanding in outsiders, and therefore may be of limited value in explicating the symbol systems or institutions of a particular group of people. Furthermore, in the context of religious education, which has a very strong tendency to portray rather loosely knit religious traditions as holistic entities, insider accounts from one segment of the tradition can be read inadvertently as universally applicable. The key issue in ethnographic interpretation has been to find a balance between the two extremes, to work out a balanced relationship between the concepts, symbols, institutions etc of 'insiders' and the vocabulary of the anthropologist - some if it technical and some if it not - used to reconstruct the insiders' world and to interpret it to others.

Some of anthropology's failures have been attempts to accommodate ethnographic method to the natural sciences. The work of Alfred Radcliffe-Brown, for example, drew heavily on Durkheim, treated social anthropology as a form of comparative sociology and was attacked for imposing a positivist interpretation on its data.[13] Others, including various types of conflict theorists (eg Marxist), have tended to impress particular ideological interpretations of a more political kind. Some approaches have recognised artistic elements in ethnography. For example, Edward Evans-Pritchard, one of Radcliffe-Brown's critics, in his later work argued that ethnography was an art, requiring competences similar to those of the historian.[14] Strict comparison of social institutions was impossible and any quest for the laws of human social behaviour was futile.[15] In different ways, and especially through their interest in literary theory and practice, anthropologists such as Claude Lévi-Strauss, Victor Turner, Mary Douglas, Edmund Leach and Clifford Geertz have blurred the boundary between art and science through their views of anthropological interpretation.

INTERPRETIVE ANTHROPOLOGY

The 'interpretive' anthropology of Clifford Geertz is particularly relevant to our purpose. For Geertz the essence of anthropological analysis lies in creating a balance between what he calls 'experience near' and 'experience distant' concepts.

> An experience-near concept is, roughly, one that someone - a patient, a subject, in our case an informant - might himself naturally and effortlessly use to define what he or his fellows see, feel, think, imagine, and so on, and which he would readily understand when similarly applied by others. An experience-distant concept is one that specialists of one sort or another - an analyst, an experimenter, an ethnographer, even a priest or an ideologist - employ to forward their scientific, philosophical, or practical aims.[16]

It is important to emphasise that Geertz is referring to concepts rather than terms. He gives 'caste' as an example of an 'experience near' concept for Hindus. The concept would be familiar to most Hindus, while the term might not be. Further some uses of the term by outsiders expressing particular interpretations of the concept might be 'experience distant'.[17] In any case, Geertz acknowledges that the distinction between 'experience near' and 'experience distant' is sometimes a matter of degree. One might compare the distinction between 'folk' terms and 'analytic' terms sometimes made by writers on ethnographic methodology.[18] The key question for Geertz is how each set of concepts should be deployed in order:

> ...to produce an interpretation of the way a people live which is neither imprisoned within their mental horizons... nor systematically deaf to the distinctive tonalities of their existence...[19]

The art of anthropological analysis is to grasp concepts that are for another people 'experience near' well enough to place them

> ...in illuminating connection with experience-distant concepts theorists have fashioned to capture the general features of social life...[20]

How can this be done? Not by empathising with the people being studied, with an ethnographer imagining himself or herself to be someone else and then seeing what he or she thought. As far as Geertz is concerned,

The ethnographer does not, and, in my opinion, largely cannot, perceive what his informants perceive. What he perceives, and that uncertainly enough, is what they perceive "with" - or "by means of," or "through" ... or whatever the word should be.[21]

The way to proceed, says Geertz is

...by searching out and analysing the symbolic forms - words, images, institutions, behaviours - in terms of which, in each place, people actually represented themselves to themselves and to one another.[22]

Geertz gives examples from his fieldwork with various groups of people in Java, Bali and Morocco showing how he discerned in each case the concept of 'person' or, in less specifically Western terms, 'the human individual'. In Geertz's view, attempting to grasp another's concept of 'person' by means of empathy usually amounts to accommodating that concept to the Western conception of a person as:

...a bounded, unique, more or less integrated motivational and cognitive universe, a dynamic center of awareness, emotion, judgment, and action organised into a distinctive whole and set contrastively both against other such wholes and against its social and natural background...[23]

All of Geertz's examples are illuminating, but a summary of one gives an idea of his mode of analysis. The key to grasping the idea of the human individual in the particular group of Javanese people he studied turned out to be two pairs of 'experience near' concepts. The first pair, *batin*, and *lair* are borrowed from Islamic (Sufi) mysticism and reworked. *Batin* is an 'inside' word referring to the emotional life of human beings generally.

It consists of the fuzzy, shifting flow of subjective feeling perceived directly in all its phenomenological immediacy but considered to be, at its roots at least, identical across all individuals, whose individuality it thus effaces.[24]

Lair, on the other hand, is an 'outside' word referring to external actions, movements, postures and speech. *Lair*, like *batin*, refers generally to human beings. 'Inward feelings' and 'outward actions' are regarded as independent realms of being that separately need to be controlled or regulated.

The other two concepts connect with the idea of control or putting into proper order. *Alus* is a rich word whose connotations include 'refined', 'civilised' and 'smooth'. By contrast the meanings of *kasar* include 'impolite', 'rough', 'coarse' and 'insensitive'. The aim is to be *alus* in both *batin* and *lair* realms of the individual. In the 'inner', *batin* realm this is achieved through religious (mainly mystical) discipline. In the 'outer', *lair* realm its is achieved through a very tight system of etiquette. Geertz shows the application of this analysis to anthropological understanding with a vivid example:

Only when you have seen, as I have, a young man whose wife - a woman he had in fact raised from childhood and who had been the centre of his life - has suddenly and inexplicably died, greeting everyone with a set smile and formal apologies for his wife's absence and trying, by mystical techniques, to flatten out, as he himself put it, the hills and valley of his emotion into an even, level plain ("that is what you have to do," he said to me, "be smooth inside and out") can you come, in the face of our own notions of the intrinsic honesty of deep feeling and the moral importance of personal sincerity, to take the possibility of such a conception of selfhood seriously and appreciate, however inaccessible it is to you, its own sort of force.[25]

I hope the point is clear, though through my summary of Geertz's summary, the 'depth' of the exercise can be barely communicated. A few more remarks on Geertz's analytical methods (methods are what they are, although he does not like the term) might make his position clearer. Although the example does not discuss directly Geertz's use of 'experience distant' concepts, the impression is given that part of his 'feeling' the way towards a grasp of 'experience near' concepts is through running parallels with, and then rejecting as inadequate, concepts from his own 'form of life'. Thus 'body' and 'soul' are mentioned in his account as being entirely inappropriate designations for *lair* and *batin*, for to look for one word expressions in one cultural setting and then match them with 'equivalents' from another would be to make a category mistake. Lists of English words are also used by Geertz to express the subtleties of meaning of 'experience near' concepts and fairly complex English sentences are required to convey this sense. Look again at Geertz's 'definition' of *batin* (above).

More important is the technique used for getting to the point where he can attempt these English interpretations. Here Geertz sees his method as a type of hermeneutics. Geertz's data analysis consists in getting a sense of the 'culture' as a whole through its parts, and getting a sense of each part - each 'symbol', whether it be a word, image, institution or behaviour - by considering it in relation to the whole.

> Hopping back and forth between the whole conceived through the parts that actualize it and the parts conceived through the whole that motivate them, we seek to turn them, by a sort of intellectual perpetual motion, into explications of one another.[26]

As Geertz acknowledges, this is a version of what Dilthey (in applying a technique from the study of religions to the social sciences) called the hermeneutic circle. Geertz regards this method as central in ethnographic interpretation, just as it is (he holds) in other forms of interpretation, such as literary, historical, psychoanalytic or Biblical. In this sense understanding someone else's way of life is akin to interpreting a poem.[27]

A final related point, which emphasises the artistry of ethnography even further, is to acknowledge the various levels of interpretation that go on in ethnographic work. For example, the ethnographer may be attempting to grasp an informant's understanding of a way of life which is neither her or his own nor that of the ethnographer. It is through 'thick description' (a term Geertz borrows from Gilbert Ryle) of a way of life, embodied in detailed field notes, that different levels of interpretation are revealed.

> ...what we call our data are really our own constructions of other people's constructions of what they and their compatriots are up to... Right down at the factual base, the hard rock, insofar as there is any, of the whole enterprise, we are already explicating.[28]

There is an admission here that even though ethnographers can get close to the insider's view, they cannot be insiders, and must be interpreting. Their activity has strong artistic elements and is more akin to literary criticism than scientific method. Despite this acknowledgement, Geertz has had his ethnographic critics, especially those who argue that he uses literary devices subtly to establish the ethnographer's authority and that he sometimes moves from particular examples to a generalised cultural stereotype.[29] Though there may be some truth in the criticisms (especially some of those directed at specific instances), Geertz's critics do not render the hermeneutic method invalid, nor do they come up with better techniques for grasping the grammar of a general cultural scene in relation to its constituent parts.

RELIGIOUS EDUCATION

What are the implications of all this for religious education? It is only possible here to give a sketch of a few ideas. First we might be more critical of concepts that tend to be taken for granted as having a universal and stable meaning. The concept of 'religion' itself and the names of some of the major 'religious systems' come to mind. Related to this is a caution against projecting concepts from one religious world view on to another, a tendency found in some phenomenological studies and commonly in curriculum materials - the 'numinous' and the 'spiritual' are but two.

Then there is the use of ethnographic and hermeneutical methods in the study of religions. In the Religious Education and Community Project we have been using these methods for some time in our studies of children from different religious and ethnic backgrounds. In our research with Hindu children, for example, we have attempted to combine insights from religious studies, ethnography and hermeneutics in giving accounts of children's personal experience, their involvement in different kinds of membership group and their relationship to the wider Hindu tradition.[30]

This methodology has also been applied to the preparation of curriculum material based on the research[31] and to the recent studies of children from Christian, Jewish, Muslim and Sikh backgrounds.[32] There are also possibilities for using ethnographic and hermeneutical methods with children in their own work in religious education.[33]

Finally, Geertz's own reservations and the criticisms he has received point to the fact that ethnographic sources should not be used alone. A hermeneutic involving reflection on the interplay between ethnographic accounts, accounts by 'insiders' and insights from other disciplines (eg history and psychology) might lead to a deeper and more critical understanding than through attempting to will oneself into another's world view.

REFERENCES

1. Schools Council (1971) p.21.

2. Burn and Hart (1988).

3. Jackson (1992).

4. Wittgenstein (1958).

5. Said (1978).

6. Kopf (1969) p.140.

7. Jackson (1987); Jackson and Killingley (1988), chapter 1.

8. Otto (1959) p.21.

9. 1926 reproduced in Waardenburg (1973) p.403.

10. 1926 in Waardenburg (1973) p.401.

11. Waardenburg (1973) p.403-4.

12. Tylor (1871)

13. Radcliffe-Brown (1958)

14. Evans-Pritchard (1961)

15. Evans-Pritchard (1962)

16. Geertz (1983) p.57.

17. Dumont (1972)

18. Spradley (1980)

19. Geertz (1983) p.57.

20. Geertz (1983) p.58.

21. Geertz (1983) p.58.

22. Geertz (1983) p.58.

23. Geertz (1983) p.59.

24. Geertz (1983) p.60.

25. Geertz (1983) p.61.

26. Geertz (1983) p.69.

27. Geertz (1983) p.70.

28. Geertz (1973) p.9.

29. Clifford and Marcus (1986)

30. Jackson and Nesbitt (1993)

31. Jackson and Nesbitt (1990)

32. These studies based in the Department of Arts Education at the University of Warwick and conducted between 1990 and 1993, have been funded by the Economic and Social Research Council (Reference number R000232489). One short report of some aspects of the study of children from Christian backgrounds is Jackson and Nesbitt (1992).

32. A brief outline of the use of some ethnographic methods with children of junior school age is Jackson (1990).

Burn, J and Hart, C (1988): *The Crisis in Religious Education*, London, Educational Research Trust.

Clifford, J and Marcus, G (eds) (1986): *Writing Culture: The Poetics and Politics of Ethnography*, Berkeley, University of California Press.

Dumont, L (1972): *Homo Hierarchicus*, London, Paladin.

Evans-Pritchard, E (1961): *Anthropology and History*, Manchester.

Evans-Pritchard, E (1962): *Essays in Social Anthropology*, London.

Geertz, C (1973): *The Interpretation of Cultures*, New York, Basic Books.

Geertz, C (1983): *Local Knowledge*, New York, Basic Books.

Jackson, R (1987): 'Changing Conceptions of Hinduism in "Timetabled Religion"' in Burghart, R (ed), *Hinduism in Great Britain*, London, Tavistock.

Jackson, R (1990): 'Children as Ethnographers' in Jackson, R and Starkings, D (eds) *The Junior RE Handbook*, Cheltenham, Stanley Thornes,.

Jackson, R (1992): 'The Misrepresentation of Religious Education' in Leicester, M and Taylor, M (eds) *Ethics, Ethnicity and Education*, London, Kogan Page.

Jackson, R and Killingley, D (1988): *Approaches to Hinduism*, London, John Murray.

Jackson, R and Nesbitt, E (1990): *Listening to Hindus*, London, Unwin Hyman.

Jackson, R and Nesbitt, E (1992): 'The Diversity of Experience in the Religious Upbringing of Children from Christian Families in Britain, *British Journal of Religious Education*, Vol 15, No 1, Autumn, pp19-28.

Jackson, R and Nesbitt, E (1993): *Hindu Children in Britain*, Stoke on Trent, Trentham Books.

Kopf, D (1969): *British Orientalism and the Bengal Renaissance*, Berkeley and Los Angeles, University of California Press.

Otto, R (1959): *The Idea of the Holy*, Harmondsworth, Pelican.

Radcliffe-Brown, A (1958): *Method in Social Anthropology*, University of Chicago Press.

Said, E (1978): *Orientalism*, London, Routledge and Kegan Paul.

Spradley, J (1980): *Participant Observation*, New York, Holt, Rinehart and Winston.

Tylor, E B (1871): *Primitive Culture*, 2 vols., London, John Murray.

Waardenburg, J (ed.)(1973): *Classical Approaches to the Study of Religion*, The Hague, Mouton, (Vol 1).

Wittgenstein, L (1958): *Philosophical Investigations*, Oxford, Blackwell.

Robert Jackson is Reader in Arts Education at the University of Warwick. Director of the Religious Education and Community Project (based at the University of Warwick), he has published widely in Religious Education and Religious Studies and is a member of the Religious Education Council of England and Wales. A jazz trombonist with the midlands band, Spicy Jazz, he teaches a course in jazz as part of Warwick's Arts Education music programme.

ROBERT GREEN

EXPLORATIONS IN MUSIC AND RELIGION

Music relates to spirituality as a matter of profound experiences not easily verbalised. The author enquires into the nature of 'meaning' in music, relating its pursuit to National Curriculum attainment targets and psychological development. He shows how historical relationships between music and religion in the West can provide a shared basis for classroom practice in music and RE, balancing personal creativity with the awareness of a heritage. As a devlopment of this, he turns to practical suggestions involving the musical exploration of children's own stories and stories drawn from the great religious traditions. Here he demonstrates a practical relationship between the National Curriculum musical concerns of composing, performing and listening and religious education's imaginative and expressive dimensions.

The Princess Royal was reported to have suggested that 'Land of Hope and Glory' on occasions be substituted for the National Anthem. The consequent rise in morale would ensure that England's rugby team were not beaten into the ground by the Scots at Murrayfield following the debilitating and passionate skirl of the pipes. A recent radio programme discussed the link between spirituality and creativity in the treatment of the mentally ill. An article by Dennis Starkings about the response of 10-12 year olds to representations of the Buddha refers to the key words being not "instruction and illustration" but rather, "evidence and exploration" and concludes that "the exploration of certain works of art can take us on a journey that runs from everyday experience to the heightened understanding and interpretation of experience in the world's great religious traditions".[1] The programme note for a concert of funky but sophisticated music composed and played by Mike Gibbs, John Scofield and a big band compared Mike Gibbs' conception of a music score with Le Corbusier's definition of a house as a machine for living: 'a space which we can inhabit and which contains and represents the sum of emotions fed into it'.

It seems that the arts and music do have a 'something', an area of experience 'which cannot easily be verbalised' as the DES 5-16(1985) Music guidelines have it. Most people seem to be aware of the 'something' in spite of the enormous variation in their ability or willingness to analyse and comprehend it. This 'something' is akin, I think, to what we call spirituality. The four examples listed in the above paragraph illustrate this 'something' and reinforce the importance of the expressive arts as a catalyst in life, in the curriculum, and for RE in particular.

Meaning in Music?

Much has been written about meaning in music. Leonard B. Meyer suggests that the division between the 'absolutists' and the 'referentialists' is not the same as the difference between the 'formalist' and the 'expressionist'. He summarises:

> One might, in other words, divide expressionists into two groups: absolute expressionists and referential expressionists. The former group believe that expressive emotional meanings arise in response to music and that these exist without reference to the extramusical world of concepts, actions and emotional states, while the latter group would assert that emotional expression is dependent upon an understanding of the referential content of music.[2]

Whatever our personal conclusions are on this matter, there is apparently no doubt about there *being* a meaning in music and both of Meyer's groups need have no difficulty with accepting the spiritual nature of an aesthetic response, which Swanwick describes as:

> primarily and always an intensified response raised into full consciousness. Aesthetic means to feel more powerfully, to perceive more clearly. Its opposite is *anaesthetic*."[3]

The attainment targets for music, as the National Curriculum document (1992) defines them - Composing, Performing, Listening and Appraisal - are of equal significance in the struggle to get to the bottom of this response. They can each serve to open young minds to the exquisite delight of touching the ineffable. A heightened response is achieved by creative activity. To witness the performance of a great musical setting of the Mass either in concert or liturgically draws responses as does the contemplation of an icon. The telling of a Hindu story through dance and vocal chanting accompanied by the Gamelan orchestra is comparable with the Passion story told by soloists, chorus and orchestra with the music of J.S.Bach. *Godspell* and *Jesus Christ Superstar* interpret and heighten responses in the same way.

Much recent work in the field of developmental psychology in music demonstrates that young children are capable of producing creative work which adults are able to interpret in sophisticated ways. Thus:

> Piagetian concrete operational thought is not essential for "participation in the artistic process"...a reasonably competent 7-year old should understand the basic metrical properties of his musical system and the appropriate scales, harmonies, cadences, and groupings, even as she should be able, given some motifs, to combine them into a musical unit that is appropriate to his culture, but is not a

complete copy of a work previously known. What is lacking is fluency in motor skills which will allow accurate performance, experience with the code, tradition and style of that culture, and a range of feeling life.[4]

Analyses of young children's composition, as by Swanwick and Tillman, make it clear that from a very early age children are producing in their work, responses that often demonstrate precocious traits that do not fit into a clearly defined age phase.[5]

MUSIC AND RELIGION - AN HISTORICAL PERSPECTIVE

Composers for centuries have written musical interpretations of biblical stories. Handel's *Israel in Egypt*, Michael Hurd's *Jonah Man Jazz*, Britten's church parables, e.g. *The Burning Fiery Furnace* or the parables' fore-runner, *Noyes Fludde*, Honegger's *King David* and even Wagner's *Parsifal* are some examples. They all enrich and interpret the story they tell using the musical style of their time. In the *St.Matthew Passion* by J.S.Bach how human is the lachrymose despair of Peter following his denial when Bach interprets the scene in the elaborately decorated aria 'Have mercy upon me' with its yearningly melancholy violin obligato.

Mahler's *Eighth Symphony*, like Elgar's *Dream of Gerontius*, takes us painfully but pleasurably through feelings and maybe philosophies that we are reluctant to approach in other contexts. Mahler said of the work:

> It is the greatest work I have yet composed and it is so different in content and form that I cannot even write about it. Imagine that the universe bursts into song. We hear no longer human voices, but those of planets and suns circling in their orbits."[6]

Later he said that the work was a great "dispenser of joy". In the symphony Mahler sets the hymn, *Veni, Creator Spiritus* for the first section but contrasts it with the massive second movement, setting the final scenes from Goethe's *Faust*. The last section, the great chorus mysticus, ends with the words, "The Indescribable, Here it is done: The Woman-soul leadeth us Upward and on !" The work has a strong uniting form and indeed there are four recognisable movements within the two sections but as Mahler said in a letter to his wife (the dedicatee of the symphony):

> It is a peculiarity of the interpretation of works of art that the rational element in them (that which is soluble by reason) is almost never their true reality, but only a veil which hides their form. Insofar as a soul needs a body an artist is bound to derive the means of creation from the rational world. But the chief thing is still the artistic conception, which no mere words can ever explain. In *Faust* everything points toward this final supreme moment, which, though beyond expression, touches the very heart of feeling.[7]

Opera further illustrates these special insights that music brings to human experience. The Oedipus myth as told by Stravinsky and Cocteau in *Oedipus Rex* with an emotionally detached text, a passionless narrator and didactic 'neo-classical' music is, nevertheless, devastatingly moving at the point when, eyeless, Oedipus is banished from the city, the inhuman use of mask only adding to the power of the relentless music with the apparently disinterested Chorus. Mark-Anthony Turnage's version of the same story,

Greek, based on Berkoff's play, by using contemporary musical techniques and vivid, often bizarre, characterisation, interprets the myth in a new way. The music in both the Stravinsky and the Turnage is the vital ingredient that takes the listener further into understanding the timeless relevance of the Greek drama.

Benjamin Britten's *War Requiem* intersperses and combines Wilfred Owen's harrowing war poetry with the liturgical requiem text. The easily recognised musical and literary links combine to present a work of great power. Shostakovich wrote his eighth string quartet after a visit to Dresden and it is often referred to as his war requiem. In his case sparse and sometimes violent music is shot through with quotes from his earlier works and Russian folk tunes. The ineffable message of both the Britten and the Shostakovich are very similar and serve to illustrate the underlying mystery of the heightened response.

A class of six year olds were played a short part of *The Death of Ase* from Grieg's music for *Peer Gynt* amongst a selection of other contrasting excerpts. They were asked for their responses in words, which of course deletes the notion of ineffability, but nevertheless it was fascinating to receive the answer for the Grieg that it is 'lonely'. It seems that a sophisticated response and possibly understanding are to be expected from listening activities as well as composing.

Music has always had a significant role at the major turning points in the development of Christianity. The Reformation and counter-Reformation not only led church leaders to criticise music's role but also aided changes in musical style. Thus Erasmus complained:

> We have introduced a laborious and theatrical kind of music into our sacred edifices, a tumultuous bawl of diverse voices ... vile love ditties...human voices vie with instruments...People flock to the sacred edifice as to a theatre to have their ears charmed.[8]

Luther, a great supporter of music in the liturgy says in the preface to John Walter's *Wittemberg Song Book* (1524):

> These songs are set for four voices for no other reason than that I wished that the young (who apart from this must be trained in music and in other proper arts) might have something to rid them of their love ditties and wanton songs... also because I am not of the opinion that all the arts should be crushed to earth and perish through the Gospel, as some bigoted persons pretend, but would willingly see them all, and especially music, servants of Him who gave and created them.[9]

It is interesting to note the views of Josquin des Pres (c.1450-1521) on teaching composition as reported in Coclico - *Musical Compendium* (1552). "Josquin did not consider all suited to learn composition; he judged that only those should be taught who were drawn to this delightful art by a special natural impulse.[10] In the twentieth century we would hope to enable all to at least have the opportunity to discover their own special impulse in the field of composition and creativity.

Zarlino in his *Foundations of Harmony* (1558) reminds us poetically of the affective nature of music writing well before the seventeenth century when the affections became a fundamental consideration for musicians, performers and theorists alike:

a dissonance causes the consonance which immediately follows it to seem more acceptable. Thus it is perceived and recognised with greater pleasure by the ear, just as after darkness light is more acceptable and delightful to the eye, and after the bitter the sweet is more luscious and palatable.[11]

The Counter Reformation was intensely concerned with the place of music in the liturgy and the celebrated Council of Trent (1545-63) reflected the important Humanist ideas which in music led to a greater concentration on setting good texts in an intelligible and interpretatively relevant way.

All things should be so ordered that the Masses, whether they be celebrated with or without singing, may reach tranquilly into the ears and hearts of those who hear them....The singing should be arranged not to give empty pleasure to the ear, but in such a way that the words may be clearly understood by all, and thus the hearts of the listeners be drawn to the desire of heavenly harmonies, in the contemplation of the joys of the blessed.[12]

The power of music and its responsible use for the further edification of the common member of the congregation has been recognised throughout the history of the church.

While looking back it is worth raising the whole issue of heritage and the balance between creative experience in education and the enabling of children or students to become aware at an early age of the wonderful palette of sounds which have been left to us from the past. It is as likely that we will experience the spiritual when hearing or performing music from the past and from a variety of cultures as it is when we are composing or improvising. In the context of the classroom it leads to many opportunities for cross-curricular work. What kind of sounds were heard in Westminster Abbey in 1680 or at Winchester in the 14th century? Why did composers write at that time ? How were they affected by the music compared to our twentieth century response ?

Religious Education and Music

Robert Jackson has suggested that the elements of Religious Education include among others "an imaginative element" and "an expressive element".[13] The arts and especially music can help to provide these elements to the mutual benefit of both. The responsibility for education is to ensure that we do not miss these elements in the rush to establish attainment targets and rigid guidelines, essential though these are. It is interesting to note that the draft music document of the National Curriculum Council makes no direct reference to the affective in music and the arts. It is all the more important then to insist that sensitivity to the affective and to mystery must be nurtured, not as an indulgence for those 'in the know', but as a privilege for everyone. In developmental and creative contexts, music and the arts are ready to enrich the individuality of the child to enable the beginnings of a spiritual response. But as Priestley comments, "Our biggest problem in schools, it seems to me, is, how on earth does one develop individuality in an institution ?"[14] And as Webster observes, "It is the case that the truth of music is more felt than said."[15]

T.S.Eliot in his essay *Poetry and Drama* discusses the function of art; it 'gives us some perception of an order in life, by imposing an order upon it'. He continues:

> It seems to me that beyond the nameable, classifiable emotions and motives of our
> conscious life when directed towards action - the part of life which prose drama
> is wholly adequate to express - there is a fringe of indefinite extent, of feeling of
> which we are only aware in a kind of temporary detachment from action. ....This
> peculiar range of sensibility can be expressed by dramatic poetry, at its moments
> of greatest intensity. At such moments, we touch the border of those feelings
> which only music can express.[16]

In education we need to provide opportunities to foster this type of creative response.
We must not to be afraid of taking the arts seriously, while having fun doing it.

PRACTICAL PERSPECTIVES

The Attainment Targets for Music - Composing, Performing, Listening and Appraising
- have direct relevance for Religious Education. Working together, mutual criticism,
delight in the finished product, rehearsing and perfecting are shared elements which
will be provided by acquiring skills and learning about creative concepts of today and
from the past. Music or the other expressive arts can mutually enrich RE and other parts
of the curriculum. But the exchange must be mutual. For example Priestley's worry
about the individual in the institutional school can be alleviated by real cross-curricular
initiatives.

In *The Junior RE Handbook* I have outlined some of the techniques used by musicians
to encourage composition in the classroom and conclude with an illustration of
performing a story through music.[17] There the example was St. Francis and the Wolf.
The following paragraphs describe other starting points for this type of work. The first
example is of a class engaging their imaginations. In this case the basic material
produced from this exercise might be developed in any part of the curriculum. The arts
and RE potential is similar in this case because of the mystery and wonder of the
children's story.

WORKING FROM A CLASS STORY....
Working with a class of six year olds on a music project that grew from a CDT starting
point, we wrote a class story.   The outline was agreed upon and the children added
the detail, i.e. what animals, plants etc. were to be found in the wood.

> In a very beautiful part of the country where the wind blows gently there is a wood
> with many trees of all kinds; oak trees with acorns, cherry blossom trees, apple
> trees and *even* a palm tree...Fruit bushes and flowers grow there. Blackberries,
> elderberries, tomatoes and *even* bananas are found there with wild roses, daffodils,
> daisies and *even* sunflowers.....Many animals live in the wood, squirrels cracking
> nuts, rabbits, a mole, foxes and *even* a jaguar. It seems that this must be an *unusual*
> wood with such a strange variety of living things in it....A small stream full of clear
> cold water runs through the wood. In a clearing in the wood where the sun shines
> brightly and the rain falls heavily is a large building. A huge water wheel is
> attached to the side of the building... Who lives there ? A man called Noah has
> lived there for so many years that nobody can remember when he first came to the

wood....In the building he makes flour for bread and cakes. He uses the water wheel to turn the huge heavy stones to grind the wheat into flour. He also sells sugar and *even* makes magical water - for there are magical diamonds in the wood.

The musical development of this story included the composing of mystical or magic music for those parts of the story that were fantastic in addition to sound collages and simple tunes for the animals and for Noah. A selection of recorded music was played to the children for them to decide the most appropriate piece for the various moods in the story. From this activity it is easy to progress to using music to accompany stories from religions, myth, legend and history.

GANESH

Another example relates to a suggestion by Clive Erricker. "In one sense religion *is* story. By this we mean that faith communities are maintained and nourished by the story within which they live. We might call this their myth. This myth is organic: it is lived out by the community in space and time. It evolves and changes in its historical and social contexts, but it also seeks to shape these contexts by providing a framework of meaning for the experiences of the believer. Another way to express this is to talk of the myth as a hermeneutical model."[18] Music will aid the interpretation of the story. Hindus go for *darshan* rather than worship to behold the image. When we experience Bach or Mahler's music we are in a sense listening to an image. The story of how Shiva and Parvati's son, Vinayaka, became Ganesh, the deity who surprises the adult westerner by his multi-faceted appearance, is a rich field for musical interpretation. The story has adventure, violence, Shiva's long journey, the elephant's sacrifice and the final creation of the benign friendly god with elephant head and four arms.

An Indian atmosphere can be created using *rag* and *tala* as a starting point for improvisation and composition in pastiche style. This may not be the preferred way to start work on the story. Perhaps to behold the image and to create sounds that express the feelings that it arouses in any suitable style may be a better way to uncover the real essence of the story. Also, composed music can be chosen. There is much popular music in the 'minimalist' style which will enhance the concentration required to 'see' the full significance of the image. The music curriculum will welcome the chance to benefit from another way into a twentieth century style. Composers include, for example, Steve Reich, John Cage, Phillip Glass, John Adams, Georgy Ligeti, Karlheinz Stockhausen and Mike Oldfield. Indeed this may lead to an critical exploration of contemplative music from Gregorian chant, Mongolian song, Russian orthodox chant to the Gamelan of the far east.

For composing and improvisation, playing ostinato patterns from the pentatonic, whole-tone and other modes and scales on a large variety of instruments will open minimalist mantra-like possibilities for all. This exercise can include work in the other expressive arts and will lead to a discussion of how it has helped us to experience and understand new ideas and concepts. It might exemplify for RE the transcendent imagination. The teacher of RE can use it to make this point.

KING DAVID

The life story of King David is full of possibilities for all three of the musical ingredients of Composing, Listening and Performing. The fight with Goliath, the witch at Endor, the death of Absalom, the anointing of Solomon as his successor can form the basis for the writing of descriptive music expressing a variety of emotions. Modern versions of the psalms, new texts devised by the students may be set in a contemporary style including folk, pop and rock. Rap style is used to tell the story of the battle and the visit to the witch as if being recounted by a contemporary storyteller.

Listening to Thomas Tompkins beautiful setting of *When David Heard That Absalom Was Dead*, to the exciting bits of Honegger's *King David* and to the coronation anthem by Handel, *Zadok the Priest*, will take on a new relevance in the context of the student's own composition. Parts of the Honegger will act as inspiration for composition especially the section with the witch. The final chorus takes the listener from the story in history towards its relevance for us today in the same way that student improvisation and composition will enhance their awareness of the importance of historical understanding.

A Parable

The parables offer a rich field for musical and dramatic exploration. The story of the traveller from Jericho to Jerusalem, set upon and then treated kindly by the Samaritan, deals with issues that suggest a contemporary treatment using contrasting musical moods, violent, compassionate and descriptive. Set in an urban environment the story can be interpreted dramatically perhaps with video using popular music, electro-acoustic music and music concrete (e.g. a collage of street sounds).

The musical, *West Side Story*, has the urban violence tempered with a moral message and, based on *Romeo and Juliet*, gives further opportunities for listening; e.g. Prokoviev and Tschaikovsky. Comparison of the Bernstein musical with the Prokoviev ballet on video will confirm the vitality and power of the message when expressed by the arts and will assist pupils to extend their own creative work.

The National Curriculum

The draft proposals for music in the National Curriculum (1991) considered the aims of music teaching in school. These are a few quotations from the document:

> Music is so much part of the background of everyday life that we tend to take it for granted. For many people, however, it is a powerful focus for a creative energy, and one which both stimulates and guides the imagination. Music education aims to develop aesthetic sensitivity and creative ability in all pupils. (Section 4.2)

> Within that framework, we consider that the main aim of music education in schools is to foster pupil's sensitivity to, and their understanding and enjoyment of, music, through an active involvement in listening, composing and performing. (Section 4.3)

> The study of music as a foundation subject should provide for the progressive development of .....*the capacity to express ideas, thoughts and feelings through music.* (Section 4.3)

The importance of cross-curricular planning is stressed in all parts of the National Curriculum documentation. Not only will it allow many aspects of the expressive curriculum more time but will demonstrate, it is to be hoped, that there is more to be gained in links between RE and music than those expressed in the music draft document.

> Music is an integral part of worship in most major religions, and can be a means of enhancing understanding of present and past doctrines and liturgies. (Section 12.11)

The spiritual, ineffable, transcendent, affective will surely be areas that will be 'enhanced' if the aim, 'to express ideas, thoughts and feelings through music' is taken as seriously as it should be. It is always worth aiming for the end of the rainbow. One texture, tune, harmony can say more than a thousand words, although a few well chosen words can do very well - as here, from Roger McGough.

sometimes
i feel like a priest
in a fish & chip queue
quietly thinking
as the vinegar runs through
how nice it would be
to buy supper for two [17]

References

1. Starkings (1991).

2. Meyer (1956) p.3.

3. Swanwick (1980) p.112.

4. Hargreaves (1986) p.83.

5. Swanwick (1988) pp.70-87.

6. Quoted in Diether (1966).

7. Quoted in Diether (1966).

8. Quoted in Robertson (1963) p.116.

9. Quoted in Strunk (1950) p.342.

10. Reese (1959) p.230.

11. Quoted in Strunk (1950) p.232.

12. Quoted in Reese (1959) p.449.

13. Jackson and Starkings (1990) pp.8 -11.

14. Priestley (1985) p.40.

15. Webster (1982) p.85.

16. Quoted in Kerman (1956) p.5.

17. See Jackson and Starkings (1990).

18. Erricker and Green (1992).

19. McGough R. the Mersey Sound, reprinted by permission of Peters Fraser & Dunlop Group Ltd.

BIBLIOGRAPHY

Diether, J (1966):   *Mahler Symphony No.8 Record Notes*, CBS.

Erricker, C. and Green, R.C (1992): "A Journey with Ganesh", *Multicultural Teaching.*

Hargreaves, D.J(1986):   *The Developmental Psychology of Music,* CUP.

Jackson R., and Starkings, D. eds (1990): *The Junior RE Handbook*, Stanley Thornes.

Kerman, J (1956):   *Opera as Drama*, Faber.

McGough, R (1967):   *The Mersey Sound*, Penguin Modern Poets.

Meyer, L.B (1956):   *Emotion and Meaning in Music*, University of Chicago.

Priestley, J (1985):   "The Spiritual in the Curriculum", in P. Souper (ed) *The Spiritual Dimension of Education*, University of Southampton.

Reese, G (1959):   *Music in the Renaissance*, Dent.

Robertson, ed. (1963):   *The Pelican History of Music Vol.2*, Penguin.

Starkings, D (1991):   "Looking into Religion", *Resource* Vol.13,No.2.

Strunk, O (1950):   *Source Readings in Music History,* Faber.

Swanwick, K (1980):   *A Basis for Music Educatio,*NFER.

Swanwick, K (1988):   *Music, Mind and Education,*Routledge.

Webster, D.H (1982):   "Spiritual Growth in Religious Education", in *Religious Education and The Imagination* , University of Hull Institute of Education.

Robert Green is a Lecturer in the Department of Arts Education at the University of Warwick. A violinist and conductor with a special interest in music as part of the expressive arts curriculum in the primary school, he is Chairman of the Music Advisory Panel of the University of Warwick Arts Centre and much in demand as an adjudicator and director of choirs and orchestras as well as for musical activities in primary schools and in-service work with teachers.

JOHN ALCOCK

SPIRITUALITY, RELIGIOUS EDUCATION AND THE DRAMATIC ARTS

'OCCASIONS FOR COMFORT AND CELEBRATION'

There are historical relationships between drama and religion in the European and other traditions. In our own time, school drama and religious education can jointly serve the personal and spiritual needs of pupils. One opportunity lies in dramatisation based on religious stories and festivals, while another lies in the exploration of contemporary personal, moral and social issues. With his account of work done in both these areas and through Theatre-in-Education, the author puts the notion of spiritual development into a realistic and practical context; and he concludes with examples of work in which the religious, the spiritual and the dramatic have been most intimately related.

Of all the arts, it could be argued that drama has had the most intimate - and yet at times the most turbulent - relationship with religious practice. In almost all faiths and cultures the manifestations of ritual and liturgy have drawn on strong theatrical traditions. History has shown, however, that drama can be regarded equally as sacred or profane, embraced at times or reviled by whatever persuasion may be termed 'the church' of its day. This chapter, then, sets out to examine the historical inter-relationship between drama and religion in the Western tradition, before going on to discuss two aspects of drama in education which may have some bearing on what may be broadly termed the ethical and the spiritual: the use of drama to explore personal, social and moral issues; drama as a means of extending individual and collective experience beyond normally perceived boundaries.

The origins of our Western theatre are generally accepted as emerging from the Theatre of Dionysus in Athens in the 5th century BCE, although, as Derek Waters points out, it may be conjectured that, from the earliest times, 'through performance of some ritual, possibly costumed, ancient man and his successors have faced the unknown, its mysteries and their fears concerning it'. [1] However, the Dionysian *Dithyramb*, a hymn of praise sung in unison by a chorus at the altar of the wine-god, offers a point of identity from which dramatic practice and religious observance may be seen to evolve. It is also the point of departure of drama into the *tragos* (tragedy) and *comos* (comedy) which gave rise to the notions of the sacred and the profane. Even today, we come across Peter Brook writing of the 'holy theatre' while Jerzy Grotowski defends 'the need for profanation'.

In English theatre the role of the medieval church is well known. The Easter *Trope*, the *Quem Quaeritis*, sung in the Abbey Church of St Gall in Switzerland, began the process of dramatisation which led to the great mystery cycles of York, Wakefield and Coventry. Like the *Dithyramb*, the *Trope* took the form of a dialogue between, in this case, a while-robed priest representing the angel at the empty tomb on the morning of the Resurrection and three choristers enacting the three Marys. As E.K.Chambers points out, the 10th century Winchester Trope Book differs little from the prompt copy of a modern stage production. Later, as ecclesiastical participants gave way to lay guilds, the secular theatre came into being. In Europe generally, as well as in England, religious drama declined with the advent of the Renaissance and the Reformation, although relics of the tradition still survive in, for example, the Oberammergau Passion Play. Whether biblically inspired modern stage musicals may be said to have their origins in the same tradition may be a matter of greater conjecture.

Other cultures, too, demonstrate the links between religious - or socio-religious, as it is sometimes termed - practice and drama. In *The Golden Bough* [2] Frazer describes the rituals and dramatic celebrations of the early civilisations of the Indus. During the Shang Dynasty in China (18th - 12th centuries BCE) ceremonial dramas emerged in which a significant feature was the role of children. Choirs of girls and boys engaged in antiphonal signing accompanied by gesture and movement. Could this be, as L.C.Arlington suggests, the first recorded example of child drama?

Incidentally, according to Peter Slade, China may also claim to be the home of the first school to teach educational drama. He records, in his book *Child Drama* [3], that the Emperor Ming Huang in the 8th century CE founded the Pear Garden, a mixed 'Youth School' of 300 students who studied what was named 'Art-Drama'. Slade goes on to say that Emperor Huang was inspired to establish his school after a 'profound mystic adventure into the Dream World', to which further reference will be made later. Slade called his own children's theatre company, an important forerunner of theatre-in-education, The Pear Tree Players.

It is perhaps appropriate, therefore, to move on at this point to consider the role of drama in education in what may be termed the narrative of religious experience. Narrative - or story - is at the basis of all culture and is the core of artistic expression, whether the content be religious or more generally anthropological. Oral traditions offer the most literal examples of story-telling but it can be equally apparent in other art forms: in art, whether it be the aboriginal cave paintings of Ayers Rock or Picasso's *Guernica*; or in music, from Vedic chant to Verdi opera. However, concentration on the use of language, spoken or sung, forms a basis for the dramatic exploration of religious narrative in any chosen tradition. This is exemplified not just in the Bible but in the *Ramayana*, the *Janam Sakhies*, the *Qur'an* and the un-numberable stories, legends and epics of cultures throughout history. A fuller exploration of this topic may be found in the *Shap Working*

Party Yearbook 1990/91 [4] which is devoted to religion and story.

Dramatisation based on religious stories and festivals has played an important part in the development of drama in education in Britain - if only in the annual school nativity play, about which anecdotes are legion. Two writers who have recorded their own experience may be referred to here: Joan Haggerty, whose book is appropriately titled *Please, Miss, Can I Play God?* [5], and Tom Stabler in *Drama in Primary Schools* [6], itself a report on the Schools Council Drama 5 - 11 Project. In his book, Stabler constantly refers to examples of dramatic activity which forge links with RE, although he expresses a certain caution about what he describes as 'straightforward classroom re-enactment of story with little further development'. The reason for this lack of development, he suggests, is that some teachers are too concerned with the outcome of drama in **performance** and not aware enough of the dramatic **process**.

An example of Stabler's own work may be seen in the BBC television documentary on Dorothy Heathcote, *Three Looms Waiting* [A]. In it, the story of Elijah, Ahab and Jezebel is enacted by children of the Hartlepools primary school of which he was head. Stabler, an unashamed devotee of the biblical epics so favoured at one time by the movie industry, did not force his young performers to articulate the unfamiliar language of the Old Testament. Instead, he encouraged them to restate the story in the immediacy of their own Cleveland idiom. The dynamics would change, therefore, with every performance but the emphasis on process meant that the children's basic comprehension of the narrative and, more importantly, its contemporary relevance for them, would remain. Stabler sums up the process when he comments:

> '... images made or recalled in drama provide raw material for its shaping and exploring power through which expression and meaning may be enhanced... This kind of work offers the possibility of a synthesis between language, feeling and thought which enriches a child's awareness and understanding of the outer world.'

It is clear, in the context of his writing, that he would consider this 'outer world' to include the spiritual.

The links between drama and RE go far beyond the evident one of dramatising biblical stories, however. Most current RE syllabuses include a consideration of contemporary personal, social and moral issues. These are, equally, the subject matter of many drama lessons. Out of this common ground it should be possible for both curriculum subjects to assist and nurture one another. Some examples may indicate the potential to be realised.

Children in a junior school in Wigan worked with Pit Prop Theatre-in-Education Company in a participatory programme entitled *Brand of Freedom* [B]. They were asked to consider, in role as Lancashire cotton workers of the 1860s, whether they should urge the British Government to support the South in the American Civil War. To do so would ensure a continued supply of cotton, thereby safeguarding their own livelihoods, but would, at the same time, be condoning the continuance of slavery in the southern states. Any feeling that America was too far away to become really concerned about was dispelled through dramatic role-play. The children were directly confronted by the character of Martha, a runaway slave, who was able to engage their sympathy and appeal to them at first hand, as well as another young woman, a fellow cotton-worker, dying of mal-nourishment. They were thus challenged, in a direct and personal way, to decide upon their moral stance.

Primary children in a Birmingham school were concerned about bullying and brought the matter to the attention of their teachers, who set about conducting their own playground and neighbourhood survey. Children and teachers then used the research and the issues it threw up in a drama project which examined the whole question of bullying, from the point of view of the perpetrators as well as the victims. Various considerations were looked at, including peer status, self-esteem and gender stereotyping. Teachers were able to use some of the work accomplished in RE lessons and, particularly, in the school assembly.

Also using their assembly as the focal point a Coventry primary school watched a class enact an Indian story, *Elephant, Monkey and the Partridge*. [7] These three animals had lived in harmony for many years in the shade and protection of a large Banyan tree but gradually they had begun to quarrel among themselves until peaceful co-existence, let alone active caring and co-operation, became impossible. The story provided a model or metaphor in which wisdom and good sense eventually prevailed and the children, following up the assembly in their lessons, discussed the need for families, societies and nations - and, indeed, schools - to draw up a code for harmonious living. As with Martha, the slave in *Brand of Freedom*, the role-playing of the three animals brought an immediacy to the narrative (and, incidentally, tempered the seriousness of the debate with not a little humour in the characterisation of the animals in the best tradition of the medieval mystery plays). Equally important was the dramatic symbol of the Banyan tree. The setting of a dramatic piece can often be of great significance (cf. the lone tree which forms the set of *Waiting for Godot*) and could, in this case, quite effectively have been a piece of constructed scenery. However, the tree was formed by members of the class combining to 'play' the many self-rooting branches which are characteristic of the Banyan, thus adding an organic dimension to the metaphor being created.

The actor as symbol as well as person is frequently illustrated in dramatic literature. This need not involve the actor's whole person. Through the use of close-up shots, films and television have made us familiar with the significance of the nervously tapping finger or the eyes widening in alarm at the off-screen presence. Among his plays for young people, Steve Eales, himself an experienced teacher, explores such a device in *Handscapes* [8] where he encourages children to observe their own hands as resources, not only for themselves but to help others. He looks at the literal and metaphorical implications of 'a helping hand' in all its aspects and the play, a good assembly piece, incidentally, stimulates language skills as well as its application for drama and RE work.

Role-play is thus able to create its own humanity and impact. It also has the facility to present different views of an issue or problem - not just by providing the opportunity for different 'actors' to take on different characters but, quite possibly, to allow the same 'actor' to play, in turn, individuals on opposite sides of the argument. A former pupil of a Midlands secondary school, reminiscing about her performance in a dramatic piece about conflict between a teenage girl and her mother, recalled how disappointed and resentful she had been at the time not be cast as the daughter but how, during rehearsals, in performance and, certainly, upon reflection, she had come to appreciate the insights the playing of the mother had given her - both in dealing with her own parents and, eventually, as a mother herself.

As one goes further into the complexities of personal and social issues, the more the moral and ethical implications become apparent. This has been illustrated by Mike Davis and Tim Long in their course-book for secondary schools *Active Replay*.[9] Perhaps 'course-book' is slightly misleading as the authors are to be congratulated on not clearly defining for which 'course' the book is intended. The role-play entitled 'Dave Marshall' does not, in fact, include the character of Dave himself, the focus being the fact that he is on a life support machine, having been declared 'brain-dead' though clinically alive. The dilemma is, therefore, explored through members of his family, a consultant neurologist and the family priest. It would, of course, be all too easy to see these last two roles as representatives of their establishments, giving the expected response. However, role-playing in depth provides the opportunity to probe the humanity of the individual behind the professional mask.

That the moral dilemma in this case should centre upon life and death may lead to a consideration of the Neti-Neti Theatre Company (London). In 1992 it undertook a national tour with its production *Grief*[10] in order to help young people in discussing the subject of bereavement, called, in a review by Michael Marland, 'one of the last taboos'. Perhaps as significant as the play's theme was its method of presentation: a mixture of naturalistic and poetic styles, the English dialogue being complemented and reinforced by Bengali and sign language. In this way, the universal nature of the experience of loss through death was emphasised.

The work of Neti-Neti, and of Pit Prop illustrated earlier, highlights an important development which has become an accepted part of educational thinking as well as of the professional theatre since the mid-sixties, namely Theatre-in-Education or TIE. Like drama and RE in schools, TIE aims to be essentially cross-curricular and to create opportunities for young people to consider all aspects of an issue. It is, of course, a largely secular debating ground but it may be worth noting, within the context of this book, that a number of TIE companies do exist in Great Britain which have a religious, including a Christian, perspective. Back to Back TIE Co. (Birmingham) has looked at the social and peer constraints on the teenage years in *Welcome to the Pressure Dome*, while Footprints (Nottingham), in *Wodgersay Reports*, has examined child and adult relationships. Neither of these companies sets out to enforce a Christian 'answer' but rather starts from its own Christian perspective to allow its young audiences to propose their own solutions.

It is generally agreed in TIE that a piece of theatre is there to stimulate potential receptivity to change of attitude rather than to try to propagandize. Whether dramatic exposition does bring about change of mind has been the subject of many studies. Currently, the evaluation and research being undertaken by Noel Dunne of the Theatre in Health Education (THE) Trust,[11] following up TIE programmes dealing with HIV and Aids, includes an element on attitude shift with regard to prejudice in, for example, gender-bias transmission. An earlier example, which may be relevant here, is provided by the experiments undertaken by Ruth Hill of the University of Chicago Divinity School in the 1930s.[12] She introduced into evening worship services dramas concerned with race, ethnicity and criminality and concluded that positive attitude change resulted, compared with 'control group' congregations who did not see or participate in the dramas. An interesting outcome, for those concerned with teaching and learning, was that positive attitude change was more significant among the participants in the dramas than among the 'audiences'. This was especially true of the criminality focused presentations - pre-echoing the work of the present-day Geese Theatre Company (New Hampshire, USA and Birmingham, England) in prisons and other detention centres.

Of particular importance to drama and TIE is the utilisation of what may be termed the *receptivity* of children and young people to the components of theatre: story, myth, magic and what has been termed 'the whole beyond'. In Slade's terms, this may be summed up in the deceptively simple word 'play'. But if drama is an extension of play, as many theorists have claimed, one must not lose sight of those shifts of awareness that take place as the child develops. The point at which the believed-in fairy story becomes the understood allegory is where, in Coleridge's phrase, 'the willing suspension of disbelief' begins - and this is an important transitional point for life, let alone for drama. The quotation itself is probably familiar enough, but it is worth pursuing it to its conclusion. 'The willing suspension', it must not be forgotten, leads on to 'the moment which constitutes poetic faith'.

These stages in receptivity are interestingly paralleled in religious experience, according to research undertaken by Theophil Thun.[13] In 1959 he studied groups of Protestant and Catholic children in Germany to ascertain their receptivity to religious concepts and practices. His conclusions, in a chronological context, provide some striking comparisons between responses to religious observance and dramatic convention. Thun's somewhat pessimistic conclusion that childhood receptivity must inevitably give way to adolescent 'religious indifference' will receive sympathetic acquiescence from many a drama practitioner, but it is the latter's lot to remain ever the aesthetic optimist.

Perhaps the clue to the justification of that optimism lies in the universality of the dramatic medium and a juxtaposition of responses may serve as a window through which to try to glimpse what James Pratt has called 'the cognitive content of the great truth'. Up to now, the discussion has been confined to the predominantly vocal, but this need not necessarily be the case. Even in Stabler's chapter on Drama and Language, quoted earlier, he makes frequent reference to the importance of movement, echoing Peter Brook's definition of theatre at the beginning of *The Empty Space*:

> 'I can take an empty space and call it a stage. A man walks across this empty space whilst someone else is watching him, and this is all that is needed for an act of theatre to be engaged.'[14]

It is the act of movement which is the commencement of the drama, not that person coming to a standstill and beginning to speak. Indeed, there are times when mime, movement and gesture are more dramatically effective than speech; when perhaps, literally, words fail. This is when other forms can come to the rescue, when, in Wittgenstein's phrase, we find ourselves 'running against the boundaries of language'. Nowhere is this more apparent than when trying to articulate the deeper, personal essence of religious experience, when drama may help to offer insights through what Brook has termed the 'theatre of the Invisible-made-Visible'.

Public testament or private meditation are equally difficult to communicate to others with exactitude, and personal experiences are often just as hard to explain to oneself. This moves the consideration of the religious into the 'spiritual', in the sense of the survey referred to by Jack Priestly, which suggests that, while only 10% of the population may regard themselves as practising any form of religion, over 70% would claim to have had an experience which is inexplicable (in normal terms) and which might be termed spiritual.[15]

Writers on drama are, on the whole, content with less metaphysical terminology. Derek Bowskill asserts that creative drama can help the child to 'soar into the world of magic and mystery' but, in context, he is talking about more than just fantasy. Keith Johnstone [16] has worked, through what he prefers to call 'spirituality', on the boundaries of conscious and unconscious experience - the hypnogogic (on the verge of sleep) and the hypnopompic (on the edge of waking). These states, in a way, suggest the duality of acceptance in the 'suspension of disbelief' or, in dramatic terms, the actor being in role while still retaining the discriminatory skill to make that role yet more convincing. A link may also be made with the 'theta train' of Zen, in which state of meditation, as Tomio Hirai has observed, dream-like images are encountered while the eyes remain wide open and wakefulness can still be verified.

It may be appropriate, at this point, to return to Peter Slade and the Emperor Huang, in order to offer some glimpses - if not quite 'making the invisible visible' - of the way in which drama has been used to explore the heightening of personal awareness in relation to normally perceived social pattern and response. That Slade's Emperor founded the Pear Garden after his 'adventure in the Dream World' offers a parallel with the Dream-work of the Senoi people of the Central Malay Peninsular, which was researched by Hendricks and Wills and made accessible to children, parents and teachers through *The Centering Book*.[17] Their conclusion is that the harmony of the lives of these people may be due, in no small measure, to the importance they give to their Dream Life, holding daily dream 'clinics' to share the creative energy of their sleep experiences.

As a follow-up to some centering exercises, a group of drama students at the University of Warwick were shown slides of the Mesa Verde in Colorado, USA. Some time in the 8th century CE, a group of native Americans created a city, complete with high-rise apartments, in the canyons and caves below the flat Mesa plateau. They ascended by day to till the fields and graze their cattle, descending at dusk to their semi-subterranean dwellings. Sometime in the 13th century they abandoned their homes in apparent haste, thought there was no sign of any invader or subsequent occupation - indeed, the place remained undisturbed until its rediscovery in 1874. The University drama studio became the Mesa for the students, who set out to build and explore their own 'Mesa environment'. They then divided into two groups, one remaining, the other going to an outdoor location. The dwellers established their society, with its patterns and culture based on centering. When the visitors returned they were not treated as invaders, being repulsed with aggression as is usual in such improvisations, but were made welcome and an impromptu festival commenced, which one student later described as 'an occasion of comfort and celebration'. [18] That, incidentally, these attitudes were at variance with what, presumably, happened historically in the Mesa Verde, was not a prior concern, as the exercise was not intended to have any ethnographic significance.

Rather, its intention was to provide an opportunity for personal and collective reflection arising from sources intended to widen perception. Nor was it intended, in a colleague's memorable phrase, to offer any 'illicit authentication of religion'.

A second, and totally contrasting example, may be predicated by a return to Thun and his investigation of receptivity in religion. Moving from childhood and adolescence he eventually arrived (1969) at a study of old age - but still found that it informed him about childhood attitudes. Early influences, it would seem, remained paramount for many, even in their 70s and 80s. And yet, old age, he concluded, was a time of looking forward as well as back. The opportunity to review one's lifetime through drama, and perhaps to anticipate one's destiny, was created by the performance artist Suzanne Lacy in her 1984 composition *Whisper, the Waves, the Wind*.[19] Set on a beach at La Jolla, California, 150 women, aged between 60 and 100 and dressed in white, processed, sat at tables and talked of aging, freedom, death and the future. At a certain point the 'audience', assembled on the cliffs above, were invited to descend and mingle and to join in their conversations. Lacy was intent, as she put it, on resurrecting 'the rituals we no longer have' through 'an ancient, communal art form'. Drama was being utilised to unite the participants, the spectators, even the sea, the sky and a few chance intruders - a US army helicopter, a skein of geese - into what Pratt has elsewhere called 'an intuitive feeling of presence'.

A final, brief example is included because it links back, coincidentally, to an earlier chapter in which Dennis Starkings refers to Gerard Manley Hopkins' *God's Grandeur*. Working with a group of secondary school students who were studying Hopkins, it was necessary to find a way to give them a sense of the intensity with which the poet perceived what he termed the *inscape* and *instress*, the uniqueness of form and energy in any natural object: not just the distinction between an oak and a beech but the primeness of an individual leaf or bud and 'the dearest freshness deep down things'. Although W.H.Gardner[20] is rather dismissive of the 'quasi-mystical illumination' which Hopkins, in his view, attached to the perception of inscape and instress, a notion of what might be termed the spiritual quality was essential to the formulation of his definition. Using a number of drama techniques, the group approached a variety of natural objects, investing them with significance in location and time, or using them as springboards for narrative, movement and sound. In resulting written work for their literature examination it was felt that the drama experience had helped some, at least, to gain insight into the spiritual dimension of Hopkins' thought.

That drama can be successful as a learning medium has been emphasised by Ann Davies, advisory drama teacher for Kent, in a video of the Kent Rural Schools' Enrichment Programme for Drama.[c] She points out that drama has often proved to be the first really creative experience for many children. The reason for this is that they are using themselves - body, voice and imagination - as a means of gaining experience. They are not being hindered, or even handicapped, by the tools of writing, the instruments of music or the implements of art.

It is hoped that teachers of RE may find, in the resources of drama and theatre, a means towards fulfilment, whether in the traditional and historical relationship between religious observance and drama, the exploration of social and moral issues, or the experience, in Brook's terms, of the 'rhythms or shapes... of the invisible'.

1. Waters (1975) pp.29-30.
2. Frazer (1911/1950) p.469.
3. Slade (1954) p.88.
4. Barnett (1990) pp.6-35.
5. Haggerty (1966) Title.
6. Stabler (1978) p.90.
7. Profitt & Bishop (1983) pp.117-118.
8. Eales (1987) pp.67-76.
9. David & Long (1989) pp.77-86.
10. Casdagli (1991) Title.
11. Dunne (1992) Report.
12. Wulff (1991) pp.165-166.
13. Ibid. pp.565-567.
14. Brook (1968) p.11.
15. Priestley (1982) p.32.
16. Johnstone (1979) pp.75-108.
17. Hendricks & Wills (1975) Title.
18. Welch (1983) Essay.
19. Tufnell & Crickmay (1990) pp.160-161.
20. Gardner (1953) p.xxi.

A   BBC TV Omnibus
B   Manchester University TV (1984)
C   KETV (1989)

---BIBLIOGRAPHY---

Banks, R A (1985):   *Drama and Theatre Arts*, London, Hodder & Stoughton.
Barnet, V (1990):   'Religion and Story' in *World Religions in Education 1990/1 Yearbook*, Cambridge, Hobson.

Brook, P (1968):   *The Empty Space*, London, Penguin.

Casdagli, P (1991):   *Grief: the Play, Writings and Workshops*, London, Casdagli, Gobey, Griffin.

Courtney, R (1968):   *Play, Drama and Thought*, London, Cassell.

Davis, M & Long, T (1989): *Active Replay*, Oxford, Blackwell.

Dunne, N (1992):   *Staffordshire HIV & Aids THE Programme*, THE Trust, Birmingham, unpublished.

Eales, S (1987):   'Handscapes', in Alcock (ed), *Playstage*, London, Methuen.

Frazer, J G (1950 edn):   *The Golden Bough*, London, Macmillan.

Gardner, W G (1953):   *Gerard Manley Hopkins*, Harmondsworth, Penguin.

Haggerty, J (1966):   *Please, Miss, Can I Play God?*, London, Methuen.

Hartnoll, P (1985):   *The Theatre: A Concise History*, London, Thames & Hudson.

Hendricks, G & Wills, R (1975): *The Centering Book*, New York, Prentice Hall.

Johnstone, K (1979):   *IMPRO: Inprovisation and the Theatre*, London, Faber.

Priestley, J (1982):   'Teaching Transcendence' in Tickner and Webster (eds), *Religious Education and the Imagination: Aspects of Education No. 28*, University of Hull.

Profitt, R & Bishop, V (1983): *Hand in Hand Assembly Book*, London, Longman.

Slade, P (1954):   *Child Drama*, University of London Press.

Stabler, T (1978):   *Drama in Primary Schools*, London, Macmillan.

Tufnell, M & Crickmay, C (1990): *Body, Space, Image*, London, Virago.

Waters, D (1975):   *A Book of Assemblies*, Richmond, Mills & Boon.

Welch, R (1983):   Essay, University of Warwick, unpublished.

Wulff, D M (1991):   *Psychology of Religion*, New York, John Wiley & Sons.

John Alcock is a former Lecturer in Drama in the Department of Arts Education at the University of Warwick, where he still teaches part-time. A published poet, he has taught Drama and English in schools, colleges and universities in England and the USA. With a special interest in community-based theatre (particularly theatre-in-education) he is currently Deputy Chair and Research Supervisor for the Theatre in Health Education Trust.

BRENDA WALL

RHYME AND REASON: RELIGIOUS EDUCATION THROUGH THE ARTS

Dissatisfied with an essentially cognitive and critical model of religious education, the author describes her pursuit of an alternative and aesthetic model allowing for personal engagement, imagination and reflection. New methods (essentially methods of 'making and doing') became possible by moving RE from the Humanities to the Expressive Arts Faculty. They were embodied in a freely chosen modular series of topics in line with the Agreed Syllabus. Having explained how the working environment was organised to permit alternatives of shared exploration and private reflection, the author describes the dynamics of individual lessons - beginning from some shared stimulus and proceeding to the engagement of heart, head and hands in making and doing something. Finally, the author justifies her approach in terms of the personal benefit to students and in relation to the values of both art and religion.

"My experience has been that most of these young people have had so much input that has not been digested that it's really a form of indigestion. And they need an area - and I think art is marvellous for this - where they can in secret, without somebody bothering them, integrate some of this material." Maria Harris [1]

Any attempt to adopt whole-heartedly an aesthetic approach to RE, and provide just such an area for the digestion of learning, involves making radical changes at the various levels of curriculum planning. It is very like discovering another rite of passage, a coming of age both theologically to recent movements in thinking, and personally as a teacher. In 1987 I chose to adopt such an approach. Until that point I had been in thrall to the current model of RE. This can be described as aiming to help students to understand religious beliefs and practices, and find their way to some search for meaning. Its chief medium is cognitive reasoning. Such a cool-headed approach was developed in reaction to previous models of RE where the level of indoctrination was becoming unacceptable.

Using this model my students did well in examinations, but I was curiously dissatisfied, and I suspect they were too. I was also becoming increasingly conscious that

179

critical examination of private beliefs - as an outsider looking on - in some way distorted those beliefs and even violated them. Trying to encourage sensitivity, I was nevertheless teaching my students to *gawp* rather than to *gaze*. I struggled to make the lessons attractive with visual aids and active learning strategies, but gradually became convinced that there must be some other mode of learning more appropriate for "treading on someone else's sacred ground". I was looking for a way that held on to the need for objectivity in learning, but also allowed for the sort of passionate engagement that Maxine Greene talks about, "if the exercise of reason is not to separate the living subject from the objects of his knowing".[2] I was also looking for a model for RE which would give the students the chance to respond also at many levels, including the sort of profound level of illumination described in The Religious Experience Research Unit's work by David Hay and Edward Robinson.[3]

During the eighties various writers were suggesting where to find a more appropriate model. Dennis Bates, Derek Webster and Brenda Lealman were writing in Britain, and Maria Harris and Sharon Parkes in the USA, all advocating the recovery of the imagination for education. Lealman suggested presenting RE in a "metaphoric mode", by using "the triggers of the imagination".[4] Agreed Syllabuses were taking note, and beginning to integrate the arts into curriculum planning. For example, the Salford Agreed Syllabus of 1987 said: "The Spiritual Dimension can be recognised in the aesthetic and creative areas of the curriculum: in dance and drama, music, art and literature". They gave as their reason for the need of a spiritual dimension the insight that learning becomes, "a shell with no kernel...and degenerates into a study of festivals".[5]

Outside RE there was a groundswell of interest in the relationship between the arts and religion. The art critic Peter Fuller became one of the catalysts for the exhibitions and publications that emerged, and the debate in the religious traditions was lively - a debate over the contemporary expression of religious themes. In the late eighties, RE educators had other things on their minds. As far as I know, no-one in Britain was devising and implementing curricula that put the ideas of the theorists into practice by adopting wholeheartedly an aesthetic approach. Instead there was a quiet growth of affective learning strategies under the umbrella of 'experiential learning'. They aimed to provide education which "frees the mind and helps students recognise what they already know".[6] I adopted and adapted many of the exercises, but the approach left me again dissatisfied and uneasy. I was uneasy at the seductive nature of the material, which deals with primary private experience. It seemed to require from me yet another sort of obedience - obedience to another person's vision of awe, wonder, insight and personal happiness. Above all it seemed to me that education of the heart needed to be integrated with education of the head, and furthermore, education of the eyes and hands.

CURRICULUM FRAMEWORKS AND PLANNING

Changes began experimentally in the simultaneous development of a new method and a revised curriculum framework. New methods were the heart of the matter - essentially an emphasis on responses through making and doing. But perhaps those teachers who may feel the dissatisfaction that I felt some years ago, may similarly be in thrall to the established approaches to RE; and so it may be most helpful if I first explain the framework that made a change of methods possible.

I began the experiment in an upper school in Leicestershire with students aged 14 to 16. I was head of an RE department that had chosen to belong to the Expressive Arts faculty rather than the Humanities Faculty. The school had a strong tradition in valuing non-examination RE, feeling that this was more appropriate for students who had presumably already acquired nine years of information and needed now to relate some of this to their own lives. Within the Expressive Arts faculty I had sympathetic encouragement, as the role of the imagination was a key principle for the sort of education that would unlock students' potential - i.e. through such dimensions as the various kinds of art work, drama, sport and awareness exercises.

Within the security of this philosophy I was able to take the radical steps of redefining RE. The forum for this was was in place, in that students had to choose a new module within the Expressive Arts every five weeks. The overall programme for RE, available across the year in a series of modules, was described under the general title of 'Pictures and People'. The concepts of the work were clearly enunciated to the whole school. An example was shown of the sort of art work involved - in order to demonstrate that it was not alarming but was within the competence of all. Students were in no doubt as to its being RE and that they would engage with interesting ideas and with people's lives and their cultural expression. This open-market situation was a risky process for teachers unused to having students decide; but one of its benefits was that the whole school knew what was going on in RE and so could to some extent understand the resulting displays. On this basis, students could opt when to do their 15 hours of RE from the individual modules on offer throughout the year.

Under the general title, 'Pictures and People', I was aware that the topic for each module had to be clearly focused - not least to satisfy the requirements of the Agreed Syllabus. And yet it had to be open-ended, inviting various interpretations and interconnections. One way of choosing a topic, and one that will be most easily recognisable from a conventional perspective, was to adopt an historical or geographical stance. For instance, the plan of the module called, 'The African Experience' encompassed more than a look at African primal religion. It included the African experience of slavery, Black Religious Movements in America, Rastafarianism, and the Christian, Jewish and Muslim components of the Ethiopian inheritance. Studying the rock churches of Ethiopia - in particular the portable altar, the minbar, was akin to discovering an important but missing relative. Another example was our work exploring one of the roots of European Christianity through 'The Celtic Experience'. The topic included an exploration of the pre-Christian dimension. Celtic skulls and carvings were studied along with the Hebridean hearth offerings. Then we looked at the early roots in Egyptian desert monasticism, and the unique mystical experience of the Christian tradition, with its inclusion of the ordinariness of life in its orbit. It was a rich field for visual and practical learning.

In such topics, understanding all the various aspects was the most obviously intended outcome but a further outcome emerged as we moved towards practical work. A linking metaphor or idea would emerge from our shared experience of objects and

181

ideas; and it was this that triggered students' formulation and expression of their personal responses in art work. In 'The Celtic Experience' for example, the constant underlying factor proved to be the notion of 'offering' or 'sacrifice'. Combining reactions of both fear and love, it led naturally to artwork, using and developing the images we had encountered. Indeed, this whole approach could be characterised as a metaphoric mode of teaching; and this suggests an alternative way of constructing topics - one that starts not from some historical or geographical focus but from some root metaphor such as the tree, the sea, the desert, doors, and mountains. Some of these will be familiar to RE teachers as themes, but all of them have some resonance in the personal experience of students and none of them belongs exlusively to RE. In an expressive arts context they speak first to the human condition, illuminate religious beliefs and practices, and trigger the integration of responses through art.

My teaching has been, I hope, both responsible and responsive. Lesson planning during the experiment was certainly no less rigorous than under previous frameworks for RE. I aimed to satisfy both explicit and implicit aims of RE, but in the event found that outcomes far exceeded these aims. Procedures were now more responsive to tangents raised by the students and by the material. In the work on the Celts the difficult subject of fear of ghosts and of the dark had a safe setting for it to be explored in context.

THE WORKING ENVIRONMENT

If making things was to become the central medium for learning (the use of ears, eyes and hands, so that students would be 'enabled' to grasp new ideas and relate them to and in their own experience) then money had to be spent in new ways. Pencils, paint-boxes, different sorts of paper, glue and scissors were ordered alongside traditional RE fare; and surprisingly, the costs compared well with a more conventional budget, once the initial purchase of a gun-stapler and a paper guillotine had been made.

The most visible change was to the layout of the room - basing the plan on the model of people's living rooms with a carpet, a coffee table in the centre, and plants and objects all around. Rarely were these disturbed. It was not therefore an art room ambience: we had to take as much care with spillages for instance, as if we were at home. All the work tables were placed against the walls so that students could work in privacy and in silence, without fear or favour arising from the terror we all feel before we begin any piece of work from scratch. The empty space in the centre of the room, with the central coffee table, became my teaching place, The layout went far to establish a relaxed atmosphere of mutuality, with the teacher as co-learner. Maria Grey has emphasised this element as 'a redemptive factor for the educational process:

> Relationships in the classroom are far from egalitarian - teachers are paid, pupils generally do not want to be there - but by focusing on the value of mutuality, the dynamic of relatedness which is called into being, both teacher and pupils can participate in a profound creative enterprise. [7]

I often sat on the floor and spread the materials around me; and students sat either in a circle on their chairs turned inward, or approached nearer to the coffee table. Not only was this a symbol of the democratic, mutual intentions of the lessons, but it also gave an unspoken message that everyone's point of view was valid, and that hence there were no predetermined right or wrong answers in the adventure that is the search for meaning in life.

THE INTRODUCTORY STIMULUS - TEACHING STUDENTS TO SEE

The primacy of words was not in question, only the priority. Each lesson began with an introduction of from ten to fifteen minutes. This often took the form of handing round objects, seeing slides, introducing concepts. A further benefit arose from the position of the coffee table. Its placement separately from the teacher's desk implicitly gave students permission to handle objects and books when they wished. Not only were we co-learners, but the actual object was our teacher. For example, passing around pieces of Romany barge art, and paying them slow and intense attention, helped us to participate in the life-world of Romany culture. We asked *how, when, where, by whom,* and eventually *why* the object was made. This seemed a different process from the use of artifacts as so far practised by RE teachers, who seem to be given little help with the essential examination of attitudes to the introduction of religious objects. Boxes of artifacts are standard issue, but the use of less ceremonial or devotional objects as well is not encouraged. The artifacts are thus out of context. Not only can this do violence to the religious sensibility being 'examined', but it can be educationally counter-productive. Clifford Longley has argued that, "it is entirely possible for too much clinical familiarity with that something else altogether masquer-ading as an approximation, to have a severely repellant effect. It is the difference between a corpse and a living person". [8]

Encounter with the art and objects of another culture (or even another family) has, I think, deeper educational gains especially for RE. An unfamilar object produces a kind of shock. We are at that moment meeting another person's life-world, summed up in the object. In order to recover our equilibrium, various reactions occur - admiring it, wanting to buy it, making either adverse, distancing comments about it or trivialising it. However, adopting a deliberate intention to be attentive to the otherness of the object brings the sort of sympathetic understanding that RE educators aim at. Martin Buber has drawn our attention to the two modes of being in the presence of anything other than our self. He talks about the I-Thou relationship, treating the other as a *thou* rather than an *it*; not in some sort of false sanctity and adulation, but robustly, by being involved in 'meeting the stranger'. [9] This is the real 'bracketing out' of which we hear in phenomenology. "Truth," as Gadamer says, " is not reached methodologically, but dialectically. In dialectic the matter encountered poses the question to which he responds." [10]

To fulfil this sort of encounter, we need a mode of class-questioning different from the 'problematic' mode of conventional RE. Syllabuses encourage questioning through the question and answer format, and this by its very nature supposes that an answer is available. Above all, life is presented as a series of problems, and students are asked to come to conclusions about life's mysteries. A magnifying glass is implicitly present in the problematic approach, rendering the sacred a potential felon, and the RE teacher can then be seen as Mr. Fixit. By contrast, teaching students to see alters the very nature of the questioning process. Questions must be open-ended, so that the experience is one of continual discovery, and of connections being made. In short, questioning must be 'sacramental' rather than 'problematic'. In their own way, students may thus appreciate what Maria Harris put so well after studying the teaching of Mary Tully:

> .....a religious education must be related to the search for truth....It is rather the truth of art, where some things are adequate and others are more adequate, and where the opposite of a profound statement may be, paradoxically, another profound statement. [11]

I discovered that such an approach revealed more about the chosen theme of the lesson than I had planned for, and that too close an adherence to limited objectives can be teaching with only half-opened eyes.

It is human to be forever curious. Questions of *when, how and where* lead, with the experience of living, to the question of *why*. The sacramental and the problematic viewpoints are not ultimately inimical to each other. It depends on the openness with which the viewpoint is held. An aesthetic approach allows the problem to be encountered in such a way that students do not have to foreclose on one solution. They are able to move forward from curiosity aroused by the introductory stimulus. Through creative engagement in making something they achieve some clarification that does not opt out of life's difficulties and mysteries.

MAKING AND DOING - THE HEART, THE HEAD AND THE HANDS

Everything came together with the essential processes of 'making and doing' - enhancing the expressiveness and sensibility of the more academically able students, and liberating those who had been alienated and depressed by a purely verbal and literary educational diet. Not only the head and heart needed engagement in RE lessons, but also the hands.

The nature of the artwork arose from class discussion of the initial stimulus. It was in discussion that students began to relate new ideas and unusual objects to their own experience and concerns - a process that was open-ended and gave rise to many interpretations and interconnections. But the really important stage was reached when all this reflectiveness took the practical form of making and doing. Whether our approach had been founded on root metaphors or had discovered them through the process of discussion, students had some key symbols on which to focus the practical stage of exploration through art. For example, the word 'doors' had already admitted many dimensions of personal and shared experience to the initial discussion. The topic enabled students to alternate objective learning with exploration of their own subjectivity. In this topic we explored *Alice in Wonderland*, the doors to reality and illusion, as well as 'death as the door to the after-life', the placing of remains under the threshold, the mezuzah, holy water stoops, and the iconostasis. Moving closer to the stage of making and doing, we studied the paintings of Howard Hodgkin. We then followed his lead to 'place' a secret imaginatively on the paper and then cover it with layers and patches of colour - each representing ways of safeguarding or revealing what that secret meant to them. Finally, we added a 'Hodgkin' frame, thus opening a door to some sense of self-worth and to the inner spiritual journey.

Students soon came to accept the radically different approach to RE lessons, eager to participate and to arrive on time. At the 'making' stage however, there was still some puzzlement and resistance to be overcome by students new to the courses. Students were anxious that they would feel embarrassed in various ways. Their secondary school experience had implicitly told them that the hands were inferior to the head as a means of acquiring knowledge. Their experience in Design Departments (increasingly technologically based) had given them little practice in making things for the pure joy of making and for no other reason than the discovery of the possibility of the transformation of materials into something else. They had a very low sense of self-esteem over their own visual literacy and art production, doubting (for example) their capacity to draw accurately. Often, their fear of failure was expressed overall as a fear of being treated like primary pupils. To help with all this, the layout of the room allowed for individual privacy during the 'making time'. From the start students were encouraged to display their own work only when and if they chose to do so - being allowed complete anonymity if that was what they preferred. Only thus could some students learn to have confidence in their work and to trust each other. Music appropriate to the work was played during the 'making time', quietening the room and assisting the atmosphere of privacy and concentration. Students were thus introduced to a wide range of music. Steve Reich and Russian orthodox singing were asked for as repeats. When students finally made their work public I felt they were taking a leap of trust in their own judgement, a wager on their own work as being meaningful to themselves and accepted as meaningful to others. It happened increasingly, so that both healthy rivalry and co-operation began to emerge.

IN CONCLUSION

Edward Robinson has proposed that initiation into the transcendent is the special role of the arts. [12] This alone would be justification for an aesthetic approach to RE teaching. In the act of making, a piece of material becomes something else that did not previously exist. Some sort of transfiguration occurs, and it seems akin to the movement of the heart from which religious belief stems. Robinson points to the unique capacity of "humans to conceive of things as being different from the way they are', and so be "open to a dimension of mystery". [13] For Robinson, "the language of mystery is the language of the imagination", and imagination is the essential means, humanly speaking, by which faith becomes possible.[14] Elsewhere, Robinson has described the peculiar nature of the encounter with the artistic process that is a sort of dialectic shock [15] It is, for him, the vital prerequisite for appreciation of, "some sense of that 'form of death' that is the necessary prelude to any awareness of the mystery, horror and beauty of life". Similarly, David Hargreaves has outlined the nature of the 'conversive' role of the arts, with his theory of the traumatic nature of aesthetic learning - saying that by, "traumatic initiation one has moved from being on the outside to being on the inside".[16] I think therefore that there may be more to my students' initial embarrassment and growing adventurousness than they have ever put into words. Not that they have been short of words.

Students' comments were various. Not everyone was convinced. One student said, "Pictures and People is O.K. I liked doing clay and video and charcoal, but talking and listening and Celtic knots was boring". On the other hand, the following two comments were more typical and were made after five weeks' work:

> I am more aware of the Celtic lives and their religion and beliefs. I now can be more confident in my drawing and not always do it slowly and carefully. I can distort faces and make them look powerful. I think about the sort of lives the Celts lived and what sort of fears the children might have had or been taught. I am glad we looked at fear, ghosts and faces. Now I know more about what and why things frighten us. I was able to say what I was frightened of and now I can control it. I really enjoyed this way of teaching RE. It is a lot better. I think they should do it in all schools.

> I enjoyed the artistic exercises as I usually only draw technical things and the work we did had more feeling and atmosphere in, and I felt I had created things rather than just drawn and shaped them.

This approach requires a lot of hard work. Resources are to be collected, galleries to be visited, images searched for, skips raided. The art work has to be introduced (perhaps, Blue Peter style ....."and here is one I made earlier"). Secondary teachers may feel initially daunted. But this approach is almost a way of life for primary teachers, and it is a very rewarding one. For every occasion when students said, "We've done this already in science (etc)", there were many when students expressed their sense of things falling into place and becoming meaningful - an experience like hitting the jack-pot. "Art," says Maria Harris, "is a unique kind of revelation, not only because of what it reveals but because it reveals what can be known in no other way." [17] Our work can provide the sort of oasis where learning can be integrated and both teacher and student refreshed and energised for further learning.

References

1. Harris (1979) pp.141-153.

2. Greene (1973) p.255.

3. Hay (1982) and Robinson (1977).

4. Lealman (1982) p.60.

5. City of Salford Education Department (1987) pp.30 and 31.

6. Hammond, Hay et. al., (1990) p.7.

7. Grey (1989) p.167.

8. Longley (1988) p.12.

9. Buber (1937).

10. Quoted in Palmer, R E (1969) p.165.

11. Harris (1971) p.199.

12. Robinson (1987) p.84.

13. Robinson (1987) pp.8 and 24.

14. Robinson (1987) pp.16 and 6.

15. Robinson (1971) p.162.

16. Hargreaves (1983) p.162.

17. Harris (1971) p.28.

BIBLIOGRAPHY

Buber, M (1937):   *I and Thou*, Edinburgh, T.& T Clark.

City of Salford Education Department (1987):   *Religious Education - Planning and Practice*, The Agreed Syllabus for The City of Salford.

Greene, M (1973):   *Teacher as Stranger - Educational Philosophy for the Modern Age* Belmont, California, Wadsworth.

Grey, M. (1989):   *Redeeming the Dream*, London, SPCK.

Hammond, J & D. Hay et al., (1990):   *New Methods in Religious Education: An Experiential Approach*, Oliver and Boyd.

Hargreaves, D H (1983):   'The teaching of Art and the Art of Teaching: Towards an Alternative View of Aesthetic Learning', in M. Hammersley and A Hargreaves (eds.), *Curriculum Practice: Some Sociological Case Studies*, Falmer Press.

Harris, M (1971):   The Aesthetic Dimensions in Redefining Religious Education, Ed.D. Thesis, Columbia University, New York.

Harris, M (1979):   'A Model of aesthetic education', in Gloria Durka and Joan-Marie Smith (eds.) *Aesthetic Dimensions of Religious Education*, Paulist Press.

Hay, D (1982):   *Exploring Inner Space*, London, Penguin Press.

Lealman, B (1982):   'The Ignorant Eye: Perception and Religious Education', *British Journal of Religious Education*, vol.4, 1982 pp.59-63.

Longley, C (1971):   'The True Art of Teaching Religion', London, *The Times*, 24th September 1988.

Palmer, R E (1969):   *Four Major Theorists in Hermeneutics*, N.W. University Press, Evanston, 1969.

Robinson, E (1971):   'Religious Education; A Shocking Business', Learning for Living, Vol.2, 1971.

Robinson, E (1977): 'The Original Vision', Religious Experience Research Unit, Manchester College, Oxford.

Robinson, E (1987): *The Language of Mystery*, London, SCM Press.

Brenda Wall has written articles on the theory and practice of an aesthetic, practical approach to RE. Having until recently taught in a Leicestershire school as an RE specialist, she now travels widely, disseminating the approach to teachers. She is currently developing an approach to spiritual growth through creativity by means of a fellowship from the Joseph Rowntree Quaker Trust. Enquiries concerning consultancy and short courses can be addressed to her at Middle Foster Place, Hepworth, Holmfirth, Huddersfield, HD7 1TN.